HAD I KNOWN

Had I Known

COLLECTED ESSAYS

BARBARA EHRENREICH

TWELVE

New York

Twelve
Hachette Book Group
1290 Avenue of the Americas, New York, NY 10104
twelvebooks.com
twitter.com/twelvebooks

The essays in this collection were previously published and may have been slightly
revised for this edition.

First Edition: March 2020

Twelve is an imprint of Grand Central Publishing. The Twelve name and logo are
trademarks of Hachette Book Group, Inc.

The publisher is not responsible for websites (or their content) that are not owned
by the publisher.

The Hachette Speakers Bureau provides a wide range of authors for speaking
events. To find out more, go to www.hachettespeakersbureau.com or call
(866) 376-6591.

Additional copyright/credits information is on page 351.

LCCN: 2019950073
ISBNs: 978-1-4555-4367-0 (hardcover), 978-1-4555-4368-7 (ebook)

Printed in the United States of America

LSC-C

10 9 8 7 6 5 4 3 2 1

CONTENTS

INTRODUCTION

Back in the fat years—two or three decades ago, when the "mainstream" media were booming—I was able to earn a living as a freelance writer. My income was meager, and I had to hustle to get it, turning out about four articles— essays, reported pieces, reviews—a month at $1 or $2 a word. One of the things I wanted to write about, in part for obvious personal reasons, was poverty and inequality, but I'd do just about anything—like, I cringe to say, "The Heartbreak Diet" for a major fashion magazine—to pay the bills.

It wasn't easy to interest glossy magazines in poverty in the 1980s and '90s. I once spent two hours over an expensive lunch—paid for, of course, by a major publication— trying to pitch to a clearly indifferent editor who finally conceded, over decaf espresso and crème brûlée, "OK, do your thing on poverty. But can you make it upscale?" (Yes, I found a way to do this.) Then there was the editor of a quite liberal magazine who responded to my pitch for a story involving blue-collar men by asking, "Hmm, but can they talk?" (Actually, my husband was one of them.)

I finally got lucky at *Harper's*, where fabled editor Lewis Lapham gave me an assignment that turned into a book, which in turn became a best seller, *Nickel and Dimed: On (Not) Getting By in America*. Thanks to the royalties and subsequent speaking fees, at last I could begin to undertake projects without concern for the pay, just because they seemed important to me. This was the writing life I had always dreamed of—adventurous, obsessively fascinating, and sufficiently remunerative that I could help support less affluent members of my family.

In the years that followed, I wrote about America's shifting class contours, the criminalization of poverty, sexual harassment, the racial wealth gap, as well as any other subject that attracted me—from the automation of war to Americans' apparent belief that they can live forever if only they eat the right combination of veggies and nuts. I paid my bills and, better yet, I was having fun.

Meanwhile, though I didn't see it at first, the world of journalism as I had known it was beginning to crumble around me. Squeezed to generate more profits for billionaire newspaper owners and new media conglomerates, newsrooms laid off reporters, who often went on to swell the crowds of hungry freelancers. Once-generous magazines shrank or slashed their freelance budgets; there were no more free lunches.

True, the internet was filled with a multiplicity of new outlets to write for, but paying writers or other "content providers" turned out not to be part of their business plan. I saw my own fees at one major news outlet drop to one-third of their value between 2004 and 2009. I heard from younger journalists who were scrambling for adjunct jobs or doing piecework in "corporate communications." But

I determined to carry on writing about the subjects that gripped me, especially poverty and inequality, even if I had to finance my efforts entirely on my own. And I felt noble for doing so.

Then, as the kids say today, I "checked my privilege." I realized that there was something wrong with an arrangement whereby a relatively affluent person, such as I had become, could afford to write about minimum-wage jobs, squirrels as an urban food source, or the penalties for sleeping in parks, while the people who were actually experiencing these sorts of things, or were in danger of experiencing them, could not.

In the last few years, I've gotten to know a number of people who are at least as qualified writers as I am, especially when it comes to the subject of poverty, but who've been held back by their own poverty. There's Darryl Wellington, for example, a local columnist (and poet) in Santa Fe who has, at times, had to supplement his tiny income by selling his plasma—a fallback that can have serious health consequences. Or Joe Williams, who, after losing an editorial job, was reduced to writing for $50 a piece for online political sites while mowing lawns and working in a sporting goods store for $10 an hour to pay for a room in a friend's house. Linda Tirado was blogging about her job as a cook at IHOP when she managed to snag a contract for a powerful book titled *Hand to Mouth* (for which I wrote the preface). Now she is working on a "multimedia mentoring project" to help other working-class journalists get published.

There are many thousands of people like these—gifted

journalists who want to address serious social issues but cannot afford to do so in a media environment that thrives by refusing to pay, or pay anywhere near adequately, its "content providers." Some were born into poverty and have stories to tell about coping with low-wage jobs, evictions, or life as a foster child. Others inhabit the once-proud urban "creative class," which now finds itself priced out of its traditional neighborhoods, like Park Slope or LA's Echo Park, scrambling for health insurance and child care, sleeping on other people's couches. They want to write—or do photography or make documentaries. They have a lot to say, but it's beginning to make more sense to apply for work as a cashier or a fry cook.

This is the real face of journalism today: not million-dollar-a-year anchorpersons, but low-wage workers and downwardly spiraling professionals who can't muster up expenses to even start on the articles, photo essays, and videos they want to do, much less find an outlet to cover the costs of doing them. You can't, as I learned from Darryl Wellington, hop on a plane to cover a police shooting in your hometown if you don't have a credit card.

This impoverishment of journalists impoverishes journalism. We come to find less and less in the media about the people who work from paycheck to paycheck, as if 80 percent of the population had quietly emigrated while the other 20 percent wasn't looking. Media outlets traditionally neglected stories about the downtrodden because they don't sit well on the same page with advertisements for diamonds and luxury homes. And now there are fewer journalists on hand at major publications to arouse the conscience of editors and other gatekeepers. Coverage of poverty accounts for less than 1 percent of American news, or, as former *Times* columnist Bob Herbert has put it: "We don't have coverage of poverty in this country. If there is a story about poor people in the *New York Times* or in the *Washington Post*, that's the exception that proves the rule. We do not cover poverty. We do not cover the poor."

As for commentary about poverty—a disproportionate share of which issues from very well-paid, established columnists like David Brooks of the *New York Times* and George Will of the *Washington Post*—all too often, it tends to reflect the historical biases of economic elites, that the poor are different than "we" are, less educated, intelligent, self-disciplined, and more inclined to make "bad lifestyle choices." If the pundits sometimes sound like Republican presidential candidates, this is not because there is a political conspiracy afoot. It's just what happens when the people who get to opine about inequality are drawn almost entirely from the top of the income distribution.

It hurts the poor and the economically precarious when they can't see themselves reflected in the collective mirror that is the media. They begin to feel that they are indeed different and somehow unworthy, compared to the "mainstream." But it also potentially hurts the rich.

In a highly polarized society like our own, the wealthy have a special stake in keeping honest journalism about class and inequality alive. Burying an aching social problem does not solve it. The rich and their philanthropies need to step up and support struggling journalists and the slender projects that try to keep them going. As Nick Hanauer, a self-proclaimed member of the 0.01 percent, warned other members of his class in 2018: "If we don't do something to fix the glaring inequities in this economy, the pitchforks are going to come for us."

At an age when most people retire—or are pushed out of the workforce into low-paid work as home health aides, valet parkers, or babysitters—I am fortunate enough to be able to keep on writing about the things that inflame my curiosity or fill me with moral outrage. But mostly I try, through a nonprofit I helped create, the Economic Hardship Reporting Project, to launch struggling journalists who otherwise might never be heard from on account of their poverty or skin color, gender or sexual orientation, youth or age. It's a great joy to me to work with people like Darryl, Joe, Linda, and so many others, and to see them begin to thrive. In the spirit of torch-passing, I dedicate this book to them.

Barbara Ehrenreich
May 2019

HAVES AND
HAVE-NOTS

NICKEL-AND-DIMED: ON (NOT) GETTING BY IN AMERICA

Harper's Magazine, 1999

At the beginning of June 1998 I leave behind everything that normally soothes the ego and sustains the body—home, career, companion, reputation, ATM card—for a plunge into the low-wage workforce. There, I become another, occupationally much diminished "Barbara Ehrenreich"—depicted on job-application forms as a divorced homemaker whose sole work experience consists of housekeeping in a few private homes. I am terrified, at the beginning, of being unmasked for what I am: a middle-class journalist setting out to explore the world that welfare mothers are entering, at the rate of approximately 50,000 a month, as welfare reform kicks in. Happily, though, my fears turn out to be entirely unwarranted: during a month of poverty and toil, my name goes unnoticed and for the most part unuttered. In this parallel universe where my father never got out of the mines and I never got through college, I am "baby," "honey," "blondie," and, most commonly, "girl."

My first task is to find a place to live. I figure that if I can earn $7 an hour—which, from the want ads, seems doable—I can afford to spend $500 on rent, or maybe, with severe economies, $600. In the Key West area, where I live, this pretty much confines me to flophouses and trailer homes—like the one, a pleasing fifteen-minute drive from town, that has no air-conditioning, no screens, no fans, no television, and, by way of diversion, only the challenge of evading the landlord's Doberman pinscher. The big problem with this place, though, is the rent, which at $675 a month is well beyond my reach. All right, Key West is expensive. But so is New York City, or the Bay Area, or Jackson Hole, or Telluride, or Boston, or any other place where tourists and the wealthy compete for living space with the people who clean their toilets and fry their hash browns.[1] Still, it is a shock to realize that "trailer trash" has become, for me, a demographic category to aspire to.

So I decide to make the common trade-off between affordability and convenience, and go for a $500-a-month efficiency thirty miles up a two-lane highway from the employment opportunities of Key West, meaning forty-five minutes if there's no road construction and I don't get caught behind some sun-dazed Canadian tourists. I hate the drive, along a roadside studded with white crosses commemorating the more effective head-on collisions, but it's a sweet little place—a cabin, more or less, set in the swampy

---

1   According to the Department of Housing and Urban Development, the "fair-market rent" for an efficiency is $551 here in Monroe County, Florida. A comparable rent in the five boroughs of New York City is $704; in San Francisco, $713; and in the heart of Silicon Valley, $808. The fair-market rent for an area is defined as the amount that would be needed to pay rent plus utilities for "privately owned, decent, safe, and sanitary rental housing of a modest (non-luxury) nature with suitable amenities."

back yard of the converted mobile home where my land-lord, an affable TV repairman, lives with his bartender girl-friend. Anthropologically speaking, a bustling trailer park would be preferable, but here I have a gleaming white floor and a firm mattress, and the few resident bugs are easily vanquished.

Besides, I am not doing this for the anthropology. My aim is nothing so mistily subjective as to "experience poverty" or find out how it "really feels" to be a long-term low-wage worker. I've had enough unchosen encounters with poverty and the world of low-wage work to know it's not a place you want to visit for touristic purposes; it just smells too much like fear. And with all my real-life assets—bank account, IRA, health insurance, multiroom home—waiting indulgently in the background, I am, of course, thoroughly insulated from the terrors that afflict the genuinely poor.

No, this is a purely objective, scientific sort of mission. The humanitarian rationale for welfare reform—as opposed to the more punitive and stringy impulses that may actually have motivated it—is that work will lift poor women out of poverty while simultaneously inflating their self-esteem and hence their future value in the labor market. Thus, whatever the hassles involved in finding child care, transportation, etc., the transition from welfare to work will end happily, in greater prosperity for all. Now there are many problems with this comforting prediction, such as the fact that the economy will inevitably undergo a downturn, eliminating many jobs. Even without a downturn, the influx of a million former welfare recipients into the low-wage labor market could depress wages by as much as 11.9 percent, according to the Economic Policy Institute (EPI) in Washington, DC.

But is it really possible to make a living on the kinds of jobs currently available to unskilled people? Mathematically, the answer is no, as can be shown by taking $6 to $7 an hour, perhaps subtracting a dollar or two an hour for child care, multiplying by 160 hours a month, and comparing the result to the prevailing rents. According to the National Coalition for the Homeless, for example, in 1998 it took, on average nationwide, an hourly wage of $8.89 to afford a one-bedroom apartment, and the Preamble Center for Public Policy estimates that the odds against a typical welfare recipient's landing a job at such a "living wage" are about 97 to 1. If these numbers are right, low-wage work is not a solution to poverty and possibly not even to homelessness.

It may seem excessive to put this proposition to an experimental test. As certain family members keep unhelpfully reminding me, the viability of low-wage work could be tested, after a fashion, without ever leaving my study. I could just pay myself $7 an hour for eight hours a day, charge myself for room and board, and total up the numbers after a month. Why leave the people and work that I love? But I am an experimental scientist by training. In that business, you don't just sit at a desk and theorize; you plunge into the everyday chaos of nature, where surprises lurk in the most mundane measurements. Maybe, when I got into it, I would discover some hidden economies in the world of the low-wage worker. After all, if 30 percent of the workforce toils for less than $8 an hour, according to the EPI, they may have found some tricks as yet unknown to me. Maybe—who knows?—I would even be able to detect in myself the bracing psychological effects of getting out of the house, as promised by the welfare wonks at places like the Heritage Foundation. Or, on the other hand, maybe there would be unexpected costs—physical, mental, or financial—to throw off all my calculations. Ideally, I should do this with two small children in tow, that being the welfare average, but mine are grown and no one is willing to lend me theirs for a month-long vacation in penury. So this is not the perfect experiment, just a test of the best possible case: an unencumbered woman, smart and even strong, attempting to live more or less off the land.

On the morning of my first full day of job searching, I take a red pen to the want ads, which are auspiciously numerous. Everyone in Key West's booming "hospitality industry" seems to be looking for someone like me—trainable, flexible, and with suitably humble expectations as to pay. I know I possess certain traits that might be advantageous—I'm white and, I like to think, well-spoken and poised—but I decide on two rules: One, I cannot use any skills derived from my education or usual work—not that there are a lot of want ads for satirical essayists anyway. Two, I have to take the best-paid job that is offered me and of course do my best to hold it; no Marxist rants or sneaking off to read novels in the ladies' room. In addition, I rule out various occupations for one reason or another: Hotel front-desk clerk, for example, which to my surprise is regarded as unskilled and pays around $7 an hour, gets eliminated because it involves standing in one spot for eight hours a day. Waitressing is similarly something I'd like to avoid, because I remember it leaving me bone tired when I was eighteen, and I'm decades of varicosities and back pain beyond that now. Telemarketing, one of the first refuges of the suddenly indigent, can be dismissed on grounds of personality. This leaves certain supermarket jobs, such as deli clerk, or housekeeping in Key West's thousands of hotel and guest rooms. Housekeeping is especially appealing, for reasons both atavistic and practical: it's what my mother did before I came along, and it can't be too different from what I've been doing part-time, in my own home, all my life.

So I put on what I take to be a respectable-looking outfit of ironed Bermuda shorts and scooped-neck T-shirt and set out for a tour of the local hotels and supermarkets. Best Western, Econo Lodge, and HoJo's all let me fill out application forms, and these are, to my relief, interested in little more than whether I am a legal resident of the United States and have committed any felonies. My next stop is Winn-Dixie, the supermarket, which turns out to have a particularly onerous application process, featuring a fifteen-minute "interview" by computer since, apparently, no human on the premises is deemed capable of representing the corporate point of view. I am conducted to a large room decorated with posters illustrating how to look "professional" (it helps to be white and, if female, permed) and warning of the slick promises that union organizers might try to tempt me with. The interview is multiple choice: Do I have anything, such as child-care problems, that might make it hard for me to get to work on time? Do I think safety on the job is the responsibility of management? Then, popping up cunningly out of the blue: How many dollars' worth of stolen goods have I purchased in the last year? Would I turn in a fellow employee if I caught him stealing? Finally, "Are you an honest person?"

Apparently, I ace the interview, because I am told that all I have to do is show up in some doctor's office tomorrow for a urine test. This seems to be a fairly general rule: if you want to stack Cheerio boxes or vacuum hotel rooms in chemically fascist America, you have to be willing to squat down and pee in front of some health worker (who has no doubt had to do the same thing herself.) The wages Winn-Dixie is offering—$6 and a couple of dimes to start with—are not enough, I decide, to compensate for this indignity.[2]

I lunch at Wendy's, where $4.99 gets you unlimited refills at the Mexican part of the Super-bar, a comforting surfeit of refried beans and "cheese sauce." A teenage employee, seeing me studying the want ads, kindly offers me an application form, which I fill out, though here, too, the pay is just $6 and change an hour. Then it's off for a round of the locally owned inns and guesthouses. At "The Palms,"

---

2   According to the *Monthly Labor Review* (November 1996), 28 percent of work sites surveyed in the service industry conduct drug tests (corporate workplaces have much higher rates), and the incidence of testing has risen markedly since the eighties. The rate of testing is highest in the South (56 percent of work sites polled), with the Midwest in second place (50 percent). The drug most likely to be detected—marijuana, which can be detected in urine for weeks—is also the most innocuous, while heroin and cocaine are generally undetectable three days after use. Prospective employees sometimes try to cheat the tests by consuming excessive amounts of liquids and taking diuretics and even masking substances available through the internet.

let's call it, a bouncy manager actually takes me around to see the rooms and meet the existing housekeepers, who, I note with satisfaction, look pretty much like me—faded ex-hippie types in shorts with long hair pulled back in braids. Mostly, though, no one speaks to me or even looks at me except to proffer an application form. At my last stop, a palatial B & B, I wait twenty minutes to meet "Max," only to be told that there are no jobs now but there should be one soon, since "nobody lasts more than a couple weeks." (Because none of the people I talked to knew I was a reporter, I have changed their names to protect their privacy and, in some cases perhaps, their jobs.)

Three days go by like this and, to my chagrin, no one out of the approximately twenty places I've applied calls me for an interview. I had been vain enough to worry about coming across as too educated for the jobs I sought, but no one even seems interested in finding out how overqualified I am. Only later will I realize that the want ads are not a reliable measure of the actual jobs available at any particular time. They are, as I should have guessed from Max's comment, the employers' insurance policy against the relentless turnover of the low-wage workforce. Most of the big hotels run ads almost continually, just to build a supply of applicants to replace the current workers as they drift away or are fired, so finding a job is just a matter of being at the right place at the right time and flexible enough to take whatever is being offered that day. This finally happens to me at one of the big discount hotel chains, where I go, as usual, for housekeeping and am sent, instead, to try out as a waitress at the attached "family restaurant," a dismal spot with a counter and about thirty tables that looks out on a parking garage and features such tempting fare as "Pollish [sic] sausage and BBQ sauce" on 95-degree days. Phillip, the dapper young West Indian who introduces himself as the manager, interviews me with about as much enthusiasm as if he were a clerk processing me for Medicare, the principal questions being what shifts can I work and when can I start. I mutter something about being woefully out of practice as a waitress, but he's already on to the uniform: I'm to show up tomorrow wearing black slacks and black shoes; he'll provide the rust-colored polo shirt with HEARTHSIDE embroidered on it, though I might want to wear my own shirt to get to work, ha ha. At the word "tomorrow," something between fear and indignation rises in my chest. I want to say, "Thank you for your time, sir, but this is just an experiment, you know, not my actual life."

So begins my career at the Hearthside, I shall call it, one small profit center within a global discount hotel chain, where for two weeks I work from 2:00 till 10:00 P.M. for $2.43 an hour plus tips.[3] In some futile bid for gentility, the management has barred employees from using the front door, so my first day I enter through the kitchen, where a red-faced man with shoulder-length blond hair is throwing

---

3 According to the Fair Labor Standards Act, employers are not required to pay "tipped employees," such as restaurant servers, more than $2.13 an hour in direct wages. However, if the sum of tips plus $2.13 an hour falls below the minimum wage, or $5.15 an hour, the employer is required to make up the difference. This fact was not mentioned by managers or otherwise publicized at either of the restaurants where I worked.

frozen steaks against the wall and yelling, "Fuck this shit!"
"That's just Jack," explains Gail, the wiry middle-aged waitress who is assigned to train me. "He's on the rag again"—
a condition occasioned, in this instance, by the fact that the
cook on the morning shift had forgotten to thaw out the
steaks. For the next eight hours, I run after the agile Gail,
absorbing bits of instruction along with fragments of personal tragedy. All food must be trayed, and the reason she's
so tired today is that she woke up in a cold sweat thinking
of her boyfriend, who killed himself recently in an upstate
prison. No refills on lemonade. And the reason he was in
prison is that a few DUIs caught up with him, that's all,
could have happened to anyone. Carry the creamers to the
table in a monkey bowl, never in your hand. And after he
was gone she spent several months living in her truck, peeing in a plastic pee bottle and reading by candlelight at
night, but you can't live in a truck in the summer, since you
need to have the windows down, which means anything
can get in, from mosquitoes on up.

At least Gail puts to rest any fears I had of appearing
overqualified. From the first day on, I find that of all the
things I have left behind, such as home and identity, what
I miss the most is competence. Not that I have ever felt utterly competent in the writing business, in which one day's
success augurs nothing at all for the next. But in my writing
life, I at least have some notion of procedure: do the research, make the outline, rough out a draft, etc. As a server,
though, I am beset by requests like bees: more iced tea here,
ketchup over there, a to-go box for table fourteen, and
where are the high chairs, anyway? Of the twenty-seven

tables, up to six are usually mine at any time, though on slow afternoons or if Gail is off, I sometimes have the whole place to myself. There is the touch-screen computer-ordering system to master, which is, I suppose, meant to minimize server-cook contact, but in practice requires constant verbal fine-tuning: "That's gravy on the mashed, OK? None on the meatloaf," and so forth—while the cook scowls as if I were inventing these refinements just to torment him. Plus, something I had forgotten in the years since I was eighteen: about a third of a server's job is "side work" that's invisible to customers—sweeping, scrubbing, slicing, refilling, and restocking. If it isn't all done, every little bit of it, you're going to face the 6:00 P.M. dinner rush defenseless and probably go down in flames. I screw up dozens of times at the beginning, sustained in my shame entirely by Gail's support— "It's OK, baby, everyone does that sometime"—because, to my total surprise and despite the scientific detachment I am doing my best to maintain, I care.

The whole thing would be a lot easier if I could just skate through it as Lily Tomlin in one of her waitress skits, but I was raised by the absurd Booker T. Washingtonian precept that says: If you're going to do something, do it well. In fact, "well" isn't good enough by half. Do it better than anyone has ever done it before. Or so said my father, who must have known what he was talking about because he managed to pull himself, and us with him, up from the mile-deep copper mines of Butte to the leafy suburbs of the Northeast, ascending from boilermakers to martinis before booze beat out ambition. As in most endeavors I have encountered in my life, doing it "better than anyone" is not a reasonable goal.

Still, when I wake up at 4:00 A.M. in my own cold sweat, I am not thinking about the writing deadlines I'm neglecting; I'm thinking about the table whose order I screwed up so that one of the boys didn't get his kiddie meal until the rest of the family had moved on to their Key Lime pies. That's the other powerful motivation I hadn't expected—the customers, or "patients," as I can't help thinking of them on account of the mysterious vulnerability that seems to have left them temporarily unable to feed themselves. After a few days at Hearthside, I feel the service ethic kick in like a shot of oxytocin, the nurturance hormone. The plurality of my customers are hardworking locals—truck drivers, construction workers, even housekeepers from the attached hotel—and I want them to have the closest to a "fine dining" experience that the grubby circumstances will allow. No "you guys" for me; everyone over twelve is "sir" or "ma'am." I ply them with iced tea and coffee refills; I return, mid-meal, to inquire how everything is; I doll up their salads with chopped raw mushrooms, summer squash slices, or whatever bits of produce I can find that have survived their sojourn in the cold-storage room mold-free.

There is Benny, for example, a short, tight-muscled sewer repairman, who cannot even think of eating until he has absorbed a half hour of air-conditioning and ice water. We chat about hyperthermia and electrolytes until he is ready to order some finicky combination like soup of the day, garden salad, and a side of grits. There are the German tourists who are so touched by my pidgin *"Wilkommen"* and *"Ist alles gut?"* that they actually tip. (Europeans, spoiled by their trade-union-ridden, high-wage welfare states, generally do not know that they are supposed to tip. Some restaurants, the Hearthside included, allow servers to "grat" their foreign customers, or add a tip to the bill. Since this amount is added before the customers have a chance to tip or not tip, the practice amounts to an automatic penalty for imperfect English.) There are the two dirt-smudged lesbians, just off their construction shift, who are impressed enough by my suave handling of the fly in the piña colada that they take the time to praise me to Stu, the assistant manager. There's Sam, the kindly retired cop, who has to plug up his tracheotomy hole with one finger in order to force the cigarette smoke into his lungs.

Sometimes I play with the fantasy that I am a princess who, in penance for some tiny transgression, has undertaken to feed each of her subjects by hand. But the non-princesses working with me are just as indulgent, even when this means flouting management rules—concerning, for example, the number of croutons that can go on a salad (six). "Put on all you want," Gail whispers, "as long as Stu isn't looking." She dips into her own tip money to buy biscuits and gravy for an out-of-work mechanic who's used up all his money on dental surgery, inspiring me to pick up the tab for his milk and pie. Maybe the same high levels of agape can be found through-out the "hospitality industry." I remember the poster deco-rating one of the apartments I looked at, which said "If you seek happiness for yourself you will never find it. Only when you seek happiness for others will it come to you," or words to that effect—an odd sentiment, it seemed to me at the time, to find in the dank one-room basement apartment of a bellhop at the Best Western. At the Hearthside, we utilize whatever bits of autonomy we have to ply our customers with the illicit calories that signal our love. It is our job as servers to assemble the salads and desserts, pouring the dressing and squirting the whipped cream. We also control the number of butter patties our customers get and the amount of sour cream on their baked potatoes. So if you wonder why Americans are so obese, consider the fact that waitresses both express their humanity and earn their tips through the covert distribution of fats.

Ten days into it, this is beginning to look like a livable lifestyle. I like Gail, who is "looking at fifty" but moves so fast she can alight in one place and then another without apparently being anywhere between them. I clown around with Lionel, the teenage Haitian busboy, and catch a few fragments of conversation with Joan, the svelte fortyish hostess and militant feminist who is the only one of us who dares to tell Jack to shut the fuck up. I even warm up to Jack when, on a slow night and to make up for a particularly unwarranted attack on my abilities, or so I imagine, he tells me about his glory days as a young man at "coronary school"—or do you say "culinary"?—in Brooklyn, where he dated a knock-out Puerto Rican chick and learned everything there is to know about food. I finish up at 10:00 or 10:30, depending on how much side work I've been able to get done during the shift, and cruise home to the tapes I snatched at random when I left my real home—Marianne Faithfull, Tracy Chapman, Enigma, King Sunny Adé, the Violent Femmes—just drained enough for the music to set my cranium resonating, but hardly dead. Midnight snack is Wheat Thins and Monterey Jack, accompanied by cheap white wine on ice and whatever AMC has to offer. To bed by 1:30 or 2:00, up at 9:00 or 10:00, read for an hour while my uniform whirls around in the landlord's washing machine, and then it's another eight hours spent following Mao's central instruction, as laid out in the Little Red Book, which was: Serve the people.

I could drift along like this, in some dreamy proletarian idyll, except for two things. One is management. If I have kept this subject on the margins thus far it is because I still flinch to think that I spent all those weeks under the surveillance of men (and later women) whose job it was to monitor my behavior for signs of sloth, theft, drug abuse, or worse. Not that managers and especially "assistant managers" in low-wage settings like this are exactly the class enemy. In the restaurant business, they are mostly former cooks or servers, still capable of pinch-hitting in the kitchen or on the floor, just as in hotels they are likely to be former clerks, and paid a salary of only about $400 a week. But everyone knows they have crossed over to the other side, which is, crudely put, corporate as opposed to human. Cooks want to prepare tasty meals, servers want to serve them graciously, but managers are there for only one reason—to make sure that money is made for some theoretical entity that exists far away in Chicago or New York, if a corporation can be said to have a physical existence at all. Reflecting on her career, Gail tells me ruefully that she had sworn, years ago, never to work for a corporation again. "They don't cut you no slack. You give and you give, and they take."

Managers can sit—for hours at a time if they want—but it's their job to see that no one else ever does, even when there's nothing to do, and this is why, for servers, slow times can be as exhausting as rushes. You start dragging out each little chore, because if the manager on duty catches you in an idle moment, he will give you something far nastier to do. So I wipe, I clean, I consolidate ketchup bottles and recheck the cheesecake supply, even tour the tables to make sure the customer evaluation forms are all standing perkily in their places—wondering all the time how many calories I burn in these strictly theatrical exercises. When, on a particularly dead afternoon, Stu finds me glancing at a *USA Today* a customer has left behind, he assigns me to vacuum the entire floor with the broken vacuum cleaner that has a handle only two feet long, and the only way to do that without incurring orthopedic damage is to proceed from spot to spot on your knees.

On my first Friday at the Hearthside there is a "mandatory meeting for all restaurant employees," which I attend, eager for insight into our overall marketing strategy and the niche (your basic Ohio cuisine with a tropical twist?) we aim to inhabit. But there is no "we" at this meeting. Phillip, our top manager except for an occasional "consultant" sent out by corporate headquarters, opens it with a sneer: "The break room—it's disgusting. Butts in the ashtrays, newspapers lying around, crumbs." This windowless little room, which also houses the time clock for the entire hotel, is where we stash our bags and civilian clothes and take our half-hour meal breaks. But a break room is not a right, he tells us. It can be taken away. We should also know that the lockers in the break room and whatever is in them can be searched at any time. Then comes gossip; there has been gossip; gossip (which seems to mean employees talking among themselves) must stop. Off-duty employees are henceforth barred from eating at the restaurant, because "other servers gather around them and gossip." When Phillip has exhausted his agenda of rebukes, Joan complains about the condition of the ladies' room and I throw in my two bits about the vacuum cleaner. But I don't see any backup coming from my fellow servers, each of whom has subsided into her own personal funk; Gail, my role model, stares sorrowfully at a point six inches from her nose. The meeting ends when Andy, one of the cooks, gets up, muttering about breaking up his day off for this almighty bullshit.

Just four days later we are suddenly summoned into the kitchen at 3:30 P.M., even though there are live tables on the floor. We all—about ten of us—stand around Phillip, who announces grimly that there has been a report of some "drug activity" on the night shift and that, as a result, we are now to be a "drug-free" workplace, meaning that all new hires will be tested, as will possibly current employees on a random basis. I am glad that this part of the kitchen is so dark, because I find myself blushing as hard as if I had been caught toking up in the ladies' room myself: I haven't been treated this way—lined up in the corridor, threatened with locker searches, peppered with carelessly aimed accusations—since junior high school. Back on the floor, Joan cracks, "Next they'll be telling us we can't have sex on the job." When I ask Stu what happened to inspire the crackdown, he just mutters about "management decisions" and takes the opportunity to upbraid Gail and me for being too generous with the rolls. From now on there's to be only one per customer, and it goes out with the dinner, not with the salad. He's also been riding the cooks, prompting Andy to come out of the kitchen and observe—with the serenity of a man whose customary implement is a butcher knife—that "Stu has a death wish today."

Later in the evening, the gossip crystallizes around the theory that Stu is himself the drug culprit, that he uses the restaurant phone to order up marijuana and sends one of the late servers out to fetch it for him. The server was caught, and she may have ratted Stu out or at least said enough to cast some suspicion on him, thus accounting for his pissy behavior. Who knows? Lionel, the busboy, entertains us for the rest of the shift by standing just behind Stu's back and sucking deliriously on an imaginary joint.

The other problem, in addition to the less-than-nurturing management style, is that this job shows no sign of being financially viable. You might imagine, from a comfortable distance, that people who live, year in and year out, on $6 to $10 an hour have discovered some survival stratagems unknown to the middle class. But no. It's not hard to get my coworkers to talk about their living situations, because housing, in almost every case, is the principal source of disruption in their lives, the first thing they fill you in on when they arrive for their shifts. After a week, I have compiled the following survey:

- Gail is sharing a room in a well-known downtown flophouse for which she and a roommate pay about $250 a week. Her roommate, a male friend, has begun hitting on her, driving her nuts, but the rent would be impossible alone.

- Claude, the Haitian cook, is desperate to get out of the two-room apartment he shares with his girlfriend and two other, unrelated, people. As far as I can determine, the other Haitian men (most of whom only speak Creole) live in similarly crowded situations.

- Annette, a twenty-year-old server who is six months pregnant and has been abandoned by her boyfriend, lives with her mother, a postal clerk.

- Marianne and her boyfriend are paying $170 a week for a one-person trailer.

- Jack, who is, at $10 an hour, the wealthiest of us, lives in the trailer he owns, paying only the $400-a-month lot fee.

- The other white cook, Andy, lives on his dry-docked boat, which, as far as I can tell from his loving descriptions, can't be more than twenty feet long. He offers to take me out on it, once it's repaired, but the offer comes with inquiries as to my marital status, so I do not follow up on it.

- Tina and her husband are paying $60 a night for a double room in a Days Inn. This is because they have no car and the Days Inn is within walking distance of the Hearthside. When Marianne, one of the breakfast servers, is tossed out of her trailer for subletting (which is against the trailer-park rules), she leaves her boyfriend and moves in with Tina and her husband.

- Joan, who had fooled me with her numerous and tasteful outfits (hostesses wear their own clothes), lives in a van she parks behind a shopping center at night and showers in Tina's motel room. The clothes are from thrift shops.[4]

It strikes me, in my middle-class solipsism, that there is gross improvidence in some of these arrangements. When Gail and I are wrapping silverware in napkins—the only task for which we are permitted to sit—she tells me she is thinking of escaping from her roommate by moving into the Days Inn herself. I am astounded: How can she even think of paying $40 to $60 a day? But if I was afraid of sounding like a social worker, I come out just sounding like a fool. She squints at me in disbelief, "And where am I supposed to get a month's rent and a month's deposit for an apartment?" I'd been feeling pretty smug about my $500 efficiency, but of course it was made possible only by the $1,300 I had allotted myself for start-up costs when I began my low-wage life: $1,000 for the first month's rent and deposit, $100 for initial groceries and cash in my pocket, $200 stuffed away for emergencies. In poverty, as in certain propositions in physics, starting conditions are everything.

There are no secret economies that nourish the poor; on

---

4 I could find no statistics on the number of employed people living in cars or vans, but according to the National Coalition for the Homeless's 1997 report "Myths and Facts About Homelessness," nearly one in five homeless people (in twenty-nine cities across the nation) is employed in a full- or part-time job.

the contrary, there are a host of special costs. If you can't put up the two months' rent you need to secure an apartment, you end up paying through the nose for a room by the week. If you have only a room, with a hot plate at best, you can't save by cooking up huge lentil stews that can be frozen for the week ahead. You eat fast food, or the hot dogs and Styrofoam cups of soup that can be microwaved in a convenience store. If you have no money for health insurance—and the Hearthside's skimpy plan kicks in only after three months—you go without routine care or prescription drugs and end up paying the price. Gail, for example, was fine until she ran out of money for estrogen pills. She is supposed to be on the company plan by now, but they claim to have lost her application form and need to begin the paperwork all over again. So she spends $9 per migraine pill to control the headaches she wouldn't have, she insists, if her estrogen supplements were covered. Similarly, Marianne's boyfriend lost his job as a roofer because he missed so much time after getting a cut on his foot for which he couldn't afford the prescribed antibiotic.

My own situation, when I sit down to assess it after two weeks of work, would not be much better if this were my actual life. The seductive thing about waitressing is that you don't have to wait for payday to feel a few bills in your pocket, and my tips usually cover meals and gas, plus something left over to stuff into the kitchen drawer I use as a bank. But as the tourist business slows in the summer heat, I sometimes leave work with only $20 in tips (the gross is higher, but servers share about 15 percent of their tips with the busboys and bartenders). With wages included, this amounts to about the minimum wage of $5.15 an hour. Although the sum in the drawer is pilling up, at the present rate of accumulation it will be more than a hundred dollars short of my rent when the end of the month comes around. Nor can I see any expenses to cut. True, I haven't gone the lentil-stew route yet, but that's because I don't have a large cooking pot, pot holders, or a ladle to stir with (which would cost about $30 at Kmart, less at thrift stores), not to mention onions, carrots, and the indispensable bay leaf. I do make my lunch almost every day—usually some slow-burning, high-protein combo like frozen chicken patties with melted cheese on top and canned pinto beans on the side. Dinner is at the Hearthside, which offers its employees a choice of BLT, fish sandwich, or hamburger for only $2. The burger lasts longest, especially if it's heaped with gut-puckering jalapeños, but by midnight my stomach is growling again.

So unless I want to start using my car as a residence, I have to find a second, or alternative, job. I call all the hotels where I filled out housekeeping applications weeks ago—the Hyatt, Holiday Inn, Econo Lodge, HoJo's, Best Western, plus a half dozen or so locally run guesthouses. Nothing. Then I start making the rounds again, wasting whole mornings waiting for some assistant manager to show up, even dipping into places so creepy that the front-desk clerk greets you from behind bulletproof glass and sells pints of liquor over the counter. But either someone has exposed my real-life housekeeping habits—which are, shall we say, mellow—or I am at the wrong end of some infallible ethnic equation: most, but by no means all, of the working housekeepers I see on my job searches are African Americans,

Spanish-speaking, or immigrants from the Central European post-Communist world, whereas servers are almost invariably white and monolingually English-speaking. When I finally get a positive response, I have been identified once again as server material. Jerry's, which is part of a well-known national family restaurant chain and physically attached here to another budget hotel chain, is ready to use me at once. The prospect is both exciting and terrifying, because, with about the same number of tables and counter seats, Jerry's attracts three or four times the volume of customers as the gloomy old Hearthside.

Picture a fat person's hell, and I don't mean a place with no food. Instead there is everything you might eat if eating had no bodily consequences—cheese fries, chicken-fried steaks, fudge-laden desserts—only here every bite must be paid for, one way or another, in human discomfort. The kitchen is a cavern, a stomach leading to the lower intestine that is the garbage and dishwashing area, from which issue bizarre smells combining the edible and the offal: creamy carrion, pizza barf, and that unique and enigmatic Jerry's scent—citrus fart. The floor is slick with spills, forcing us to walk through the kitchen with tiny steps, like Susan McDougal in leg irons. Sinks everywhere are clogged with scraps of lettuce, decomposing lemon wedges, waterlogged toast crusts. Put your hand down on any counter and you risk being stuck to it by the film of ancient syrup spills, and this is unfortunate, because hands are utensils here, used for scooping up lettuce onto salad plates, lifting out pie slices, and even moving hash browns from one plate to another. The regulation poster in the single unisex restroom admonishes us to wash our hands thoroughly and even offers instructions for doing so, but there is always some vital substance missing—soap, paper towels, toilet paper—and I never find all three at once. You learn to stuff your pockets with napkins before going in there, and too bad about the customers, who must eat, though they don't realize this, almost literally out of our hands.

The break room typifies the whole situation: there is none, because there are no breaks at Jerry's. For six to eight hours in a row, you never sit except to pee. Actually, there are three folding chairs at a table immediately adjacent to the bathroom, but hardly anyone ever sits here, in the very rectum of the gastro-architectural system. Rather, the function of the peritoilet area is to house the ashtrays in which servers and dishwashers leave their cigarettes burning at all times, like votive candles, so that they don't have to waste time lighting up again when they dash back for a puff. Almost everyone smokes as if his or her pulmonary well-being depended on it—the multinational mélange of cooks, the Czech dishwashers, the servers, who are all native-born American—creating an atmosphere in which oxygen is only an occasional pollutant. My first morning at Jerry's, when the hypoglycemic shakes set in, I complain to one of my fellow servers that I don't understand how she can go so long without food. "Well, I don't understand how you can go so long without a cigarette," she responds in a tone of reproach—because work is what you do for others; smoking is what you do for yourself. I don't know why the anti-smoking crusaders have never grasped the element of defiant self-nurturance that makes the habit so endearing to its victims—as if, in the American workplace, the only thing people have to call their own is the tumors they are nourishing and the spare moments they devote to feeding them.

Now, the Industrial Revolution is not an easy transition, especially when you have to zip through it in just a couple of days. I have gone from craft work straight into the factory, from the air-conditioned morgue of the Hearthside directly into the flames. Customers arrive in human waves, sometimes disgorged fifty at a time from their tour buses, peckish and whiny. Instead of two "girls" on the floor at once, there can be as many as six of us running around in our brilliant pink-and-orange Hawaiian shirts. Conversations, either with customers or fellow employees, seldom last more than twenty seconds at a time. On my first day, in fact, I am hurt by my sister servers' coldness. My mentor for the day is an emotionally uninflected twenty-three-year-old, and the others, who gossip a little among themselves about the real reason someone is out sick today and the size of the bail bond someone else has had to pay, ignore me completely. On my second day, I find out why. "Well, it's good to see you again," one of them says in greeting. "Hardly anyone comes back after the first day." I feel powerfully vindicated—a survivor—but it would take a long time, probably months, before I could hope to be accepted into this sorority.

I start out with the beautiful, heroic idea of handling the two jobs at once, and for two days I almost do it: the breakfast/lunch shift at Jerry's, which goes till 2:00, arriving at the Hearthside at 2:10, and attempting to hold out until 10:00. In the ten minutes between jobs, I pick up a spicy chicken sandwich at the Wendy's drive-through window, gobble it down in the car, and change from khaki slacks to black, from Hawaiian to rust polo. There is a problem, though. When during the 3:00 to 4:00 P.M. dead time I finally sit down to wrap silver, my flesh seems to bond to the seat. I try to refuel with a purloined cup of soup, as I've seen Gail and Joan do dozens of times, but a manager catches me and hisses "No eating!" though there's not a customer around to be offended by the sight of food making contact with a server's lips. So I tell Gail I'm going to quit, and she hugs me and says she might just follow me to Jerry's herself.

But the chances of this are minuscule. She has left the flophouse and her annoying roommate and is back to living in her beat-up old truck. But, guess what? she reports to me excitedly later that evening: Phillip has given her permission to park overnight in the hotel parking lot, as long as she keeps out of sight, and the parking lot should be totally safe, since it's patrolled by a hotel security guard! With the Hearthside offering benefits like that, how could anyone think of leaving?

Gail would have triumphed at Jerry's, I'm sure, but for me it's a crash course in exhaustion management. Years ago, the kindly fry cook who trained me to waitress at a Los Angeles truck stop used to say: Never make an unnecessary trip; if you don't have to walk fast, walk slow; if you don't have to walk, stand. But at Jerry's the effort of distinguishing necessary from unnecessary and urgent from whenever would itself be too much of an energy drain. The only thing to do is to treat each shift as a one-time-only emergency: you've got fifty starving people out there, lying scattered on the battlefield, so get out there and feed them! Forget that you will have to do this again tomorrow, forget that you will have to be alert enough to dodge the drunks on the drive home tonight—just burn, burn, burn! Ideally, at some point you enter what servers call "a rhythm" and psychologists term a "flow state," in which signals pass from the sense organs directly to the muscles, bypassing the cerebral cortex, and a Zen-like emptiness sets in. A male server from the Hearthside's morning shift tells me about the time he "pulled a triple"—three shifts in a row, all the way around the clock—and then got off and had a drink and met this girl, and maybe he shouldn't tell me this, but they had sex right then and there, and it was like, beautiful.

But there's another capacity of the neuromuscular system, which is pain. I start tossing back drugstore-brand ibuprofen pills as if they were vitamin C, four before each shift, because an old mouse-related repetitive-stress injury in my upper back has come back to full-spasm strength, thanks to the tray carrying. In my ordinary life, this level of disability might justify a day of ice packs and stretching. Here I comfort myself with the Aleve commercial in which the cute blue-collar guy asks: If you quit after working four hours, what would your boss say? And the not-so-cute blue-collar guy, who's lugging a metal beam on his back, answers: He'd fire me, that's what. But fortunately, the commercial tells us, we workers can exert the same kind of authority over our painkillers that our bosses exert over us. If Tylenol doesn't want to work for more than four hours, you just fire its ass and switch to Aleve.

True, I take occasional breaks from this life, going home now and then to catch up on e-mail and for conjugal visits (though I am careful to "pay" for anything I eat there), seeing *The Truman Show* with friends and letting them buy my ticket. And I still have those what-am-I-doing-here moments at work, when I get so homesick for the printed word that I obsessively reread the six-page menu. But as the days go by, my old life is beginning to look exceedingly strange. The e-mails and phone messages addressed to my former self come from a distant race of people with exotic concerns and far too much time on their hands. The neighborly market I used to cruise for produce now looks forbiddingly like a Manhattan yuppie emporium. And when I sit down one morning in my real home to pay bills from my past life, I am dazzled by the two- and three-figure sums owed to outfits like Club Body Tech and Amazon.com.

Management at Jerry's is generally calmer and more "professional" than at the Hearthside, with two exceptions. One is Joy, a plump, blowsy woman in her early thirties, who once kindly devoted several minutes to instructing me in the correct one-handed method of carrying trays but whose moods change disconcertingly from shift to shift and even within one. Then there's B.J., aka B.J.-the-bitch, whose contribution is to stand by the kitchen counter and yell, "Nita, your order's up, move it!" or "Barbara, didn't you see you've got another table out there? Come on, girl!" Among other things, she is hated for having replaced the whipped-cream squirt cans with big plastic whipped-cream-filled baggies that have to be squeezed with both hands—because, reportedly, she saw or thought she saw employees trying to inhale the propellant gas from the squirt cans, in the hope that it might be nitrous oxide. On my third night, she pulls me aside abruptly and brings her face so close that it looks as if she's planning to butt me with her forehead. But instead of saying, "You're fired," she says, "You're doing fine." The only trouble is I'm spending time chatting with customers: "That's how they're getting you." Furthermore I am letting them "run me," which means harassment by sequential demands: you bring the ketchup and they decide they want extra Thousand Island; you bring that and they announce they now need a side of fries; and so on into distraction. Finally she tells me not to take her wrong. She tries to say things in a nice way, but you get into a mode, you know, because everything has to move so fast.[5]

I mumble thanks for the advice, feeling like I've just been stripped naked by the crazed enforcer of some ancient sumptuary law: No chatting for you, girl. No fancy service ethic allowed for the serfs. Chatting with customers is for the beautiful young college-educated servers in the downtown carpaccio joints, the kids who can make $70 to $100 a night. What had I been thinking? My job is to move

---

5   In *Workers in a Lean World: Unions in the International Economy* (Verso, 1997), Kim Moody cites studies finding an increase in stress-related workplace injuries and illness between the mid-1980s and the early 1990s. He argues that rising stress levels reflect a new system of "management by stress," in which workers in a variety of industries are being squeezed to extract maximum productivity, to the detriment of their health.

orders from tables to kitchen and then trays from kitchen to tables. Customers are, in fact, the major obstacle to the smooth transformation of information into food and food into money—they are, in short, the enemy. And the painful thing is that I'm beginning to see it this way myself. There are the traditional asshole types—frat boys who down multiple Buds and then make a fuss because the steaks are so emaciated and the fries so sparse—as well as the variously impaired—due to age, diabetes, or literacy issues—who require patient nutritional counseling. The worst, for some reason, are the Visible Christians—like the ten-person table, all jolly and sanctified after Sunday-night service, who run me mercilessly and then leave me $1 on a $92 bill. Or the guy with the crucifixion T-shirt (SOMEONE TO LOOK UP TO) who complains that his baked potato is too hard and his iced tea too icy (I cheerfully fix both) and leaves no tip. As a general rule, people wearing crosses or WWJD? (What Would Jesus Do?) buttons look at us disapprovingly no matter what we do, as if they were confusing waitressing with Mary Magdalene's original profession.

I make friends, over time, with the other "girls" who work my shift: Nita, the tattooed twenty-something who taunts us by going around saying brightly, "Have we started making money yet?" Ellen, whose teenage son cooks on the graveyard shift and who once managed a restaurant in Massachusetts but won't try out for management here because she prefers being a "common worker" and not "ordering people around." Easy-going fiftyish Lucy, with the raucous laugh, who limps toward the end of the shift because of something that has gone wrong with her leg, the exact nature of which cannot be determined without health insurance. We talk about the usual girl things—men, children, and the sinister allure of Jerry's chocolate peanut-butter cream pie—though no one, I notice, ever brings up anything potentially expensive, like shopping or movies. As at the Hearthside, the only recreation ever referred to is partying, which requires little more than some beer, a joint, and a few close friends. Still, no one here is homeless, or cops to it anyway, thanks usually to a working husband or boyfriend. All in all, we form a reliable mutual-support group: If one of us is feeling sick or overwhelmed, another one will "bev" a table or even carry trays for her. If one of us is off sneaking a cigarette or a pee,[6] the others will do their best to conceal her absence from the enforcers of corporate rationality.

But my saving human connection—my oxytocin receptor, as it were—is George, the nineteen-year-old, fresh-off-the-boat Czech dishwasher. We get to talking when he asks me, tortuously, how much cigarettes cost at Jerry's. I do my best to explain that they cost over a dollar more here than

---

6 Until April 1998, there was no federally mandated right to bathroom breaks. According to Marc Linder and Ingrid Nygaard, authors of *Void Where Prohibited: Rest Breaks and the Right to Urinate on Company Time* (Cornell University Press, 1997), "The right to rest and void at work is not high on the list of social or political causes supported by professional or executive employees, who enjoy personal workplace liberties that millions of factory workers can only daydream about....While we were dismayed to discover that workers lacked an acknowledged legal right to void at work, [the workers] were amazed by outsiders' naïve belief that their employers would permit them to perform this basic bodily function when necessary....A factory worker, not allowed a break for six-hour stretches, voided into pads worn inside her uniform; and a kindergarten teacher in a school without aides had to take all twenty children with her to the bathroom and line them up outside the stall door when she voided."

at a regular store and suggest that he just take one from the half-filled packs that are always lying around on the break table. But that would be unthinkable. Except for the one tiny earring signaling his allegiance to some vaguely alternative point of view, George is a perfect straight arrow—crew-cut, hardworking, and hungry for eye contact. "Czech Republic," I ask, "or Slovakia?" and he seems delighted that I know the difference. "Václav Havel," I try, "Velvet Revolution, Frank Zappa?" "Yes, yes, 1989," he says, and I realize we are talking about history.

My project is to teach George English. "How are you today, George?" I say at the start of each shift. "I am good, and how are you today, Barbara?" I learn that he is not paid by Jerry's but by the "agent" who shipped him over—$5 an hour, with the agent getting the dollar or so difference between that and what Jerry's pays dishwashers. I learn also that he shares an apartment with a crowd of other Czech "dishers," as he calls them, and that he cannot sleep until one of them goes off for his shift, leaving a vacant bed. We are having one of our ESL sessions late one afternoon when B.J. catches us at it and orders "Joseph" to take up the rubber mats on the floor near the dishwashing sinks and mop underneath. "I thought your name was George," I say loud enough for B.J. to hear as she strides off back to the counter. Is she embarrassed? Maybe a little, because she greets me back at the counter with "George, Joseph—there are so many of them!" I say nothing, neither nodding nor smiling, and for this I am punished later when I think I am ready to go and she announces that I need to roll fifty more sets of silverware and isn't it time

I mixed up a fresh four-gallon batch of blue-cheese dressing? May you grow old in this place, B.J., is the curse I beam out at her when I am finally permitted to leave. May the syrup spills glue your feet to the floor.

I make the decision to move closer to Key West. First, because of the drive. Second and third, also because of the drive: gas is eating up $4 to $5 a day, and although Jerry's is as high-volume as you can get, the tips average only 10 percent, and not just for a newbie like me. Between the base pay of $2.15 an hour and the obligation to share tips with the busboys and dishwashers, we're averaging only about $7.50 an hour. Then there is the $30 I had to spend on the regulation tan slacks worn by Jerry's servers—a setback it could take weeks to absorb. (I had combed the town's two downscale department stores hoping for something cheaper but decided in the end that these marked-down Dockers, originally $49, were more likely to survive a daily washing.) Of my fellow servers, everyone who lacks a working husband or boyfriend seems to have a second job: Nita does something at a computer eight hours a day; another welds. Without the forty-five-minute commute, I can picture myself working two jobs and having the time to shower between them.

So I take the $500 deposit I have coming from my landlord, the $400 I have earned toward the next month's rent, plus the $200 reserved for emergencies, and use the $1,100 to pay the rent and deposit on trailer number 46 in the Overseas Trailer Park, a mile from the cluster of budget hotels that constitute Key West's version of an industrial park. Number 46 is about eight feet in width and shaped like a barbell inside, with a narrow region—because of the sink and the stove—separating the bedroom from what might optimistically be called the "living" area, with its two-person table and half-sized couch. The bathroom is so small my knees rub against the shower stall when I sit on the toilet, and you can't just leap out of the bed, you have to climb down to the foot of it in order to find a patch of floor space to stand on. Outside, I am within a few yards of a liquor store, a bar that advertises "free beer tomorrow," a convenience store, and a Burger King—but no supermarket or, alas, laundromat. By reputation, the Overseas park is a nest of crime and crack, and I am hoping at least for some vibrant multicultural street life. But desolation rules night and day, except for a thin stream of pedestrian traffic heading for their jobs at the Sheraton or 7-Eleven. There are not exactly people here but what amounts to canned labor, being preserved from the heat between shifts.

In line with my reduced living conditions, a new form of ugliness arises at Jerry's. First we are confronted—via an announcement on the computers through which we input orders—with the new rule that the hotel bar is henceforth off-limits to restaurant employees. The culprit, I learn through the grapevine, is the ultra-efficient gal who trained me—another trailer-home dweller and a mother of three. Something had set her off one morning, so she slipped out for a nip and returned to the floor impaired. This mostly hurts Ellen, whose habit it is to free her hair from its rubber band and drop by the bar for a couple of Zins before heading home at the end of the shift, but all of us feel the chill.

Then the next day, when I go for straws, for the first time I find the dry-storage room locked. Ted, the portly assistant manager who opens it for me, explains that he caught one of the dishwashers attempting to steal something, and, unfortunately, the miscreant will be with us until a replacement can be found—hence the locked door. I neglect to ask what he had been trying to steal, but Ted tells me who he is—the kid with the buzz cut and the earring. You know, he's back there right now.

I wish I could say I rushed back and confronted George to get his side of the story. I wish I could say I stood up to Ted and insisted that George be given a translator and allowed to defend himself, or announced that I'd find a lawyer who'd handle the case pro bono. The mystery to me is that there's not much worth stealing in the dry-storage room, at least not in any fenceable quantity: "Is Gyorgi here, and am having 200—maybe—250 ketchup packets. What do you say?" My guess is that he had taken—if he had taken anything at all—some Saltines or a can of cherry-pie mix, and that the motive for taking it was hunger.

So why didn't I intervene? Certainly not because I was held back by the kind of moral paralysis that can pass as journalistic objectivity. On the contrary, something new—something loathsome and servile—had infected me, along with the kitchen odors that I could still sniff on my bra when I finally undressed at night. In real life I am moderately brave, but plenty of brave people shed their courage in concentration camps, and maybe something similar goes on in the infinitely more congenial milieu of the low-wage American workplace. Maybe, in a month or two more at

Jerry's, I might have regained my crusading spirit. Then again, in a month or two I might have turned into a different person altogether—say, the kind of person who would have turned George in.

But this is not something I am slated to find out. When my month-long plunge into poverty is almost over, I finally land my dream job—housekeeping. I do this by walking into the personnel office of the only place I figure I might have some credibility, the hotel attached to Jerry's, and confiding urgently that I have to have a second job if I am to pay my rent and, no, it couldn't be front-desk clerk. "All right," the personnel lady fairly spits, "So it's housekeeping," and she marches me back to meet Maria, the housekeeping manager, a tiny, frenetic Hispanic woman who greets me as "babe" and hands me a pamphlet emphasizing the need for a positive attitude. The hours are nine in the morning till whenever, the pay is $6.10 an hour, and there's one week of vacation a year. I don't have to ask about health insurance once I meet Carlotta, the middle-aged African-American woman who will be training me. Carla, as she tells me to call her, is missing all of her top front teeth.

On that first day of housekeeping and last day of my entire project—although I don't yet know it's the last—Carla is in a foul mood. We have been given nineteen rooms to clean, most of them "checkouts," as opposed to "stay-overs," that require the whole enchilada of bed-stripping, vacuuming, and bathroom-scrubbing. When one of the rooms that had been listed as a stay-over turns out to be a checkout, Carla calls Maria to complain, but of course to no avail. "So make up the motherfucker," Carla orders me, and I do the beds while she sloshes around the bathroom. For four hours without a break I strip and remake beds, taking about four and a half minutes per queen-sized bed, which I could get down to three if there were any reason to. We try to avoid vacuuming by picking up the larger specks by hand, but often there is nothing to do but drag the monstrous vacuum cleaner—it weighs about thirty pounds—off our cart and try to wrestle it around the floor. Sometimes Carla hands me the squirt bottle of "BAM" (an acronym for something that begins, ominously, with "butyric"; the rest has been worn off the label) and lets me do the bathrooms. No service ethic challenges me here to new heights of performance. I just concentrate on removing the pubic hairs from the bathtubs, or at least the dark ones that I can see.

I had looked forward to the breaking-and-entering aspect of cleaning the stay-overs, the chance to examine the secret, physical existence of strangers. But the contents of the rooms are always banal and surprisingly neat—zipped up shaving kits, shoes lined up against the wall (there are no closets), flyers for snorkeling trips, maybe an empty wine bottle or two. It is the TV that keeps us going, from *Jerry* to *Sally* to *Hawaii Five-O* and then on to the soaps. If there's something especially arresting, like "Won't Take No for an Answer" on *Jerry*, we sit down on the edge of a bed and giggle for a moment as if this were a pajama party instead of a terminally dead-end job. The soaps are the best, and Carla turns the volume up full blast so that she won't miss anything from the bathroom or while the vacuum is on. In room 503, Marcia confronts Jeff about

Lauren. In 505, Lauren taunts poor cuckolded Marcia. In 511, Helen offers Amanda $10,000 to stop seeing Eric, prompting Carla to emerge from the bathroom to study Amanda's troubled face. "You take it, girl," she advises. "I would for sure."

The tourists' rooms that we clean and, beyond them, the far more expensively appointed interiors in the soaps, begin after a while to merge. We have entered a better world—a world of comfort where every day is a day off, waiting to be filled up with sexual intrigue. We, however, are only gate-crashers in this fantasy, forced to pay for our presence with backaches and perpetual thirst. The mirrors, and there are far too many of them in hotel rooms, contain the kind of person you would normally find pushing a shopping cart down a city street—bedraggled, dressed in a damp hotel polo shirt two sizes too large, and with sweat dribbling down her chin like drool. I am enormously relieved when Carla announces a half-hour meal break, but my appetite fades when I see that the bag of hot-dog rolls she has been carrying around on our cart is not trash salvaged from a checkout but what she has brought for her lunch.

When I request permission to leave at about 3:30, another housekeeper warns me that no one has so far succeeded in combining housekeeping at the hotel with serving at Jerry's: "Some kid did it once for five days, and you're no kid." With that helpful information in mind, I rush back to number 46, down four Advils (the name brand this time), shower, stooping to fit into the stall, and attempt to compose myself for the oncoming shift. So much for what Marx termed the "reproduction of labor power," meaning the things a worker has to do just so she'll be ready to work again. The only unforeseen obstacle to the smooth transition from job to job is that my tan Jerry's slacks, which had looked reasonably clean by 40-watt bulb last night when I handwashed my Hawaiian shirt, prove by daylight to be mottled with ketchup and ranch-dressing stains. I spend most of my hour-long break between jobs attempting to remove the edible portions with a sponge and then drying the slacks over the hood of my car in the sun.

I can do this two-job thing, is my theory, if I can drink enough caffeine and avoid getting distracted by George's ever more obvious suffering.[7] The first few days after being caught, he seemed not to understand the trouble he was in, and our chirpy little conversations had continued. But the last couple of shifts he's been listless and unshaven, and tonight he looks like the ghost we all know him to be, with dark half-moons hanging from his eyes. At one point, when I am briefly immobilized by the task of filling little paper cups with sour cream for baked potatoes, he comes over and looks as if he'd like to explore the limits of our shared vocabulary, but I am called to the floor for a table. I re-solve to give him all my tips that night, and to hell with

---

7   In 1996 the number of persons holding two or more jobs averaged 7.8 million, or 6.2 percent of the workforce. It was about the same rate for men and for women (6.1 versus 6.2), though the kinds of jobs differ by gender. About two-thirds of multiple jobholders work one job full-time and the other part-time. Only a heroic minority—4 percent of men and 2 percent of women—work two full-time jobs simultaneously (From John F. Stinson Jr., "New Data on Multiple Jobholding Available from the CPS," in the *Monthly Labor Review,* March 1997).

the experiment in low-wage money management. At eight, Ellen and I grab a snack together standing at the mephitic end of the kitchen counter, but I can only manage two or three mozzarella sticks and lunch had been a mere handful of McNuggets. I am not tired at all, I assure myself, though it may be that there is simply no more "I" left to do the tiredness monitoring. What I would see, if I were more alert to the situation, is that the forces of destruction are already massing against me. There is only one cook on duty, a young man named Jesus ("Hay-Sue," that is) and he is new to the job. And there is Joy, who shows up to take over in the middle of the shift, wearing high heels and a long, clingy white dress and fuming as if she'd just been stood up in some cocktail bar.

Then it comes, the perfect storm. Four of my tables fill up at once. Four tables is nothing for me now, but only so long as they are obligingly staggered. As I bev table 27, tables 25, 28, and 24 are watching enviously. As I bev 25, 24 glowers because their bevs haven't even been ordered. Twenty-eight is four yuppyish types, meaning everything on the side and agonizing instructions as to the chicken Caesars. Twenty-five is a middle-aged black couple, who complain, with some justice, that the iced tea isn't fresh and the tabletop is sticky. But table 24 is the meteorological event of the century: ten British tourists who seem to have made the decision to absorb the American experience entirely by mouth. Here everyone has at least two drinks— iced tea and milk shake, Michelob and water (with lemon slice, please)—and a huge, promiscuous orgy of breakfast specials, mozz sticks, chicken strips, quesadillas, burgers with cheese and without, sides of hash browns with cheddar, with onions, with gravy, seasoned fries, plain fries, banana splits. Poor Jesus! Poor me! Because when I arrive with their first tray of food—after three prior trips just to refill bevs—Princess Di refuses to eat her chicken strips with her pancake-and-sausage special, since, as she now reveals, the strips were meant to be an appetizer. Maybe the others would have accepted their meals, but Di, who is deep into her third Michelob, insists that everything else go back while they work on their starters. Meanwhile, the yuppies are waving me down for more decaf and the black couple looks ready to summon the NAACP.

Much of what happened next is lost in the fog of war. Jesus starts going under. The little printer on the counter in front of him is spewing out orders faster than he can rip them off, much less produce the meals. Even the invincible Ellen is ashen from stress. I bring table 24 their reheated main courses, which they immediately reject as either too cold or fossilized by the microwave. When I return to the kitchen with their trays (three trays in three trips), Joy confronts me with arms akimbo: "What is this?" She means the food—the plates of rejected pancakes, hash browns in assorted flavors, toasts, burgers, sausages, eggs. "Uh, scrambled with cheddar," I try, "and that's…" "NO," she screams in my face. "Is it a traditional, a super-scramble, an eye-opener?" I pretend to study my check for a clue, but entropy has been up to its tricks, not only on the plates but in my head, and I have to admit that the original order is beyond reconstruction. "You don't know an eye-opener from a traditional?" she demands in outrage. All I know, in fact, is that my legs have lost interest in the current venture and have announced their intention to fold. I am saved by a yuppie (mercifully not one of mine) who chooses this moment to charge into the kitchen to bellow that his food is twenty-five minutes late. Joy screams at him to get the hell out of her kitchen, please, and then turns on Jesus in a fury, hurling an empty tray across the room for emphasis.

I leave. I don't walk out, I just leave. I don't finish my side work or pick up my credit-card tips, if any, at the cash register or, of course, ask Joy's permission to go. And the surprising thing is that you *can* walk out without permission, that the door opens, that the thick tropical night air parts to let me pass, that my car is still parked where I left it. There is no vindication in this exit, no fuck-you surge of relief, just an overwhelming dank sense of failure pressing down on me and the entire parking lot. I had gone into this venture in the spirit of science, to test a mathematical proposition, but somewhere along the line, in the tunnel vision imposed by long shifts and relentless concentration, it became a test of myself, and clearly I have failed. Not only had I flamed out as a housekeeper/server, I had even forgotten to give George my tips, and, for reasons perhaps best known to hardworking, generous people like Gail and Ellen, this hurts. I don't cry, but I am in a position to realize, for the first time in many years, that the tear ducts are still there, and still capable of doing their job.

*   *   *

When I moved out of the trailer park, I gave the key to number 46 to Gail and arranged for my deposit to be transferred to her. She told me that Joan is still living in her van and that Stu had been fired from the Hearthside. I never found out what happened to George.

In one month, I had earned approximately $1,040 and spent $517 on food, gas, toiletries, laundry, phone, and utilities. If I had remained in my $500 efficiency, I would have been able to pay the rent and have $22 left over (which is $78 less than the cash I had in my pocket at the start of the month). During this time I bought no clothing except for the required slacks and no prescription drugs or medical care (I did finally buy some vitamin B to compensate for the lack of vegetables in my diet). Perhaps I could have saved a little on food if I had gotten to a supermarket more often, instead of convenience stores, but it should be noted that I lost almost four pounds in four weeks, on a diet weighted heavily toward burgers and fries.

How former welfare recipients and single mothers will (and do) survive in the low-wage workforce, I cannot imagine. Maybe they will figure out how to condense their lives—including child-raising, laundry, romance, and meals—into the couple of hours between full-time jobs. Maybe they will take up residence in their vehicles, if they have one. All I know is that I couldn't hold two jobs and I couldn't make enough money to live on with one. And I had advantages unthinkable to many of the long-term poor—health, stamina, a working car, and no children to care for and support. Certainly nothing in my experience contradicts the conclusion of Kathryn Edin and Laura

Lein, in their recent book *Making Ends Meet: How Single Mothers Survive Welfare and Low-Wage Work*, that low-wage work actually involves more hardship and deprivation than life at the mercy of the welfare state. In the coming months and years, economic conditions for the working poor are bound to worsen, even without the almost inevitable recession. As mentioned earlier, the influx of former welfare recipients into the low-skilled workforce will have a depressing effect on both wages and the number of jobs available. A general economic downturn will only enhance these effects, and the working poor will of course be facing it without the slight, but nonetheless often saving, protection of welfare as a backup.

The thinking behind welfare reform was that even the humblest jobs are morally uplifting and psychologically buoying. In reality they are likely to be fraught with insult and stress. But I did discover one redeeming feature of the most abject low-wage work—the camaraderie of people who are, in almost all cases, far too smart and funny and caring for the work they do and the wages they're paid. The hope, of course, is that someday these people will come to know what they're worth, and take appropriate action.

HOW YOU CAN SAVE WALL STREET

Mother Jones, 1988

Way back when the Dow Jones first melted down, dozens of important men in pinstriped suits gathered outside the White House to chant: "Wake up, sir! Give us leadership! Quickly, please, before we go back to our fortieth-story offices and hurl our well-nourished bodies onto the Street!" This was foolish, and not just because President Reagan was tied up in his office, memorizing the names of his close friends and cabinet members.

It was foolish because in a free-enterprise system, the economy is none of the president's business. In fact, that is the very definition of the free-enterprise system, which should perhaps be called the "free-president system," since it leaves the president free of all responsibility for the economically anguished, whether they appear at the White House gates in pinstripes or overalls or secondhand blankets.

A free-enterprise economy depends only on *markets*, and, according to the most advanced mathematical macroeconomic theory, markets depend only on *moods*: specifically, the mood of the men in the pinstripes, also known as the Boys on the Street. When the Boys are in a good mood, the market thrives; when they get scared or sullen, it is time for each one of us to look into the retail apple business. For as Franklin Delano Roosevelt once said, "We have nothing to be moody about except a bad mood itself, especially when it strikes someone richer than us."

And what is responsible for the mood of the Boys on the Street? Their wives, their valets, their blood-sugar levels? No; *you* are responsible, because in free enterprise, individual is paramount. What you do in the next few hours will determine whether a few thousand key men on Wall Street have, as we like to say, a nice day. And if *they* don't have a nice day, it'll be 1933 all over again, and you might as well head to the freight yards and check into a nice clean boxcar before the crowd gets there.

Abbie Hoffman had the right idea in 1967, when he and some fellow Yippies gathered in the gallery of the New York Stock Exchange and tossed dollar bills into the pit. At the time, this gesture was widely interpreted as guerrilla theater—some crazed radical attempt at social satire. Actually, it was a desperate and earnest effort to save the economy by propitiating the gods of the market—that is, the Boys in the pit—with their favorite substance. And it worked! They were pleased! They picked up the bills and used them to wipe the perspiration from their furrowed brows. Then they smiled; and they bought low, and they sold high, and the economy surged ahead.

I would say, do it again—change your savings into small bills and toss them like confetti at the men in the pit. Only today it wouldn't work, because although dollars fall very fast, these days they are practically weightless, and the Boys on the Street might be depressed to be in a blizzard of paper worth only pennies in yen or Deutsche Marks. No, you have to be more clever these days, more subtle—which is why I have prepared the following guidelines on What You Can Do to Stabilize World Markets and Guarantee Global Prosperity:

Rule 1: Spend. Now is the time to buy everything you have ever needed or wanted, from a two-dollar porn magazine to a dwarf-shaped hitching post for the front lawn. The reason is that every dollar you spend is a vote of confidence for our free-enterprise economy. Every dollar you spend helps employ someone—in the pornography or lawn-statuary industry or wherever—so that they, too, are enabled to spend. Then the men on Wall Street, sensing the groundswell of confidence around them, will feel happy and confident themselves. Except that…

Reckless consumer spending created our scandalous $2.5 trillion level of personal debt, which alarms certain key men in Tokyo and Bonn, who in turn are likely to call the men on Wall Street and say, "Whaddya got going there, fellas, a Third-World country?" which will bring gloom to Wall Street and penury to the rest of us. Which brings us to:

Rule 2: Save. Sell all your belongings and put the money into a bank, where it will quickly become available to the Boys on the Street for the purposes of leveraged buyouts, corporate takeovers, and other activities that keep them distracted. If you feel queasy about giving up your furniture to provide a larger kitty for those jumpy fellows on the Street, stuff all your assets into a cookie jar. This will help drive up interest rates and make America a more attractive investment to Bonn. However...

The merest upward flutter of interest rates could savage the bond market and reduce the Boys on the Street to craven terror, so it would probably be better to:

Rule 3: Invest all assets in an export-oriented industry—such as nuclear missiles or infant-formula mix. This will shift the balance of trade in our favor and bring cheer to the Boys on the Street. If you have trouble thinking of something that American corporations still know how to produce that someone in the world still might want to buy, remember the pioneering example of pet rocks and the great untapped market of southern Sudan. But be careful not to:

Shift the balance of trade so far in our favor that you upset Toshiba and Mercedes, which means Tokyo and Bonn, so...

"But wait!" you say. "Why should 200 million people pander to the mood swings of a few thousand addicted gamblers?" But that's free enterprise, friends: freedom to gamble and freedom to lose. And the great thing—the truly democratic thing about it—is that you don't even have to be a player to lose.

S&M AS PUBLIC POLICY

The Guardian, 1993

Welfare may turn out to be the domestic equivalent of Saddam Hussein. Already, leading pundits have declared it to be a crucial test of Bill Clinton's manhood: Will he be tough enough to crack down on those lazy sluts who insist on living off government funds, as legions of tweed-jacketed policy wonks demand? Or will he cave in to the welfare wimps—such as, presumably, Donna Shalala—with their squeamish aversion to mass starvation? Meanwhile, no one seems to have noticed that there is an ingenious, low-cost solution that has the potential to please both sides: Allow welfare recipients to continue to collect their miserly checks, but require that they submit, periodically, to public floggings.

Distasteful? Perhaps, but punishment has become a major cultural theme of our time. Consider Madonna's oeuvre, with its emphasis on bondage and whips. Or listen to the nation's leading pundits, as they jump up and down, much like masochists at a sex orgy, demanding that Clinton give us "pain and sacrifice!" On account of the deficit, the reasoning goes, what America needs now is a good sound "spankie." And who better to take the punishment than a social group that has no money, no friends in high places, and not a speck of political clout?

Everyone from neoliberal to neoconservative agrees that something must be done. It's not so much the money (welfare consumes only 1 percent of the federal budget) as the principle of the thing. In dozens of universities and think tanks, scholarly males grow apoplectic at the thought of fifteen-year-olds using pregnancy to get their first rent-free studio apartments. Hence the widespread excitement over Clinton's campaign proposal to limit welfare to two years, during which the recipients will be treated to job training and child care, and after which they will have to scavenge for food as they may.

But a program of welfare plus floggings makes far more sense in every way. First, it will be no less effective at curing poverty than any amount of job training and forced work experience. For decades now, welfare recipients have been subjected to dozens of workfare and work-incentive programs. They have been taught how to dress for job interviews, how to find their way through the want ads, how to process words and tote up numbers. The effects, as now even the most ardent welfare hawks acknowledge, have been negligible: only minuscule gains in income and an inevitable drift back to the welfare rolls. This is not because welfare recipients are incorrigibly lazy. In a labor market where 18 percent of workers already toil full time, year-round, to earn less than poverty-level wages, there are few vacant jobs that offer a living wage, especially women with child-care problems.

Second, the welfare-plus-floggings program will be far cheaper than any work program so far devised. The conservative estimate is that it would cost $50 billion a year to ready the welfare population for the labor market—roughly twice what is spent on welfare in its present form—and that about half of this sum will be spent on child care. So what will really be accomplished by getting welfare recipients trained and out of their houses? The ten million children on welfare, who are now cared for by their mothers at home, will instead be cared for by other poor women called child-care workers—while the mothers take up data entry and burger flipping. The net result, needless to say, will be a surge of commuting among the preschool set.

But the real beauty of the welfare-plus-floggings approach is that it will provide an outlet for the punitive rage now directed at the down-and-out. In a curious inversion of the Sermon on the Mount, no social group attracts more ire than the vaguely termed "underclass." The need to punish the poor is, of course, already built into the present welfare system, which insists that recipients travel from one government office to another, usually with children in tow, and submit to intimate investigations of their finances, sleeping arrangements, and housekeeping habits. Often this bureaucratic harassment reaches fiendish proportions, driving many poor women from the dole. But imagine the much more vivid effect that could be achieved by the actual drawing of blood!

Madonna aside, sadomasochism is entirely consistent with recent political trends. For twelve years now, we've had presidents who have understood the primary function of government to be punishment in one form or another. All available funds have been channeled into the military, which rushes about the world like a schoolmistress armed with a birch rod. Bad countries—like Grenada, Panama, Libya, Iraq—are soundly whipped and sent to stand in their corners. Why, even as he was dragged from the Oval Office, George Bush managed to lash out once again at Saddam—with a "spanking," as *Time* magazine so insightfully put it.

Domestically, too, the punishment theme has been strictly adhered to. While all other domestic functions of government have withered away, the prison system has expanded to the point where the United States is second only to Russia in the percentage of its citizens incarcerated. For poor males, we have prison; for poor females, welfare—and there's no reason why one sex's punishment should be any less onerous than the other's.

It's not that the welfare recipients have done anything wrong. On the contrary, they've been neglected by underfunded schools; abused, in many cases, by husbands and boyfriends; and left to fend for their children in trailer camps or cities that resemble Mogadishu.

But we all know that "welfare reform" means, in plain English, that someone has got to be punished. Programs that throw women off welfare into unemployment or poverty-level jobs will punish, ultimately, their children. Hence the brilliance of the flogging approach: It will make the hawks and the wonks feel much better—without starving a single child.

GOING TO EXTREMES:
CEOS VS. SLAVES

The Nation, 2007

Recent findings shed new light on the increasingly unequal terrain of American society. Starting at the top executive level, you may have thought, as I did, that the guys in the C suites operated as a team—or, depending on your point of view, a pack or gang—each getting his fair share of the take. But no, the rising tide in executive pay does not lift all yachts equally. The latest pay gap to worry about is the one between the CEO and his—or very rarely her—third in command.

According to a study by Carola Frydman of the Massachusetts Institute of Technology and Raven E. Saks at the Federal Reserve, thirty to forty years ago the CEOs of major companies earned 80 percent more, on average, than the third-highest-paid executives. By the early part of the twenty-first century, however, the gap between the CEO and the third in command had ballooned up to 260 percent.

Now take a look at what's happening at the very bottom of the economic spectrum, where you might have pictured low-wage workers trudging between food banks or mendicants dwelling in cardboard boxes. It turns out, though, that the bottom is a lot lower than that. In May 2007, a millionaire couple in a woodsy Long Island suburb was charged with keeping two Indonesian domestics as slaves for five years, during which the women were paid $100 a month, fed very little, forced to sleep on mats on the floor, and subjected to beatings, cigarette burns, and other torments.

This is hardly an isolated case. If the new "top" involves pay in the tens or hundreds of millions, a private jet, and a few acres of Marin County, the new bottom is slavery. Some of America's slaves are captive domestics like the Indonesian women on Long Island. Others are sweatshop or restaurant workers, and at least ten thousand are sex slaves lured from their home countries to American brothels by the promise of respectable jobs.

CEOs and slaves: These are the extreme ends of American class polarization. But a parallel splitting is going on in many of the professions. Top-ranked college professors, for example, enjoy salaries of several hundred thousand a year, often augmented by consulting fees and earnings from their patents or biotech companies. At the other end of the professoriate, you have adjunct teachers toiling away for about $5,000 a semester or less, with no benefits or chance of tenure. There was a story a few years ago about an adjunct who commuted to his classes from a homeless shelter in Manhattan, and adjuncts who moonlight as waitresses or cleaning ladies are legion.

Similarly, the legal profession, which is topped by law firm partners billing hundreds of dollars an hour, now has a new proletariat of temp lawyers working for $19–25 an hour in sweatshop conditions. On sites like http:// temporaryattorney.blogspot.com/, temp lawyers report working twelve hours a day, six days a week, in crowded basements with inadequate sanitary facilities. According to an article in *American Lawyer*, a legal temp at a major New York firm reported being "corralled in a windowless basement room littered with dead cockroaches" where six out of seven exits were blocked.

Contemplating the violent and increasing polarization of American society, one cannot help but think of "dark energy," the mysterious force that is propelling the galaxies apart from one another at a speed far greater than can be accounted for by the energy of the original big bang. Cosmic bodies seem to be repelling one another, much as a CEO must look down at his CFO and COO, etc., and think, "They're getting too close. I've got to make more, more, more!"

The difference is that the galaxies don't need one another and are free to go their separate ways nonchalantly. But the CEO presumably depends on his fellow executives, just as the star professor relies on adjuncts to do his or her teaching and the law firm partner is enriched by the sweated labor of legal temps. For all we know, some of those CEOs go home to sip their single malts in mahogany-walled dens that have been cleaned by domestic slaves.

Why is it so hard for the people at the top to graciously acknowledge their dependency on the labor of others? We need some sort of gravitational force to counter the explosive distancing brought about by greed—before our economy imitates the universe and blows itself to smithereens.

ARE ILLEGAL IMMIGRANTS
THE PROBLEM?

Barbara's Blog, 2006

I've been reading with mixed feelings an exchange on my website's forum on the subject of illegal immigration. One contributor writes that "The first step is to deport the illegal aliens and those overstaying their visas. This should open up millions of jobs." He—well, he says he's a male in his mid-thirties—must have been watching Lou Dobbs's strident series on "Our Broken Borders," which blames about 51 percent of our economic woes on illegal immigrants. Though, to give Dobbs his due, he does pin the other 49 percent on "big corporations."

I've traveled across the US-Mexican border, and it didn't seem too broken to me. Peer through the giant fence that runs right to the Pacific Ocean in Tijuana and you see what looks like an armed encampment: That's America, the "land of opportunity," as viewed from the poorer parts of the world. On the way back north, it took fifty minutes to make our way through the US border checkpoint, waiting in bumper-to-bumper traffic as gaunt peddlers, many carrying babies on their backs, went from car to car selling trinkets and snacks.

The amazing thing is that so many Mexicans (and other Latin Americans) risk the border crossing and the hostile culture of the United States—a fact you're reminded of as soon as you enter California and see the first "human crossing" warning signs. These show a silhouetted family running together, reminding you that it's parents and children, not deer, you're likely to collide with just north of the fence.

Now we've been given a glimpse into the lives of one of the biggest categories of illegal Latino immigrants, the day laborers who do jobs like construction, moving, and landscaping. According to a 2006 study, carried out by researchers at three major US universities, about three-fourths of the day laborers in this country lack legal documents. Not surprisingly, they live miserably. Their median earnings are $700 a month, most have no access to health care, and half of them said they'd been stiffed by bosses at one time or another and gone unpaid for their work.

That's what makes undocumented workers so attractive to unscrupulous US employers: When you rip them off, they have no recourse at all. So my first, knee-jerk response to Lou Dobbs et al. would be: If you don't want undocumented immigrants competing with Americans for jobs, stop the *exploitation* of the immigrants and make sure they work under the same laws and regulations as anyone else.

The real surprise in the study is that 49 percent of the day laborers interviewed said they were usually hired not by contractors or companies of any kind, and certainly not "big corporations," but by American homeowners. I'd heard Bay Buchanan (sister of Pat) on Lou Dobbs's show fulminating about the "big corporations" that are hiring all the illegal immigrants, but in fact it's the guy next door who needs his house painted or his lawn mowed.

So there's a sickening level of hypocrisy here. In the last few years, we've seen anti-immigrant protests at day-laborer hiring sites—street corners or, very often, Home Depot parking lots—from Burbank, California, to Suffolk County, Long Island. But how many of those righteous protestors have employed undocumented immigrants themselves, if not as construction and lawn workers, then as nannies or maids?

But I do agree with one forum contributor when he writes: "I get very tired of ivory tower 'professional' types who dismiss the impact of these workers because they're just doing 'jobs nobody else wants to do.'" There's Jimmy, for example, a friend from Buffalo who hasn't had steady employment since he was laid off from an auto plant in the nineties. Now he's getting ready to move to South Florida, where there's still a shortage of workers to repair hurricane damage. His plan? Get a job, or at least hang out at Home Depot, where the pay is low and the possibilities of advancement are negligible—so he might be spotted by potential employers.

With the catastrophic ongoing layoffs in the auto industry, we can expect more American citizens to join the immigrants congregating in Home Depot parking lots. They'll have a choice: to treat the immigrants as competitors and enemies or to band together with them, as coworkers, to fight for better wages and working conditions for all.

Of course, I hope they'll choose the latter. One image haunts me from my border crossing: a thin brown man in tattered clothes trying to sell handmade wooden crosses to the Americans crawling along in their cars. He was carrying one of the larger ones on his back.

WHAT'S SO GREAT ABOUT GATED COMMUNITIES?

Huffington Post, 2007

nother Utopia seems to be biting the dust. The socialist kibbutzim of Israel have vanished or gone increasingly capitalist, and now the paranoid residential ideal represented by gated communities may be in serious trouble. Never exactly cool—remember Jim Carrey in *The Truman Show*?—these pricey enclaves of the white upper-middle class are becoming hotbeds of disillusionment.

At the annual meeting of the American Anthropological Association in Washington in 2007, incoming association president Setha Low painted a picture so dispiriting that the audience guffawed in schadenfreude. The gated community residents Low interviewed had fled from ethnically challenging cities, but they have not managed to escape from their fear. One resident reported that her small daughter has developed a severe case of xenophobia, no doubt communicated by her parents: "We were driving next to a truck with some day laborers and equipment in the back, and we stopped beside them at the light. She [her daughter] wanted to move because she was afraid those people were going to come and get her. They looked scary to her."

Leaving aside the sorry spectacle of homeowners living in fear of their landscapers, there is actually something to worry about. According to Low, gated communities are no less crime-prone than open ones, and Gopal Ahluwalia, senior vice president of research at the National Association of Home Builders, confirms this: "There are studies indicating that there are no differences in the crime in gated communities and nongated communities." The security guards often wave people on in, especially if they look like they're on a legitimate mission—such as the faux moving truck that entered a Fort Myers gated community last spring and left with a houseful of furniture. Or the crime comes from within, as at the Hilton Head Plantation community in South Carolina, where a rash of crime committed by resident teenagers has led to the imposition of a curfew.

Most recently, America's gated communities have been blighted by foreclosures. Yes, even people who were able to put together the down payment on a half-million-dollar house can be ambushed by adjustable-rate mortgages and forced down from the upper- to the lower-middle class. *Newsweek* reports that foreclosures are devastating the gated community of Black Mountain Vistas in Henderson, Nevada, where "yellow patches [now] blot the spartan lawns and phone books lie on front porches, their covers bleached from weeks under the desert sun." Similarly, according to the *Orlando Sentinel*, "Countless homeowners overwhelmed by their mortgages are taking off and leaving behind algae-filled swimming pools and knee-high weeds" in one local gated community.

So for people who sought not just prosperity but perfection, here's another sad end to the American dream, or at least their ethnically cleansed version thereof: boarded-up McMansions, plastic baggies scudding over overgrown lawns, and, in the Orlando case, a foreclosure-induced infestation of snakes. You can turn away the immigrants, the African Americans, the teenagers, and other suspect groups, but there's no fence high enough to keep out the repo man.

All right, some gated communities are doing better than others, and not all of their residents are racists. The communities that allow owners to rent out their houses or that offer homes at middle-class prices of $250,000 or so are more likely to contain a mix of classes and races. The only gated community I have ever visited consisted of dull row houses protected by a slacker guard and a fence, and my host was a writer of modest means and liberal inclinations. But all these places suffer from the delusion that security lies behind physical barriers.

Before we turn all of America into a gated community, with a seven-hundred-mile steel fence running along the southern border, we should consider the mixed history of exclusionary walls. Ancient and medieval European towns huddled behind massive walls, only to face ever more effective catapults, battering rams, and other siege engines. More recently, the Berlin Wall, which the East German government described fondly as a protective "antifascism wall," fell to a rebellious citizenry. Israel, increasingly sealed behind its anti-Palestinian checkpoints and wall, faced an outbreak of neo-Nazi crime in September—coming, strangely enough, from within.

But the market may have the last word on America's internal gated communities. "Hell is a gated community," announced the *Sarasota Herald-Tribune* last June, reporting that market research by the big home builder Pulte Homes found that no one under fifty wants to live in them, so its latest local development would be ungated. Security, or at least the promise of security, may be one consideration. But there's another old-fashioned American imperative at work here, which ought to bear on our national policies as well. As my Montana forebears would have put it: *Don't fence me in!*

IS IT NOW A CRIME TO BE POOR?

New York Times, 2009

I t's too bad so many people are falling into poverty at a time when it's almost illegal to be poor. You won't be arrested for shopping in a Dollar Store, but if you are truly, deeply, in-the-streets poor, you're well advised not to engage in any of the biological necessities of life—like sitting, sleeping, lying down, or loitering. City officials boast that there is nothing discriminatory about the ordinances that afflict the destitute, most of which go back to the dawn of gentrification in the '80s and '90s. "If you're lying on a sidewalk, whether you're homeless or a millionaire, you're in violation of the ordinance," a city attorney in St. Petersburg, Florida, said in June, echoing Anatole France's immortal observation that "The law, in its majesty equality, forbids the rich as well as the poor to sleep under bridges."

In defiance of all reason and compassion, the criminalization of poverty has actually been intensifying as the recession generates ever more poverty. So concludes a new study from the National Law Center on Homelessness and Poverty, which found that the number of ordinances against the publicly poor has been rising since 2006, along with ticketing and arrests for more "neutral" infractions like jaywalking, littering, or carrying an open container of alcohol.

The report lists America's ten "meanest" cities—the largest of which are Honolulu, Los Angeles, and San Francisco—but new contestants are springing up every day. The City Council in Grand Junction, Colorado, has been considering a ban on begging, and at the end of June, Tempe, Arizona, carried out a four-day crackdown on the indigent. How do you know when someone is indigent? As a Las Vegas statute puts it, "An indigent person is a person whom a reasonable ordinary person would believe to be entitled to apply for or receive" public assistance.

That could be me before the blow-drying and eyeliner, and it's definitely Al Szekely at any time of day. A grizzled sixty-two-year-old, he inhabits a wheelchair and is often found on G Street in Washington—the city that is ultimately responsible for the bullet he took in the spine in Fu Bai, Vietnam, in 1972. He had been enjoying the luxury of an indoor bed until last December, when the police swept through the shelter in the middle of the night looking for men with outstanding warrants.

It turned out that Mr. Szekely, who is an ordained minister and does not drink, do drugs, or curse in front of ladies, did indeed have a warrant—for not appearing in court to face a charge of "criminal trespassing" (for sleeping on a sidewalk in a Washington suburb). So he was dragged out of the shelter and put in jail. "Can you imagine?" asked Eric Sheptock, the homeless advocate (himself a shelter resident) who introduced me to Mr. Szekely. "They arrested a homeless man in a shelter for being homeless."

The viciousness of the official animus toward the indigent can be breathtaking. A few years ago, a group called Food Not Bombs started handing out free vegan food to hungry people in public parks around the nation. A number of cities, led by Las Vegas, passed ordinances forbidding the sharing of food with the indigent in public places, and several members of the group were arrested. A federal judge just overturned the antisharing law in Orlando, Florida, but the city is appealing. And now Middletown, Connecticut, is cracking down on food sharing.

If poverty tends to criminalize people, it is also true that criminalization inexorably impoverishes them. Scott Lovell, another homeless man I interviewed in Washington, earned his record by committing a significant crime— by participating in the armed robbery of a steakhouse when he was fifteen. Although Mr. Lovell dresses and speaks more like a summer tourist from Ohio than a felon, his criminal record has made it extremely difficult for him to find a job.

For Al Szekely, the arrest for trespassing meant a further descent down the circles of hell. While in jail, he lost his slot in the shelter and now sleeps outside the Verizon Center sports arena, where the big problem, in addition to the security guards, is mosquitoes. His stick-thin arms are covered with pink crusty sores, which he treats with a regimen of frantic scratching.

For the not-yet-homeless, there are two main paths to criminalization—one involving debt and the other skin color. Anyone of any color or prerecession financial status can fall into debt, and although we pride ourselves on the abolition of debtors' prison, in at least one state, Texas, people who can't afford to pay their traffic fines may be made to "sit out their tickets" in jail.

Often the path to legal trouble begins when one of your creditors has a court issue a summons for you, which you fail to honor for one reason or another. (Maybe your address has changed or you never received it.) Now you're in contempt of court. Or suppose you miss a payment and, before you realize it, your car insurance lapses; then you're stopped for something like a broken headlight. Depending on the state, you may have your car impounded or face a steep fine—again, exposing you to a possible summons. "There's just no end to it once the cycle starts," said Robert Solomon of Yale Law School. "It just keeps accelerating."

By far the most reliable way to be criminalized by poverty is to have the wrong-color skin. Indignation runs high when a celebrity professor encounters racial profiling, but for decades whole communities have been effectively "profiled" for the suspicious combination of being both dark-skinned and poor, thanks to the "broken windows" or "zero tolerance" theory of policing popularized by Rudy Giuliani, when he was mayor of New York City, and his police chief William Bratton.

Flick a cigarette in a heavily patrolled community of color and you're littering; wear the wrong-color T-shirt and you're displaying gang allegiance. Just strolling around in a dodgy neighborhood can mark you as a potential suspect, according to *Let's Get Free: A Hip-Hop Theory of Justice*, an eye-opening new book by Paul Butler, a former federal prosecutor in Washington. If you seem at all evasive, which I suppose is like looking "overly anxious" in an airport, Butler writes, the police "can force you to stop just to investigate why you don't want to talk to them." And don't get grumpy about it or you could be "resisting arrest."

There's no minimum age for being sucked into what the Children's Defense Fund calls "the cradle-to-prison pipeline." In New York City, a teenager caught in public housing without an ID—say, while visiting a friend or relative—can be charged with criminal trespassing and wind up in juvenile detention, Mishi Faruqee, the director of youth justice programs for the Children's Defense Fund of New York, told me. In just the past few months, a growing number of cities have taken to ticketing and sometimes handcuffing teenagers found on the streets during school hours.

In Los Angeles, the fine for truancy is $250; in Dallas, it can be as much as $500—crushing amounts for people living near the poverty level. According to the Los Angeles Bus Riders Union, an advocacy group, twelve thousand students were ticketed for truancy in 2008.

Why does the Bus Riders Union care? Because it estimates that 80 percent of the "truants," especially those who are black or Latino, are merely late for school, thanks to the way that overfilled buses whiz by them without stopping. I met people in Los Angeles who told me they keep their children home if there's the slightest chance of their being late. It's an ingenious antitruancy policy that discourages parents from sending their youngsters to school.

The pattern is to curtail financing for services that might help the poor while ramping up law enforcement: Starve school and public transportation budgets, then make truancy illegal. Shut down public housing, then make it a crime to be homeless. Be sure to harass street vendors when there are few other opportunities for employment. The experience of the poor, and especially poor minorities, comes to resemble that of a rat in a cage scrambling to avoid erratically administered electric shocks.

And if you should make the mistake of trying to escape via a brief marijuana-induced high, it's "gotcha" all over again, because that, of course, is illegal, too. One result is our staggering level of incarceration, the highest in the world. Today the same number of Americans—2.3 million—reside in prison as in public housing.

Meanwhile, the public housing that remains has become ever more prisonlike, with residents subjected to drug testing and random police sweeps. The safety net, or what's left of it, has been transformed into a dragnet.

Some of the community organizers I've talked to around the country think they know why "zero tolerance" policing has ratcheted up since the recession began. Leonardo Vilchis of the Union de Vecinos, a community organization in Los Angeles, suspects that "Poor people have become a source of revenue" for recession-starved cities, and that the police can always find a violation leading to a fine. If so, this is a singularly demented fund-raising strategy. At a congressional hearing in June, the president of the National Association of Criminal Defense Lawyers testified about the pervasive "overcriminalization of crimes that are not a risk to public safety," like sleeping in a cardboard box or jumping turnstiles, which lead to expensively clogged courts and prisons.

A Pew Center study found states spending a record $51.7 billion on corrections, an amount that the center judged, with an excess of moderation, to be "too much."

But will it be enough—the collision of rising prison populations that we can't afford and the criminalization of poverty—to force us to break the mad cycle of poverty and punishment? With the number of people in poverty increasing (some estimates suggest it's up to 45 million to 50 million, from 37 million in 2007), several states are beginning to ease up on the criminalization of poverty—for example, by sending drug offenders to treatment rather than jail, shortening probation and reducing the number of people locked up for technical violations like missed court appointments. But others are tightening the screws: not only increasing the number of "crimes" but also charging prisoners for their room and board—ensuring that they'll be released with potentially criminalizing levels of debt.

Maybe we can't afford the measures that would begin to alleviate America's growing poverty—affordable housing, good schools, reliable public transportation, and so forth. I would argue otherwise, but for now I'd be content with a consensus that, if we can't afford to truly help the poor, neither can we afford to go on tormenting them.

A HOMESPUN SAFETY NET

New York Times, 2009

I f nothing else, the recession is serving as a stress test for the American safety net. How prepared have we been for sudden and violent economic dislocations of the kind that leave millions homeless and jobless? So far, despite some temporary expansions of food stamps and unemployment benefits by the Obama administration, the recession has done for the government safety net pretty much what Hurricane Katrina did for the Federal Emergency Management Agency: It's demonstrated that you can be clinging to your roof with the water rising, and chances are that no one will come to helicopter you out.

Take the case of Kristen and Joe Parente, Delaware residents who had always imagined that people turned to government for help only if "they didn't want to work." Their troubles began well before the recession, when Joe, a fourth-generation pipe fitter, sustained a back injury that left him unfit for even light lifting. He fell into depression for several months, then rallied to ace a state-sponsored retraining course in computer repairs—only to find those skills no longer in demand. The obvious fallback was disability benefits, but—catch-22—when Joe applied he was told he could not qualify without presenting a recent MRI scan. This would cost $800 to $900, which the Parentes do not have, nor has Joe, unlike the rest of the family, been able to qualify for Medicaid.

When Joe and Kristen married as teenagers, the plan had been for Kristen to stay home with the children. But with Joe out of action and three children to support by the middle of this decade, Kristen went to work as a waitress, ending up, in 2008, in a "pretty fancy place on the water." Then the recession struck and in January she was laid off.

Kristen is bright, pretty, and, to judge from her command of her own small kitchen, capable of holding down a dozen tables with precision and grace. In the past she'd always been able to land a new job within days; now there was nothing. Like most laid-off people, she failed to meet the fiendishly complex and sometimes arbitrary eligibility requirements for unemployment benefits. Their car started falling apart.

So in early February, the Parentes turned to the desperate citizen's last resort—Temporary Assistance for Needy Families. Still often called "welfare," the program does not offer cash support to stay-at-home parents as did its predecessor, Aid to Families with Dependent Children. Rather, it provides supplemental income for working parents, based on the sunny assumption that there would always be plenty of jobs for those enterprising enough to get them.

After Kristen applied, nothing happened for six weeks— no money, no phone calls returned. At school, the Parentes' seven-year-old's class was asked to write out what wish they would ask of a genie, should one appear. Brianna's wish was for her mother to find a job because there was nothing to eat in the house, an aspiration that her teacher deemed too disturbing to be posted on the wall with the other children's.

Not until March did the Parentes begin to receive food stamps and some cash assistance. Meanwhile, they were finding out why some recipients have taken to calling the assistance program "Torture and Abuse of Needy Families." From the start, the experience has been "humiliating," Kristen said. The caseworkers "treat you like a bum—they act like every dollar you get is coming out of their own paychecks."

Nationally, according to Kaaryn Gustafson, an associate professor at the University of Connecticut Law School, "applying for welfare is a lot like being booked by the police." There may be a mug shot, fingerprinting, and long interrogations as to one's children's paternity. The ostensible goal is to prevent welfare fraud, but the psychological impact is to turn poverty itself into a kind of crime.

Delaware does not require fingerprints, but the Parentes discovered that they were each expected to apply for forty jobs a week, even though no money was offered for gas, tolls, or babysitting. In addition, Kristen had to drive thirty-five miles a day to attend "job readiness" classes, which she said were "a joke."

With no jobs to be found, Kristen was required to work as a volunteer at a community agency. (God forbid anyone should use government money to let her stay home with her children!) In exchange for $475 a month plus food stamps, the family submits to various forms of "monitoring" to keep them on the straight and narrow. One result is that Kristen lives in constant terror of doing something that would cause the program to report her to Child Protective Services. She worries that the state will remove her children "automatically" if program workers discover that her five-year-old son shares a bedroom with his sisters. No one, of course, is offering to subsidize a larger apartment in the name of child "protection."

It's no secret that the temporary assistance program was designed to repel potential applicants, and at this it has been stunningly successful. The theory is that government assistance encourages a debilitating "culture of poverty," marked by laziness, promiscuity, and addiction, and curable only by a swift cessation of benefits. In the years immediately after welfare "reform," about one and a half million people disappeared from the welfare rolls—often because they'd been "sanctioned" for, say, failing to show up for an appointment with a caseworker. Stories of an erratic and punitive bureaucracy get around, so the recession of 2001 produced no uptick in enrollment, nor, until very recently, did the current recession. As Mark Greenberg, a welfare expert at the Georgetown School of Law, put it, the program has been "strikingly unresponsive" to rising need.

People far more readily turn to food stamps, which have seen a 19 percent surge in enrollment since the recession began. But even these can carry a presumption of guilt or criminal intent. Four states—Arizona, California, New York, and Texas—require that applicants undergo fingerprinting. Furthermore, under a national program called Operation Talon, food stamp offices share applicants' personal data with law enforcement agencies, making it hazardous for anyone who might have an outstanding warrant—for failing to show up for a court hearing on an unpaid debt, for example—to apply.

As in the aftermath of Hurricane Katrina, the most reliable first responders are not government agencies, but family and friends. Kristen and Joe first moved in with her mother and four siblings, and in the weeks before the government came through with a check, she borrowed money from the elderly man whose house she cleans every week, who himself depends on Social Security.

I've never encountered the kind of "culture of poverty" imagined by the framers of welfare reform, but there is a tradition among the American working class of mutual aid, no questions asked. My father, a former miner, advised me as a child that if I ever needed money to "go to a poor man." He liked to tell the story of my great-grandfather, John Howes, who worked in the mines long enough to accumulate a small sum with which to purchase a plot of farmland. But as he was driving out of Butte, Montana, in a horse-drawn wagon, he picked up an Indian woman and her child, and their hard-luck story moved him to give her all his money, turn his horse around and go back to the darkness and danger of the mines.

In her classic study of an African-American community in the late '60s, the anthropologist Carol Stack found rich networks of reciprocal giving and support, and when I worked at low-wage jobs in the 1990s, I was amazed by the generosity of my coworkers, who offered me food, help with my work, and even once a place to stay. Such informal networks—and random acts of kindness—put the official welfare state, with its relentless suspicions and grudging outlays, to shame.

But there are limits to the generosity of relatives and friends. Tensions can arise, as they did between Kristen and her mother, which is what led the Parentes to move to their current apartment in Wilmington. Sandra Smith, a sociologist at the University of California, Berkeley, finds that poverty itself can deplete entire social networks, leaving no one to turn to. While the affluent suffer from "compassion fatigue," the poor simply run out of resources.

At least one influential theory of poverty contends that the poor are *too* mutually dependent, and that this is one of their problems. This perspective is outlined in the book *Bridges Out of Poverty*, cowritten by Ruby K. Payne, a motivational speaker who regularly addresses schoolteachers, social service workers, and members of low-income communities. She argues that the poor need to abandon their dysfunctional culture and emulate the more goal-oriented middle class. Getting out of poverty, according to Payne, is much like overcoming drug addiction, and often requires cutting off contact with those who choose to remain behind: "In order to move from poverty to middle class...an individual must give up relationships for achievement, at least for some period of time." The message from the affluent to the down-and-out: Neither we nor the government is going to do much to help you—and you better not help one another, either. It's every man (or woman or child) for himself.

In the meantime, Kristen has discovered a radically different approach to dealing with poverty. The community agency she volunteered at is Acorn (the Association of Community Organizations for Reform Now), the grassroots organization of low-income people that achieved national notoriety during the 2008 presidential campaign when Republicans attacked it for voter registration fraud (committed by temporary Acorn canvassers and quickly corrected by staff members). Kristen made such a good impression that she was offered a paid job in May, and now, with only a small supplement from the government, she works full time for Acorn, organizing protests against Walgreens for deciding to stop filling Medicaid prescriptions in Delaware, and, in late June, helping turn out thousands of people for a march on Washington to demand universal health insurance.

So the recession tossed Kristen from routine poverty into destitution, and from there, willy-nilly, into a new life as a community organizer and a grassroots leader. I wish I could end the story there, but the Parentes' landlord has just informed them that they'll have to go, because he's decided to sell the building, and they don't have money for a security deposit on a new apartment. "I thought we were good for six months here," Kristen told me, "but every time I let down my guard I just get slammed again."

DEAD, WHITE, AND BLUE: THE GREAT DIE-OFF OF AMERICA'S BLUE-COLLAR WHITE PEOPLE

Guernica, 2015

The white working class, which usually inspires liberal concern only for its paradoxical, Republican-leaning voting habits, has recently become newsworthy for something else: According to economist Anne Case and Angus Deaton, the winner of the latest Nobel Prize in economics, its members in the forty-five- to fifty-four-year-old age group are dying at an immoderate rate. While the life span of affluent white people continues to lengthen, the life span of poor white people has been shrinking. As a result, in just the last four years, the gap between poor white men and wealthier ones has widened by up to four years. The *New York Times* summed up the Deaton and Case study with this headline: "Income Gap, Meet the Longevity Gap."

This was not supposed to happen. For almost a century, the comforting American narrative was that better nutrition and medical care would guarantee longer lives for all. So the great blue-collar die-off has come out of the blue and is, as the *Wall Street Journal* says, "startling."

It was especially not supposed to happen to white people

who, in relation to people of color, have long had the advantage of higher earnings, better access to health care, safer neighborhoods, and, of course, freedom from the daily insults and harms inflicted on the darker-skinned. There has also been a major racial gap in longevity—5.3 years between white and black men and 3.8 years between white and black women—though, hardly noticed, it has been narrowing for the last two decades. Only white people are now dying off in unexpectedly large numbers in middle age, their excess deaths accounted for by suicide, alcoholism, and drug (usually opiate) addiction.

There are some practical reasons why white people are likely to be more efficient than black people at killing themselves. For one thing, they are more likely to be gun owners, and white men favor gunshots as a means of suicide. For another, doctors, undoubtedly acting in part on stereotypes of nonwhite people as drug addicts, are more likely to prescribe powerful opiate painkillers to white people than to people of color. (I've been offered enough oxycodone prescriptions over the years to stock a small illegal business.)

Manual labor—from waitressing to construction work—tends to wear the body down quickly, from knees to back and rotator cuffs, and when Tylenol fails, the doctor may opt for an opiate just to get you through the day.

The Wages of Despair

But something more profound is going on here, too. As *New York Times* columnist Paul Krugman puts it, the "diseases" leading to excess white working-class deaths are those of "despair," and some of the obvious causes are economic. In the last few decades, things have not been going well for working-class people of any color.

I grew up in an America where a man with a strong back—and, better yet, a strong union—could reasonably expect to support a family on his own without a college degree. In 2015, those jobs are long gone, leaving only the kind of work once relegated to women and people of color available in areas like retail, landscaping, and delivery-truck driving. This means that those in the bottom 20 percent of the white income distribution face material circumstances like those long familiar to poor black people, including erratic employment and crowded, hazardous living spaces.

White privilege was never, however, simply a matter of economic advantage. As the great African-American scholar W. E. B. Du Bois wrote in 1935, "It must be remembered that the white group of laborers, while they received a low wage, were compensated in part by a sort of public and psychological wage."

Some of the elements of this invisible wage sound almost quaint today, like Du Bois's assertion that white working-class people were "admitted freely with all classes of white people to public functions, public parks, and the best schools." Today, there are few public spaces that are not open, at least legally speaking, to black people, while the "best" schools are reserved for the affluent—mostly white and Asian American, along with a sprinkling of other people of color to provide the fairy dust of "diversity." While white Americans have lost ground economically, black people have made gains, at least in the de jure sense. As a result, the "psychological wage" awarded to white people has been shrinking.

For most of American history, government could be counted on to maintain white power and privilege by enforcing slavery and later segregation. When the federal government finally weighed in on the side of desegregation, working-class white people were left to defend their own diminishing privilege by moving rightward toward the likes of Alabama Governor (and later presidential candidate) George Wallace and his many white pseudo-populist successors down to Donald Trump.

At the same time, the day-to-day task of upholding white power devolved from the federal government to the state and then local level, specifically to local police forces, which, as we know, have taken it up with such enthusiasm as to become both a national and international scandal. The *Guardian*, for instance, now keeps a running tally of the number of Americans (mostly black) killed by cops (as of this moment, 1,209 for 2015), while black protest, in the form of the Black Lives Matter movement and a wave of on-campus demonstrations, has largely recaptured the moral high ground formerly occupied by the civil rights movement.

The culture, too, has been inching bit by bit toward racial equality, if not, in some limited areas, black ascendency. If the stock image of the early twentieth century "Negro" was the minstrel, the role of rural simpleton in popular culture has been taken over in this century by the characters in *Duck Dynasty* and *Here Comes Honey Boo Boo*. At least in the entertainment world, working-class white people are now regularly portrayed as moronic, while black people are often hyperarticulate, street-smart, and sometimes as wealthy as Kanye West. It's not easy to maintain the usual sense of white superiority when parts of the media are squeezing laughs from the contrast between savvy black people and rural white bumpkins, as in the Tina Fey comedy *Unbreakable Kimmy Schmidt*. White, presumably upper-middle-class people generally conceive of these characters and plot lines, which, to a child of white working-class parents like myself, sting with condescension.

Of course, there was also the election of the first black president. White, native-born Americans began to talk of "taking our country back." The more affluent ones formed the Tea Party; less affluent ones often contented themselves with affixing Confederate flag decals to their trucks.

On the American Downward Slope

All of this means that the maintenance of white privilege, especially among the least privileged white people, has become more difficult and so, for some, more urgent than ever. Poor white people always had the comfort of knowing that someone was worse off and more despised than they were; racial subjugation was the ground under their feet, the rock they stood upon, even when their own situation was deteriorating.

If the government, especially at the federal level, is no longer as reliable an enforcer of white privilege, then it's grassroots initiatives by individuals and small groups that are helping to fill the gap—perpetrating the microaggressions that roil college campuses, the racial slurs yelled from pickup trucks, or, at a deadly extreme, the shooting up of a black church renowned for its efforts in the civil rights era. Dylann Roof, the Charleston killer who did just that, was a jobless high school dropout and reportedly a heavy user of alcohol and opiates. Even without a death sentence hanging over him, Roof was surely headed toward an early demise.

Acts of racial aggression may provide their white perpetrators with a fleeting sense of triumph, but they also take a special kind of effort. It takes effort, for instance, to target a black runner and swerve over to insult her from your truck; it takes such effort—and a strong stomach—to paint a racial slur in excrement on a dormitory bathroom wall. College students may do such things in part out of a sense of economic vulnerability, the knowledge that as soon as school is over their college-debt payments will come due. No matter the effort expended, however, it is especially hard to maintain a feeling of racial superiority while struggling to hold onto one's own place near the bottom of an undependable economy.

While there is no medical evidence that racism is toxic to those who express it—after all, generations of wealthy slave owners survived quite nicely—the combination of downward mobility and racial resentment may be a potent invitation to the kind of despair that leads to suicide in one form or another, whether by gunshots or drugs. You can't break a glass ceiling if you're standing on ice.

It's easy for the liberal intelligentsia to feel righteous in their disgust for lower-class white racism, but the college-educated elite that produces the intelligentsia is in trouble, too, with diminishing prospects and an ever-slipperier slope for the young. Whole professions have fallen on hard times, from college teaching to journalism and the law. One of the worst mistakes this relative elite could make is to try to pump up its own pride by hating on those—of any color or ethnicity—who are falling even faster.

HEALTH

WELCOME TO CANCERLAND

Harper's Magazine, 2001

I was thinking of it as one of those drive-by mammograms, one stop in a series of mundane missions including post office, supermarket, and gym, but I began to lose my nerve in the changing room, and not only because of the kinky necessity of baring my breasts and affixing tiny x-ray opaque stars to the tip of each nipple. I had been in this place only four months earlier, but that visit was just part of the routine cancer surveillance all good citizens of HMOs or health plans are expected to submit to once they reach the age of fifty, and I hadn't really been paying attention then. The results of that earlier session had aroused some "concern" on the part of the radiologist and her confederate, the gynecologist, so I am back now in the role of a suspect, eager to clear my name, alert to medical missteps and unfair allegations. But the changing room, really just a closet off the stark windowless space that houses the mammogram machine, contains something far worse. I notice for the first time now an assumption about who I am, where I am going, and what I will need when I get there. Almost all of the eye-level space has been filled with photocopied bits of cuteness and sentimentality: pink ribbons, a cartoon about a woman with iatrogenically flattened breasts, an "Ode to a Mammogram," a list of the "Top Ten Things Only Women Understand" ("Fat Clothes" and "Eyelash Curlers" among them), and, inescapably, right next to the door, the poem "I Said a Prayer for You Today," illustrated with pink roses.

It goes on and on, this mother of all mammograms, cutting into gym time, dinnertime, and lifetime generally. Sometimes the machine doesn't work, and I get squished into position to no purpose at all. More often, the x-ray is successful but apparently alarming to the invisible radiologist, off in some remote office, who calls the shots and never has the courtesy to show her face with an apology or an explanation. I try pleading with the technician: I have no known risk factors, no breast cancer in the family, I had my babies relatively young and nursed them both. I eat right, drink sparingly, work out, and doesn't that count for something? But she just gets this tight little professional smile on her face, either out of guilt for the torture she's inflicting or because she already knows something that I am going to be sorry to find out for myself. For an hour and a half the procedure is repeated: the squishing, the snapshot, the technician bustling off to consult the radiologist and returning with a demand for new angles and more definitive images. In the intervals while she's off with the doctor I read the *New York Times* right down to the personally irrelevant sections like theater and real estate, eschewing the stack of women's magazines provided for me, much as I ordinarily enjoy a quick read about sweatproof eyeliners and "fabulous sex tonight," because I have picked up this warning vibe in the changing room, which, in my increasingly anxious state, translates into: Femininity is death. Finally there is nothing left to read but one of the free local weekly newspapers, where I find, buried deep in the classifieds, something even more unsettling than the growing prospect of major disease—a classified ad for a "breast cancer teddy bear" with a pink ribbon stitched to its chest.

Yes, atheists pray in their foxholes—in this case, with a yearning new to me and sharp as lust, for a clean and honorable death by shark bite, lightning strike, sniper fire, car crash. Let me be hacked to death by a madman, is my silent supplication—anything but suffocation by the pink sticky sentiment embodied in that bear and oozing from the walls of the changing room.

My official induction into breast cancer comes about ten days later with the biopsy, which, for reasons I cannot ferret out of the surgeon, has to be a surgical one, performed on an outpatient basis but under general anesthesia, from which I awake to find him standing perpendicular to me, at the far end of the gurney, down near my feet, stating gravely, "Unfortunately, there is a cancer." It takes me all the rest of that drug-addled day to decide that the most heinous thing about that sentence is not the presence of cancer but the absence of me—for I, Barbara, do not enter into it, even as a location, a geographical reference point. Where I once was—not a commanding presence perhaps but nonetheless a standard assemblage of flesh and words and gesture—"there is a cancer." I have been replaced by *it*, is the surgeon's implication. This is what I am now, medically speaking.

In my last act of dignified self-assertion, I request to see the pathology slides myself. This is not difficult to arrange in our small-town hospital, where the pathologist turns out to be a friend of a friend, and my rusty PhD in cell biology (Rockefeller University, 1968) probably helps. He's a jolly fellow, the pathologist, who calls me "hon" and sits me down at one end of the dual-head microscope while he mans the other and moves a pointer through the field. These are the cancer cells, he says, showing up blue because of their overactive DNA. Most of them are arranged in staid semicircular arrays, like suburban houses squeezed into a cul-de-sac, but I also see what I know enough to know I do not want to see: the characteristic "Indian files" of cells on the march. The "enemy," I am supposed to think—an image to save up for future exercises in "visualization" of their violent deaths at the hands of the body's killer cells, the lymphocytes and macrophages. But I am impressed, against all rational self-interest, by the energy of these cellular conga lines, their determination to move on out from the backwater of the breast to colonize lymph nodes, bone marrow, lungs, and brain. These are, after all, the fanatics of Barbaraness, the rebel cells that have realized that the genome they carry, the genetic essence of me, has no further chance of normal reproduction in the postmenopausal body we share, so why not just start multiplying like bunnies and hope for a chance to break out?

It has happened, after all; some genomes have achieved immortality through cancer. When I was a graduate student, I once asked about the strain of tissue-culture cells labeled "HeLa" in the heavy-doored room maintained at body temperature. "HeLa," it turns out, refers to Henrietta Lacks, an African-American woman whose tumor was the progenitor of all HeLa cells, and whose unwitting contribution to science has only recently been recognized. She died; they live, and will go on living until someone gets tired of them or forgets to change their tissue-culture medium and leaves them to starve. Maybe this is what my rebel cells have in mind, and I try beaming them a solemn warning: The chances of your surviving me in tissue culture are nil. Keep up this selfish rampage and you go down, every last one of you, along with the entire Barbara enterprise. But what kind of a role model am I, or are multicellular human organisms generally, for putting the common good above mad anarchistic individual ambition? There is a reason, it occurs to me, why cancer is our metaphor for so many runaway social processes, like corruption and "moral decay": We are no less out of control ourselves.

After the visit to the pathologist, my biological curiosity drops to a lifetime nadir. I know women who followed up their diagnoses with weeks or months of self-study, mastering their options, interviewing doctor after doctor, assessing the damage to be expected from the available treatments. But I can tell from a few hours of investigation that the career of a breast-cancer patient has been pretty well mapped out in advance for me: You may get to negotiate the choice between lumpectomy and mastectomy, but lumpectomy is commonly followed by weeks of radiation, and in either case if the lymph nodes turn out, upon dissection, to be

invaded—or "involved," as it's less threateningly put—
you're doomed to chemotherapy, meaning baldness, nausea,
mouth sores, immunosuppression, and possible anemia.
These interventions do not constitute a "cure" or anything
close, which is why the death rate from breast cancer has
changed very little since the 1930s, when mastectomy was
the only treatment available. Chemotherapy, which became
a routine part of breast-cancer treatment in the eighties,
does not confer anywhere near as decisive an advantage
as patients are often led to believe, especially in postmenopausal women like myself—a two or three percentage
point difference in ten-year survival rates,[1] according to
America's best-known breast-cancer surgeon at the time,
Dr. Susan Love. I know these bleak facts, or sort of know
them, but in the fog of anesthesia that hangs over those
first few weeks, I seem to lose my capacity for self-defense.
The pressure is on, from doctors and loved ones, to do
something right away—kill it, get it out now. The endless
exams, the bone scan to check for metastases, the high-
tech heart test to see if I'm strong enough to withstand
chemotherapy—all these blur the line between selfhood
and thing-hood anyway, organic and inorganic, me and it.
As my cancer career unfolds, I will, the helpful pamphlets
explain, become a composite of the living and the dead—an
implant to replace the breast, a wig to replace the hair. And
then what will I mean when I use the word "I"? I fall into

---

1   In the United States, one in eight women will be diagnosed with breast cancer
at some point. The chances of her surviving for five years are 86.8 percent. For a
black woman this falls to 72 percent; and for a woman of any race whose cancer
has spread to the lymph nodes, to 77.7 percent.

a state of unreasoning passive aggressivity: They diagnosed this, so it's their baby. They found it, let them fix it.

I could take my chances with "alternative" treatments, of course, like punk novelist Kathy Acker, who succumbed to breast cancer in 1997 after a course of alternative therapies in Mexico, or actress and ThighMaster promoter Suzanne Somers, who made tabloid headlines by injecting herself with mistletoe brew. Or I could choose to do nothing at all beyond mentally exhorting my immune system to exterminate the traitorous cellular faction. But I have never admired the "natural" or believed in the "wisdom of the body." Death is as "natural" as anything gets, and the body has always seemed to me like a Siamese twin dragging along behind me, a hysteric really, dangerously overreacting, in my case, to everyday allergens and minute ingestions of sugar. I will put my faith in science, even if this means that the dumb old body is about to be transmogrified into an evil clown—puking, trembling, swelling, surrendering significant parts, and oozing postsurgical fluids. The surgeon—a more genial and forthcoming one this time—can fit me in; the oncologist will see me. Welcome to Cancerland.

Fortunately, no one has to go through this alone. Thirty years ago, before Betty Ford, Rose Kushner, Betty Rollin, and other pioneer patients spoke out, breast cancer was a dread secret, endured in silence and euphemized in obituaries as a "long illness." Something about the conjuncture of "breast," signifying sexuality and nurturance, and that other word, suggesting the claws of a devouring crustacean, spooked almost everyone. Today, however, it's the biggest disease on the cultural map, bigger than AIDS, cystic fibrosis, or spinal injury, bigger even than those more pro-lific killers of women—heart disease, lung cancer, and stroke. There are roughly hundreds of websites devoted to it, not to mention newsletters, support groups, a whole genre of first-person breast-cancer books; even, for a while, a glossy, upper-middle-brow, monthly magazine, *Mamm*. There are four major national breast-cancer organizations, of which the mightiest, in financial terms, is the Susan G. Komen Foundation, headed by breast-cancer veteran and Bush's nominee for ambassador to Hungary Nancy Brinker. Komen organizes the annual Race for the Cure, which at-tracts about a million people—mostly survivors, friends, and family members. Its website provides a microcosm of the new breast-cancer culture, offering news of the races, message boards for accounts of individuals' struggles with the disease, and a "marketplace" of breast-cancer-related products to buy.

More so than in the case of any other disease, breast-cancer organizations and events feed on a generous flow of corporate support. Nancy Brinker relates how her early attempts to attract corporate interest in promoting breast cancer "awareness" were met with rebuff. A bra manufac-turer, importuned to affix a mammogram-reminder tag to his product, more or less wrinkled his nose. Now breast cancer has blossomed from wallflower to the most popular girl at the corporate charity prom. While AIDS goes beg-ging and low-rent diseases like tuberculosis have no friends at all, breast cancer has been able to count on Revlon, Avon, Ford, Tiffany, Pier 1, Estée Lauder, Ralph Lauren, Lee Jeans, Saks Fifth Avenue, JCPenney, Boston Market,

Wilson athletic gear—and I apologize to those I've omitted. You can "shop for the cure" during the week when Saks donates 2 percent of sales to a breast-cancer fund; "wear denim for the cure" during Lee National Denim Day, when for a $5 donation you get to wear blue jeans to work. You can even "invest for the cure," in the Kinetics Asset Management's new no-load Medical Fund, which specializes entirely in businesses involved in cancer research.

If you can't run, bike, or climb a mountain for the cure—all of which endeavors are routine beneficiaries of corporate sponsorship—you can always purchase one of the many products with a breast-cancer theme. There are 2.2 million American women in various stages of their breast-cancer careers, who, along with anxious relatives, make up a significant market for all things breast-cancer-related. Bears, for example: I have identified four distinct lines, or species, of these creatures, including "Carol," the Remembrance Bear; "Hope," the Breast Cancer Research Bear, which wears a pink turban as if to conceal chemotherapy-induced baldness; the "Susan Bear," named for Nancy Brinker's deceased sister, Susan; and the new Nick & Nora Wish Upon a Star Bear, available, along with the Susan Bear, at the Komen Foundation website's "marketplace."

And bears are only the tip, so to speak, of the cornucopia of pink-ribbon-themed breast-cancer products. You can dress in pink-beribboned sweatshirts, denim shirts, pajamas, lingerie, aprons, loungewear, shoelaces, and socks; accessorize with pink rhinestone brooches, angel pins, scarves, caps, earrings, and bracelets; brighten up your home with breast-cancer candles, stained-glass pink-ribbon candleholders, coffee mugs, pendants, wind chimes, and night-lights; pay your bills with special BreastChecks or a separate line of Checks for the Cure. "Awareness" beats secrecy and stigma, of course, but I can't help noticing that the existential space in which a friend has earnestly advised me to "confront [my] mortality" bears a striking resemblance to the mall.

This is not, I should point out, a case of cynical merchants exploiting the sick. Some of the breast-cancer tchotchkes and accessories are made by breast-cancer survivors themselves, such as "Janice," creator of the "Daisy Awareness Necklace," among other things, and in most cases a portion of the sales goes to breast-cancer research. Virginia Davis of Aurora, Colorado, was inspired to create the "Remembrance Bear" by a friend's double mastectomy and sees her work as more of a "crusade" than a business. This year she expects to ship 10,000 of these teddies, which are manufactured in China, and send part of the money to the Race for the Cure. If the bears are infantilizing—as I try ever so tactfully to suggest that this is how they may, in rare cases, be perceived—so far no one has complained. "I just get love letters," she tells me, "from people who say, 'God bless you for thinking of us.'"

The ultrafeminine theme of the breast-cancer "marketplace"—the prominence, for example, of cosmetics and jewelry—could be understood as a response to the treatments' disastrous effects on one's looks. But the infantilizing trope is a little harder to account for, and teddy bears are not its only manifestation. A tote bag distributed to breast-cancer patients by the Libby Ross Foundation (through places such as the Columbia Presbyterian Medical Center) contains, among other items, a tube of Estée Lauder Perfumed Body Crème, a hot-pink satin pillowcase, an audiotape "Meditation to Help You with Chemotherapy," a small tin of peppermint pastilles, a set of three small inexpensive rhinestone bracelets, a pink-striped "journal and sketchbook," and—somewhat jarringly—a small box of crayons. Marla Willner, one of the founders of the Libby Ross Foundation, told me that the crayons "go with the journal—for people to express different moods, different thoughts…" though she admitted she has never tried to write with crayons herself. Possibly the idea is that regression to a state of childlike dependency puts one in the best frame of mind with which to endure the prolonged and toxic treatments. Or it may be that, in some versions of the prevailing gender ideology, femininity is by its nature incompatible with full adulthood—a state of arrested development. Certainly men diagnosed with prostate cancer do not receive gifts of Matchbox cars.

But I, no less than the bear huggers, need whatever help I can get, and start wading out into the web in search of practical tips on hair loss, lumpectomy versus mastectomy, how to select a chemotherapy regimen, what to wear after surgery and what to eat when the scent of food sucks. There is, I soon find, far more than I can usefully absorb, for thousands of the afflicted have posted their stories, beginning with the lump or bad mammogram, proceeding through the agony of the treatments; pausing to mention the sustaining forces of family, humor, and religion; and ending, in almost all cases, with warm words of encouragement for the neophyte. Some of these are no more than a paragraph long—brief waves from sister sufferers; others offer almost hour-by-hour logs of breast-deprived, chemotherapized lives:

> **Tuesday, August 15, 2000**: Well, I survived my 4th chemo. Very, very dizzy today. Very nauseated, but no barfing! It's a first....I break out in a cold sweat and my heart pounds if I stay up longer than 5 minutes.

> **Friday, August 18, 2000**:...By dinnertime, I was full-out nauseated. I took some meds and ate a rice and vegetable bowl from Trader Joe's. It smelled and tasted awful to me, but I ate it anyway....Rick brought home some Kern's nectars and I'm drinking that. Seems to have settled my stomach a little bit.

I can't seem to get enough of these tales, reading on with panicky fascination about everything that can go wrong—septicemia, ruptured implants, startling recurrences a few years after the completion of treatments, "mets" (metastases) to vital organs, and—what scares me most in the short term—"chemo brain," or the cognitive deterioration that sometimes accompanies chemotherapy. I compare myself with everyone, selfishly impatient with those whose conditions are less menacing, shivering over those who have reached Stage IV ("There is no Stage V," as the main character in the play *Wit*, who has ovarian cancer, explains), constantly assessing my chances.

Feminism helped make the spreading breast-cancer sisterhood possible, and this realization gives me a faint feeling of belonging. Thirty years ago, when the disease went hidden behind euphemism and prostheses, medicine was a solid patriarchy, women's bodies its passive objects of labor. The women's health movement, in which I was an activist in the seventies and eighties, legitimized self-help and mutual support, and encouraged women to network directly, sharing their stories, questioning the doctors, banding together. It is hard now to recall how revolutionary these activities once seemed, and probably few participants in breast-cancer chat rooms and on breast-cancer message boards realize that when postmastectomy patients first proposed meeting in support groups in the mid-1970s, the American Cancer Society responded with a firm and fatherly "no." Now no one leaves the hospital without a brochure directing her to local support groups and, at least in my case, a follow-up call from a social worker to see whether I am safely ensconced in one. This cheers me briefly, until I realize that if support groups have won the stamp of medical approval this may be because they are no longer perceived as seditious.

In fact, aside from the dilute sisterhood of the cyber (and actual) support groups, there is nothing very feminist—in an ideological or activist sense—about the mainstream of breast-cancer culture today. Let me pause to qualify: You can, if you look hard enough, find plenty of genuine, self-identified feminists within the vast pink sea of the breast-cancer crusade, women who are militantly determined to "beat the epidemic" and insistent on more user-friendly approaches to treatment. It was feminist health activists who led the campaign, in the seventies and eighties, against the most savage form of breast-cancer surgery—the Halsted radical mastectomy, which removed chest muscle and lymph nodes as well as breast tissue and left women permanently disabled. It was the women's health movement that put a halt to the surgical practice, common in the seventies, of proceeding directly from biopsy to mastectomy without ever rousing the patient from anesthesia. More recently, feminist advocacy groups such as the San Francisco–based Breast Cancer Action and the Cambridge-based Women's Community Cancer Project helped blow the whistle on "high-dose chemotherapy," in which the bone marrow was removed prior to otherwise lethal doses of chemotherapy and later replaced—to no good effect, as it turned out.

Like everyone else in the breast-cancer world, the feminists want a cure, but they even more ardently demand to know the cause or causes of the disease without which we will never have any means of prevention. "Bad" genes of the inherited variety are thought to account for fewer than 10 percent of breast cancers, and only 30 percent of women diagnosed with breast cancer have any known risk factor (such as delaying childbearing or the late onset of menopause) at all. Bad lifestyle choices like a fatty diet have, after brief popularity with the medical profession, been largely ruled out. Hence suspicion should focus on environmental carcinogens, the feminists argue, such as plastics, pesticides (DDT and PCBs, for example, though banned in this country, are still used in many countries that grow the produce we eat), and the industrial runoff in our groundwater. No carcinogen has been linked definitely to human breast cancer yet, but many have been found to cause the disease in mice, and the inexorable increase of the disease in industrialized nations—about 1 percent a year between the 1950s and the 1990s—further hints at environmental factors, as does the fact that women migrants to industrialized countries quickly develop the same breast-cancer rates as those who are native born. Their emphasis on possible ecological factors, which is not shared by groups such as Komen and the American Cancer Society, puts the feminist breast-cancer activists in league with other, frequently rambunctious, social movements—environmental and anticorporate.

But today theirs are discordant voices in a general chorus of sentimentality and good cheer; after all, breast cancer would hardly be the darling of corporate America if its complexion changed from pink to green. It is the very blandness of breast cancer, at least in mainstream perceptions, that makes it an attractive object of corporate charity and a way for companies to brand themselves friends of the middle-aged female market. With breast cancer, "There was no concern that you might actually turn off your audience because of the lifestyle or sexual connotations that AIDS has," Amy Langer, director of the National Alliance of Breast Cancer Organizations, told the *New York Times* in 1996. "That gives corporations a certain freedom and a certain relief in supporting the cause." Or as Cindy Pearson, director of the National Women's Health Network, the organizational progeny of the women's health movement, puts it more caustically: "Breast cancer provides a way of doing something for women, without being feminist."

In the mainstream of breast-cancer culture, one finds very little anger, no mention of possible environmental causes, few complaints about the fact that, in all but the more advanced, metastasized cases, it is the "treatments," not the disease, that cause illness and pain. The stance toward existing treatments is occasionally critical—in *Mamm*, for example—but more commonly grateful; the overall tone, almost universally upbeat. The Breast Friends website, for example, features a series of inspirational quotes: "Don't cry over anything that can't cry over you," "I can't stop the birds of sorrow from circling my head, but I can stop them from building a nest in my hair," "When life hands out lemons, squeeze out a smile," "Don't wait for your ship to come in…Swim out to meet it," and much more of that ilk. Even in the relatively sophisticated *Mamm*, a columnist bemoans not cancer or chemotherapy but the end of chemotherapy, and humorously proposes to deal with her separation anxiety by pitching a tent outside her oncologist's office. So pervasive is the perkiness of the breast-cancer world that unhappiness requires a kind of apology, as when "Lucy," whose "long-term prognosis is not good," starts her personal narrative on breastcancertalk.org by telling us that her story "is not the usual one, full of sweetness and hope, but true nevertheless."

There is, I discover, no single noun to describe a woman with breast cancer. As in the AIDS movement, upon which breast-cancer activism is partly modeled, the words "patient" and "victim," with their aura of self-pity and passivity, have been ruled un-PC. Instead, we get verbs: Those who are in the midst of their treatments are described as "battling" or "fighting," sometimes intensified with "bravely" or "fiercely"—language suggestive of Katharine Hepburn with her face to the wind. Once the treatments are over, one achieves the status of "survivor," which is how the women in my local support group identify themselves, AA-style, as we convene to share war stories and rejoice in our "survivorhood": "Hi, I'm Kathy and I'm a three-year survivor." For those who cease to be survivors and join the more than 40,000 American women who succumb to breast cancer each year—again, no noun applies. They are said to have "lost their battle" and may be memorialized by photographs carried at races for the cure—our lost, brave sisters, our fallen soldiers. But in the overwhelmingly Darwinian culture that has grown up around breast cancer, martyrs count for little; it is the "survivors" who merit constant honor and acclaim. They, after all, offer living proof that expensive and painful treatments may in some cases actually work.

Scared and medically weakened women can hardly be expected to transform their support groups into bands of activists and rush out into the streets, but the equanimity of breast-cancer culture goes beyond mere absence of anger to what looks, all too often, like a positive embrace of the disease. As "Mary" reports, on the Bosom Buds message board:

> I really believe I am a much more sensitive and thoughtful person now. It might sound funny but I was a real worrier before. Now I don't want to waste my energy on worrying. I enjoy life so much more now and in a lot of aspects I am much happier now.

Or this from "Andee":

This was the hardest year of my life but also in many ways the most rewarding. I got rid of the baggage, made peace with my family, met many amazing people, learned to take very good care of my body so it will take care of me, and reprioritized my life.

Cindy Cherry, quoted in the *Washington Post*, goes further:

If I had to do it over, would I want breast cancer? Absolutely. I'm not the same person I was, and I'm glad I'm not. Money doesn't matter anymore. I've met the most phenomenal people in my life through this. Your friends and family are what matter now.

The First Year of the Rest of Your Life, a collection of brief narratives with a foreword by Nancy Brinker and a share of the royalties going to the Komen Foundation, is filled with such testimonies to the redemptive powers of the disease: "I can honestly say I am happier now than I have ever been in my life—even before the breast cancer." "For me, breast cancer has provided a good kick in the rear to get me started rethinking my life." "I have come out stronger, with a new sense of priorities. Never a complaint about lost time, shattered sexual confidence, or the long-term weakening of the arms caused by lymph-node dissection and radiation. What does not destroy you, to paraphrase Nietzsche, makes you a spunkier, more evolved, sort of person.

The effect of this relentless brightsiding is to transform breast cancer into a rite of passage—not an injustice or a tragedy to rail against, but a normal marker in the life cycle, like menopause or graying hair. Everything in mainstream breast-cancer culture serves, no doubt inadvertently, to tame and normalize the disease: The diagnosis may be disastrous, but there are those cunning pink rhinestone angel pins to buy and races to train for. Even the heavy traffic in personal narratives and practical tips, which I found so useful, bears an implicit acceptance of the disease and the current barbarous approaches to its treatment: You can get so busy comparing attractive head scarves that you forget to question a form of treatment that temporarily renders you both bald and immuno-incompetent. Understood as a rite of passage, breast cancer resembles the initiation rites so exhaustively studied by Mircea Eliade: First there is the selection of the initiates—by age in the tribal situation, by mammogram or palpation here. Then come the requisite ordeals—scarification or circumcision within traditional cultures, surgery and chemotherapy for the cancer patient. Finally, the initiate emerges into a new and higher status— an adult and a warrior—or, in the case of breast cancer, a "survivor."

And in our implacably optimistic breast-cancer culture, the disease offers more than the intangible benefits of spiritual upward mobility. You can defy the inevitable disfigurements and come out, on the survivor side, actually prettier, sexier, more femme. In the lore of the disease— shared with me by oncology nurses as well as by survivors— chemotherapy smooths and tightens the skin; helps you lose weight; and, when your hair comes back, it will be fuller, softer, easier to control, and perhaps a surprising new color. These may be myths, but for those willing to get with the prevailing program, opportunities for self-improvement abound. The American Cancer Society offers the "Look Good...Feel Better" program, "dedicated to teaching women cancer patients beauty techniques to help restore their appearance and self-image during cancer treatment." Thirty thousand women participate a year, each copping a free makeover and bag of makeup donated by the Cosmetic, Toiletry, and Fragrance Association, the trade association of the cosmetics industry. As for that lost breast: After reconstruction, why not bring the other one up to speed? Of the more than 50,000 mastectomy patients who opt for reconstruction each year, 17 percent go on, often at the urging of their plastic surgeons, to get additional surgery so that the remaining breast will "match" the more erect and perhaps larger new structure on the other side.

Not everyone goes for cosmetic deceptions, and the question of wigs versus baldness, reconstruction versus undisguised scar, defines one of the few real disagreements in breast-cancer culture. On the more avant-garde, upper-middle-class side, *Mamm* magazine—which features literary critic Eve Kosofsky Sedgwick as a columnist—tends to favor the "natural" look. Here, mastectomy scars can be "sexy" and baldness something to celebrate. The January 2001 cover story features women who "looked upon their baldness not just as a loss, but also as an opportunity: to indulge their playful sides...to come in contact, in new ways, with their truest selves." One decorates her scalp with temporary tattoos of peace signs, panthers, and frogs; another expresses herself with a shocking purple wig; a third reports that unadorned baldness makes her feel "sensual, powerful, able to re-create myself with every new day." But no hard feelings toward those who choose to hide their condition under wigs or scarves; it's just a matter, *Mamm* tells us, of "different aesthetics." Some go for pink ribbons; others will prefer the Ralph Lauren Pink Pony breast-cancer motif. But everyone agrees that breast cancer is a chance for creative self-transformation—a makeover opportunity, in fact.

Now, cheerfulness, up to and including delusion and false hope, has a recognized place in medicine. There is plenty of evidence that depressed and socially isolated people are more prone to succumb to diseases, cancer included, and a diagnosis of cancer is probably capable of precipitating serious depression all by itself. To be told by authority figures that you have a deadly disease, for which no real cure exists, is to enter a liminal state fraught with perils that go well beyond the disease itself. Consider the phenomenon of "voodoo death"—described by ethnographers among, for example, Australian aborigines—in which a person who has been condemned by a suitably potent curse obligingly shuts down and dies within a day or two. Cancer diagnoses could, and in some cases probably do, have the same kind of fatally dispiriting effect. So, it could be argued, the collectively pumped-up optimism of breast-cancer culture may be just what the doctor ordered. Shop for the Cure, dress in pink-ribbon regalia, organize a run or hike—whatever gets you through the night.

But in the seamless world of breast-cancer culture, where one website links to another—from personal narratives and grassroots endeavors to the glitzy level of corporate sponsors and celebrity spokespeople—cheerfulness is more or less mandatory, dissent a kind of treason. Within this tightly knit world, attitudes are subtly adjusted, doubters gently brought back to the fold. In *The First Year of the Rest of Your Life*, for example, each personal narrative is followed by a study question or tip designed to counter the slightest hint of negativity—and they are very slight hints indeed, since the collection includes no harridans, whiners, or feminist militants:

> Have you given yourself permission to acknowledge you have some anxiety or "blocks" and to ask for help for your emotional well-being?
>
> Is there an area in your life of unresolved internal conflict? Is there an area where you think you might want to do some "healthy mourning"?
>
> Try keeping a list of the things you find "good about today."

As an experiment, I post a statement on the Komen.org message board, under the subject line "angry," briefly listing my own heartfelt complaints about debilitating treatments, recalcitrant insurance companies, environmental carcinogens, and, most daringly, "sappy pink ribbons." I receive a few words of encouragement in my fight with the insurance company, which has taken the position that my biopsy was a kind of optional indulgence, but mostly a chorus of rebukes. "Suzy" writes to say, "I really dislike saying you have a bad attitude toward all of this, but you do, and it's not going to help you in the least." "Mary" is a bit more tolerant, writing, "Barb, at this time in your life, it's so important to put all your energies toward a peaceful, if not happy, existence. Cancer is a rotten thing to have happen and there are no answers for any of us as to why. But to live your life, whether you have one more year or 51, in anger and bitterness is such a waste...I hope you can find some peace. You deserve it. We all do. God bless you and keep you in His loving care. Your sister, Mary."

"Kitty," however, thinks I've gone around the bend: "You need to run, not walk, to some counseling...Please, get yourself some help and I ask everyone on this site to pray for you so you can enjoy life to the fullest."

I do get some reinforcement from "Gerri," who has been through all the treatments and now finds herself in terminal condition: "I am also angry. All the money that is raised, all the smiling faces of survivors who make it sound like it is OK to have breast cancer. IT IS NOT OK!" But Gerri's message, like the others on the message board, is posted under the mocking heading "What does it mean to be a breast-cancer survivor?"

"Culture" is too weak a word to describe all this. What has grown up around breast cancer in just the last fifteen years more nearly resembles a cult—or, given that it numbers more than two million women, their families, and friends—perhaps we should say a full-fledged religion. The products—teddy bears, pink-ribbon brooches, and so forth—serve as amulets and talismans, comforting the sufferer and providing visible evidence of faith. The personal narratives serve as testimonials and follow the same general arc as the confessional autobiographies required of seventeenth-century Puritans: First there is a crisis, often involving a sudden apprehension of mortality (the diagnosis or, in the old Puritan case, a stern word from on high); then comes a prolonged ordeal (the treatment or, in the religious case, internal struggle with the Devil); and finally, the blessed certainty of salvation, or its breast-cancer equivalent, survivorhood. And like most recognized religions, breast cancer has its great epideictic events, its pilgrimages and mass gatherings where the faithful convene and draw strength from their numbers. These are the annual races for a cure, attracting a total of about a million people at more than eighty sites—70,000 of them at the largest event, in Washington, DC, which in recent years has been attended by Dan and Marilyn Quayle and Al and Tipper Gore. Everything comes together at the races: Celebrities and corporate sponsors are showcased; products are hawked; talents, like those of the "Swinging, Singing Survivors" from Syracuse, New York, are displayed. It is at the races, too, that the elect confirm their special status. As one participant wrote in the *Washington Post*:

I have taken my "battle scarred" breasts to the Mall, donned the pink shirt, visor, pink shoelaces, etc. and walked proudly among my fellow veterans of the breast cancer war. In 1995, at the age of 44, I was diagnosed and treated for Stage II breast cancer. The experience continues to redefine my life.

Feminist breast-cancer activists, who in the early nineties were organizing their own mass outdoor events—demonstrations, not races—to demand increased federal funding for research, tend to keep their distance from these huge, corporate-sponsored, pink gatherings. Ellen Leopold, for example—a member of the Women's Community Cancer Project in Cambridge and author of *A Darker Ribbon: Breast Cancer, Women, and Their Doctors in the Twentieth Century*—has criticized the races as an inefficient way of raising money. She points out that the Avon Breast Cancer Crusade, which sponsors three-day, sixty-mile walks, spends more than a third of the money raised on overhead and advertising, and Komen may similarly fritter away up to 25 percent of its gross. At least one corporate-charity insider agrees. "It would be much easier and more productive," says Rob Wilson, an organizer of charitable races for corporate clients, "if people, instead of running or riding, would write out a check to the charity."

To true believers, such criticisms miss the point, which is always, ultimately, "awareness." Whatever you do to publicize the disease—wear a pink ribbon, buy a teddy bear, attend a race—reminds other women to come forward for their mammograms. Hence, too, they would argue, the cult of the "survivor": If women neglect their annual screenings, it must be because they are afraid that a diagnosis amounts to a death sentence. Beaming survivors, proudly displaying their athletic prowess, are the best possible advertisement for routine screening mammograms, early detection, and the ensuing round of treatments. Yes, miscellaneous businesses—from tiny distributors of breast-cancer wind chimes and note cards to major corporations seeking a woman-friendly image—benefit in the process, not to mention the breast-cancer industry itself, the estimated $12–16 billion-a-year business in surgery, "breast health centers," chemotherapy "infusion suites," radiation treatment centers, mammograms, and drugs ranging from anti-emetics (to help you survive the nausea of chemotherapy) to tamoxifen (the hormonal treatment for women with estrogen-sensitive tumors). But what's to complain about? Seen through pink-tinted lenses, the entire breast-cancer enterprise—from grassroots support groups and websites to the corporate providers of therapies and sponsors of races—looks like a beautiful example of synergy at work: Cult activities, paraphernalia, and testimonies encourage women to undergo the diagnostic procedures, and since a fraction of these diagnoses will be positive, this means more members for the cult as well as more customers for the corporations, both those that provide medical products and services and those that offer charitable sponsorships.

But this view of a life-giving synergy is only as sound as the science of current detection and treatment modalities, and, tragically, that science is fraught with doubt, dissension, and what sometimes looks very much like denial. Routine screening mammograms, for example, are the major goal of "awareness," as when Rosie O'Donnell exhorts us to go out and "get squished." But not all breast-cancer experts are as enthusiastic. At best the evidence for the salutary effects of routine mammograms—as opposed to breast self-examination—is equivocal, with many respectable large-scale studies showing a vanishingly small impact on overall breast-cancer mortality. For one thing, there are an estimated two to four false positives for every cancer detected, leading thousands of healthy women to go through unnecessary biopsies and anxiety. And even if mammograms were 100 percent accurate, the admirable goal of "early" detection is more elusive than the current breast-cancer dogma admits. A small tumor, detectable only by mammogram, is not necessarily young and innocuous; if it has not spread to the lymph nodes, which is the only form of spreading detected in the common surgical procedure of lymph-node dissection, it may have already moved on to colonize other organs via the bloodstream. David Plotkin, director of the Memorial Cancer Research Foundation of Southern California, concludes that the benefits of routine mammography "are not well established; if they do exist, they are not as great as many women hope." Alan Spievack, a surgeon recently retired from the Harvard Medical School, goes further, concluding from his analysis of dozens of studies that routine screening mammography is, in the words of famous British surgeon Dr. Michael Baum, "one of the greatest deceptions perpetrated on the women of the Western world."

Even if foolproof methods for early detection existed,[2] they would, at the present time, serve only as portals to treatments offering dubious protection and considerable collateral damage. Some women diagnosed with breast

---

2   Some improved prognostic tools, involving measuring a tumor's growth rate and the extent to which it is supplied with blood vessels, are being developed but are not yet in use.

cancer will live long enough to die of something else, and some of these lucky ones will indeed owe their longevity to a combination of surgery, chemotherapy, radiation, and/ or anti-estrogen drugs such as tamoxifen. Others, though, would have lived untreated or with surgical excision alone, either because their cancers were slow-growing or because their bodies' own defenses were successful. Still others will die of the disease no matter what heroic, cell-destroying therapies are applied. The trouble is, we do not have the means to distinguish between these three groups. So for many of the thousands of women who are diagnosed each year, Plotkin notes, "The sole effect of early detection has been to stretch out the time in which the woman bears the knowledge of her condition." These women do not live longer than they might have without any medical intervention, but more of the time they do live is overshadowed with the threat of death and wasted in debilitating treatments.

To the extent that current methods of detection and treatment fail or fall short, America's breast-cancer cult can be judged as an outbreak of mass delusion, celebrating survivorhood by downplaying mortality and promoting obedience to medical protocols known to have limited efficacy. And although we may imagine ourselves to be well past the era of patriarchal medicine, obedience is the message behind the infantilizing theme in breast-cancer culture, as represented by the teddy bears, the crayons, and the prevailing pinkness. You are encouraged to regress to a little-girl state, to suspend critical judgment, and to accept whatever measures the doctors, as parent surrogates, choose to impose.

Worse, by ignoring or underemphasizing the vexing issue

of environmental causes, the breast-cancer cult turns women into dupes of what could be called the Cancer Industrial Complex: the multinational corporate enterprise that with one hand doles out carcinogens and disease and, with the other, offers expensive, semitoxic pharmaceutical treatments. Breast Cancer Awareness Month, for example, is sponsored by AstraZeneca (the manufacturer of tamoxifen), which, until a corporate reorganization in 2000, was a leading producer of pesticides, including acetochlor, classified by the EPA as a "probable human carcinogen." This particularly nasty conjuncture of interests led the environmentally oriented Cancer Prevention Coalition (CPC) to condemn Breast Cancer Awareness Month as "a public relations invention by a major polluter which puts women in the position of being unwitting allies of the very people who make them sick." Although AstraZeneca no longer manufactures pesticides, CPC has continued to criticize the breast-cancer crusade—and the American Cancer Society—for its unquestioning faith in screening mammograms and careful avoidance of environmental issues. In a June 12, 2001, press release, CPC chairman Samuel S. Epstein, MD, and the well-known physician activist Quentin Young castigated the American Cancer Society for its "longstanding track record of indifference and even hostility to cancer prevention… Recent examples include issuing a joint statement with the Chlorine Institute justifying the continued global use of persistent organochlorine pesticides, and also supporting the industry in trivializing dietary pesticide residues as avoidable risks of childhood cancer. ACS policies are further exemplified by allocating under 0.1 percent of its $700 million annual budget to environmental and occupational causes of cancer."

In the harshest judgment, the breast-cancer cult serves as an accomplice in global poisoning—normalizing cancer, prettying it up, even presenting it, perversely, as a positive and enviable experience.

When, my three months of chemotherapy completed, the oncology nurse calls to congratulate me on my "excellent bloodwork results," I modestly demur. I didn't do anything, I tell her, anything but endure—marking the days off on the calendar, living on Protein Revolution canned vanilla health shakes, escaping into novels and work. Courtesy restrains me from mentioning the fact that the tumor markers she's tested for have little prognostic value, that there's no way to know how many rebel cells survived chemotherapy and may be carving out new colonies right now. She insists I should be proud; I'm a survivor now and entitled to recognition at the Relay for Life being held that very evening in town.

So I show up at the middle-school track where the relay's going on just in time for the Survivors' March: About 100 people, including a few men, since the funds raised will go to cancer research in general, are marching around the track eight to twelve abreast while a loudspeaker announces their names and survival times and a thin line of observers, mostly people staffing the raffle and food booths, applauds. It could be almost any kind of festivity, except for the distinctive stacks of cellophane-wrapped pink Hope Bears for sale in some of the booths. I cannot help but like the kinky small-town gemütlichkeit of the event, especially when the audio system strikes up that universal anthem of solidarity, "We Are Family," and a few people of various ages start twisting to the music on the jerry-rigged stage. But the money raised is going far away, to the American Cancer Society, which will not be asking us for our advice on how to spend it.

I approach a woman I know from other settings, one of our local intellectuals, as it happens, decked out here in a pink-and-yellow survivor T-shirt and with an American Cancer Society "survivor medal" suspended on a purple ribbon around her neck. "When do you date your survivorship from?" I ask her, since the announced time, five and a half years, seems longer than I recall. "From diagnosis or the completion of your treatments?" The question seems to annoy or confuse her, so I do not press on to what I really want to ask: At what point, in a downwardly sloping breast-cancer career, does one put aside one's survivor regalia and admit to being, in fact, a die-er? For the dead are with us even here, though in much diminished form. A series of paper bags, each about the right size for a junior burger and fries, line the track. On them are the names of the dead, and inside each is a candle that will be lit later, after dark, when the actual relay race begins.

My friend introduces me to a knot of other women in survivor gear, breast-cancer victims all, I learn, though of course I would not use the V-word here. "Does anyone else have trouble with the term 'survivor'?" I ask, and, surprisingly, two or three speak up. It could be "unlucky," one tells me; it "tempts fate," says another, shuddering slightly. After all, the cancer can recur at any time, either in the breast or in some more strategic site. No one brings up my own objection to the term, though: that the mindless triumphalism of "survivorhood" denigrates the dead and the dying. Did we who live "fight" harder than those who've died? Can we claim to be "braver," better, people than the dead? And why is there no room in this cult for some gracious acceptance of death, when the time comes, which it surely will, through cancer or some other misfortune?

No, this is not my sisterhood. For me at least, breast cancer will never be a source of identity or pride. As my dying correspondent Gerri wrote: "IT IS NOT OK!" What it is, along with cancer generally or any slow and painful way of dying, is an abomination, and, to the extent that it's human-made, also a crime. This is the one great truth that I bring out of the breast-cancer experience, which did not, I can now report, make me prettier or stronger, more feminine or spiritual—only more deeply angry. What sustained me through the "treatments" is a purifying rage, a resolve, framed in the sleepless nights of chemotherapy, to see the last polluter, along with, say, the last smug health insurance operative, strangled with the last pink ribbon. Cancer or no cancer, I will not live that long, of course. But I know this much right now for sure: I will not go into that last good night with a teddy bear tucked under my arm.

THE NAKED TRUTH
ABOUT FITNESS

Lear's, 1990

The conversation has all the earmarks of a serious moral debate. The man is holding out for the pleasures of this life, few as they are and short as it is. The woman (we assume his wife, since they are having breakfast together and this is a prime-time television commercial) defends the high road of virtue and self-denial. We know there will be a solution, that it will taste like fresh-baked cookies and will simultaneously lower cholesterol, fight osteoporosis, and melt off unwholesome flab. We *know* this. What we have almost forgotten to wonder about is this: Since when is breakfast cereal a *moral* issue?

Morality is no longer a prominent feature of civil society. In the 1980s, politicians abandoned it, Wall Street discarded it, televangelists defiled it. Figuratively speaking, we went for the sucrose rush and forgot the challenge of fiber. But only figuratively. For as virtue drained out of our public lives, it reappeared in our cereal bowls, our exercise regimens, and our militant responses to cigarette smoke, strong drink, and greasy food.

We redefined virtue as health. And considering the probable state of our souls, this was not a bad move. By relocating the seat of virtue from the soul to the pecs, the abs, and the coronary arteries, we may not have become the most virtuous people on earth, but we surely became the most desperate for grace. We spend $5 billion a year on our health-club memberships, $2 billion on vitamins, nearly $1 billion on home-exercise equipment, and $6 billion on sneakers to wear out on our treadmills and StairMasters. We rejoice in activities that leave a hangover of muscle pain and in foods that might, in more temperate times, have been classified as fodder. To say we want to be healthy is to gravely understate the case. We want to be *good*.

Consider my own breakfast cereal, a tasteless, colorless substance that clings to the stomach lining with the avidity of Krazy Glue. Quite wisely, the box makes no promise of good taste or visual charm. Even the supposed health benefits are modestly outlined in tiny print. No, the incentive here is of a higher nature. "It is the right thing to do," the manufacturer intones on the back of the box, knowing that, however alluring our temptations to evil, we all want to do the right thing.

The same confusion of the moral and the physical pervades my health club. "Commit to get fit!" is the current slogan, the verb reminding us of the moral tenacity that has become so elusive in our human relationships. In the locker room we sound like the inmates of a miraculously rehabilitative women's prison, always repenting, forever resolving: "I shouldn't have had that doughnut this morning." "I wasn't here for two weeks and now I'm going to pay the price." Ours is a hierarchy of hardness. The soft, the slow, the easily tired rate no compassion, only the coldest of snubs.

Health is almost universally recognized as a *kind* of virtue. At least, most cultures strong enough to leave an ethnographic trace have discouraged forms of behavior that are believed to be unhealthy. Nevertheless, most of us recognize that health is not an accomplishment so much as it is a *potential*. My upper-body musculature, developed largely on Nautilus machines, means that I probably *can* chop wood or unload trucks, not that I ever *will*. Human cultures have valued many things—courage, fertility, craftsmanship, and deadly aim among them—but ours is almost alone in valuing not the deed itself but the mere capacity to perform it.

So what is it that drives us to run, lift, strain, and monitor our metabolisms as if we were really accomplishing something—something pure, that is, and noble? Sociologist Robert Crawford argues that outbreaks of American "healthism" coincide with bouts of middle-class anxiety. It was near the turn of the century, a time of economic turmoil and violent labor struggles, that white-collar Americans embarked on their first 1980s-style health craze. They hiked, rode bikes, lifted weights, and otherwise heeded Teddy Roosevelt's call for "the strenuous life." They filtered their water and fussed about bran (though sweets were heavily favored as a source of energy). On the loonier fringe, they tried "electric belts," vibrating chairs, testicle supporters, "water cures," prolonged mastication, and copious enemas—moralizing all the while about "right living" and "the divine laws of health."

Our own health-and-fitness craze began in another period of economic anxiety—the 1970s, when the economy slid into "stagflation" and a college degree suddenly ceased to guarantee a career above the cab-driving level. In another decade—say, the 1930s or the 1960s—we might have mobilized for economic change. But the 1970s was the era of *How to Be Your Own Best Friend* and *Looking Out for Number One*, a time in which it seemed more important, or more feasible, to reform our bodies than to change the world. Bit by bit and with the best of intentions, we began to set aside the public morality of participation and protest for the personal morality of health.

Our fascination with fitness has paid off. Fewer Americans smoke; they drink less hard liquor, eat more fiber and less fat. Our rate of heart disease keeps declining, our life expectancy is on the rise. We are less dependent on doctors, more aware of our own responsibility for our health. No doubt we feel better, too, at least those of us who have the means and the motivation to give up bourbon for Evian and poker for racquetball. I personally am more confident and probably more durable as a fitness devotee than I ever was in my former life as a chairwarmer.

But there's a difference between health and healthism, between health as a reasonable goal and health as a transcendent value. By confusing health and virtue, we've gotten testier, less tolerant, and ultimately less capable of confronting the sources of disease that do *not* lie within our individual control. Victim blaming, for example, is an almost inevitable side effect of healthism. If health is our personal responsibility, the reasoning goes, then disease must be our *fault*.

I think of the friend—a thoroughly intelligent, compassionate, and (need I say?) ultrafit person—who called to tell me that her sister was facing surgery for a uterine tumor. "I can't understand it," my friend confided. "I'm sure she's been working out." *Not quite enough* was the implication, despite the absence of even the frailest connection between fibroids and muscle tone. But like sixteenth-century Christians, we've come to see every illness as a punishment for past transgressions. When Chicago mayor Harold Washington died of a heart attack, some eulogizers offered baleful mutterings about his penchant for unreformed, high-cholesterol, soul food. When we hear of someone getting cancer, we mentally scan their lifestyle for the fatal flaw—fatty foods, smoking, even "repressed anger."

There are whole categories of disease that cannot, in good conscience, be blamed on the lifestyles or moral shortcomings of their victims. An estimated 25,000 cancer deaths a year, for example, result from exposure to the pesticides applied so lavishly in agribusiness. Ten thousand Americans are killed every year in industrial accidents; an estimated 20,000 more die from exposure to carcinogens in the workplace—asbestos, toxic solvents, radiation. These deaths are preventable, but not with any amount of oat bran or low-impact aerobics. Environmental and occupational diseases will require a far more rigorous social and political regimen of citizen action, legislation, and enforcement.

Even unhealthy lifestyles can have "environmental" as well as personal origins. Take the matter of diet and smoking. It's easy for the middle-class fiber enthusiast to look down on the ghetto dweller who smokes cigarettes and spends her food stamps on Doritos and soda pop. But in low-income neighborhoods convenience stores and fast-food joints are often the only sources of food, while billboards and TV commercials are the primary sources of nutritional "information." Motivation is another problem. It's one thing to give up smoking and sucrose when life seems long and promising, quite another when it might well be short and brutal.

Statistically speaking, the joggers and bran eaters are concentrated in the white-collar upper-middle class. Blue- and pink-collar people still tend to prefer Bud to Evian and meat loaf to poached salmon. And they still smoke—at a rate of 51 percent, compared with 35 percent for people in professional and managerial occupations. These facts should excite our concern: Why not special cardiovascular-fitness programs for the assembly-line worker as well as the executive? Reduced-rate health-club memberships for truck drivers and typists? Nutritional supplements for the down-and-out? Instead, healthism tends to reinforce long-standing prejudices. If healthy habits are an expression of moral excellence, then the working class is not only "tacky," ill-mannered, or whatever else we've been encouraged to believe—it's morally deficient.

Thus, perversely, does healthism ease the anxieties of the affluent. No amount of straining against muscle machines can save laid-off workers; no aerobic exercises can reduce the price of a private-school education. But fitness *can* give its practitioners a sense of superiority over the potbellied masses. On the other side of victim blaming is an odious mood of self-congratulation: "We" may not be any smarter or more secure about our futures. But surely we are more disciplined and pure.

In the end, though—and the end does come—no one is well served by victim blaming. The victim isn't always "someone else," someone fatter, lazier, or more addicted to smoke and grease. The fact is that we do die, all of us, and that almost all of us will encounter disease, disability, and considerable discomfort either in the process or along the way. The final tragedy of healthism is that it leaves us so ill prepared for the inevitable. If we believe that health is a sign of moral purity and anything less is a species of sin, then death condemns us all as failures. Longevity is not a resoundingly interesting lifetime achievement, just as working out is not exactly a life's work.

Somehow, we need to find our way back to being healthy without being health*ist*. Health is great. It makes us bouncier and probably happier. Better yet, it can make us fit *for* something: strong enough to fight the big-time polluters, for example, the corporate waste dumpers; tough enough to take on economic arrangements that condemn so many to poverty and to dangerous occupations; lean and powerful enough to demand a more nurturing, less anxiety-ridden social order.

Health is good. But it is not, as even the ancient and athletic Greeks would have said, *the* good.

GOT GREASE?

Los Angeles Times, 2002

I t's not only the stock market that has the upper classes biting their fingernails. In the last few years, the low-fat, high-carb way of life that was central to the self-esteem of the affluent has been all but discredited. If avarice was the principal vice of the bourgeoisie, a commitment to low fat was its counterbalancing virtue. You can bet, for example, that those CEOs who cooked the books and ransacked their companies' assets did not start the day with two eggs over easy, a rasher of bacon, and a side of hash browns. No, unbuttered low-fat muffins and delicate slices of melon fueled the crimes of Wall Street: Grease was for proles.

But that dogma no longer holds up. A large number of nutritionists now deny that the low-fat approach will make you slim and resistant to heart disease. As we know, the onset of the American epidemic of obesity coincided precisely with the arrival of the antifat campaign in the 1980s, accompanied by a cornucopia of low-fat cookies, cakes, potato chips, and frozen pot-roast dinners. Millions of Americans began to pig out on "guilt-free" feasts of ungarnished carbs—with perverse and often debilitating results, especially among those unable to afford health club memberships and long hours on the elliptical trainer.

I have confirmed these findings with my own scientific study, which draws on a sample of exactly two: Jane Brody, the *New York Times* health columnist and tireless opponent of all foodstuffs other than veggies and starch, and me. It was Brody, more than anyone else, who promoted the low-fat way of life to the masses, from the eighties on, with headlines like "Our Excessive Protein Intake Can Hurt Liver, Kidneys, Bone," "Fill Up on Bread to Lose Weight," and "Chemicals in Food Less Harmful Than Fat."

As she revealed in a 1999 column, Brody was herself raised on a high-carb, low-fat diet of "shredded wheat, oatmeal, challah, Jewish rye and bagels," the last, presumably, unblemished by the customary "shmear" of cream cheese. I, meanwhile, was raised on a diet that might strain even an Inuit's gallbladder. We ate eggs every morning, meat for lunch, and meat again for dinner, invariably accompanied by gravy or at least pan drippings. We buttered everything from broccoli to brownies and would have buttered butter itself if it were not for the problems of traction presented by the butter-butter interface.

And how did Brody and I exit from our dietarily opposite childhoods? She, by her own admission, was a veritable butterball by her mid-twenties—a size 14 at just under five feet tall. I, at five-foot-seven, weighed in at a gaunt and geeky 110 pounds.

Fast-forwarding to the present, we assume Brody is now admirably trim, if only because of her exercise regimen, since otherwise she wouldn't have dared to promote the low-fat dogma in person. For my part, I no longer butter my brownies, perhaps in part because of Brody's tireless preaching. But the amount of fat she recommends for an entire day—one tablespoon—wouldn't dress a small salad for me or lubricate a single Triscuit. I still regard bread as a vehicle for butter and chicken as an excuse for gravy or, when served cold, mayonnaise. The result? I'm a size 6 and have a cholesterol level that an envious doctor once denounced as "too low." Case closed.

But if that doesn't convince you, there's now a solid medical explanation for why the low-fat, high-carb approach is actually fattening. A meal of carbs—especially those derived from sugar and refined flour—is followed by a surge of blood sugar, then, as insulin is released in response, a sudden collapse, leaving you often light-headed, cranky, headachy, and certainly hungrier than before you ate. Fats and protein can make you fat, too, of course, if ingested in sufficient quantity, but at least they fulfill the conventional role of anything designated as a foodstuff, which is to say that they leave you feeling like you've actually eaten something.

As long as people want to lose weight, we'll probably have dueling diet doctors. But now that it's apparent that the prevailing low-fat wisdom is bunk, why would anyone opt for a diet with a mouthfeel that mimics sawdust?

Perhaps because facts don't matter when a dogma so flattering to the affluent is at stake. In the last couple of decades, the low-fat way of life has become an important indicator of social rank, along with whole-grain—as opposed to white—bread and natural fibers versus polyester. If you doubt this, consider the multiple meanings of grease, as in *greaser* and *greasy spoon*. Among the nutritionally correct upper-middle-class people of my acquaintance, a dinner of French bread and pasta has long been considered a suitable offering for guests—followed by a plate of bone-dry biscotti. And don't bother asking for the butter.

What has made the low-fat dogma especially impervious to critique, though, is the overclass identification of low-fat with virtue and fat with the long-suspected underclass tendency to self-indulgence. Low-fat is the flip side of avarice for a reason: Thanks to America's deep streak of Puritanism—perhaps mixed with a dollop of democratic idealism—ours has been a culture in which everyone wants to be rich but no one wants to be known as a "fat cat." We might be hogging the earth's resources, the affluent seem to be saying, but at least we're not indulging the ancient human craving for fat. So the low-fat diet has been the hair shirt under the fur coat—the daily deprivation that offsets the endless greed.

I wouldn't go so far as to blame the financial shenanigans of the last few years on Brody, but clearly there is a connection. The long-term effects of a low-fat, low-protein diet are easy to guess—a perpetual feeling of insatiety, a relentless, gnawing hunger for more. No doubt, for many thousands of low-fat, high-earning people, money became a substitute, however unfulfilling, for dietary fat. The effect was naturally strongest in Silicon Valley, where dot-commania collided with the northern California, Berkeley-based carbo cult, to disastrous effect. That "irrational exuberance" of the late nineties was in fact the giddiness of hypoglycemia, induced by a diet of boutique muffins and $5-a-loaf "artisan bread."

My advice to the fat-deprived execs: Take a break from the markets and go out and get yourself a bacon cheeseburger and fries or, if you still have a few bucks to toss around, a nice pancetta-rich plate of spaghetti carbonara. Eat every last drop. Then lean back, with the grease dripping down your chin, smile at the people around you, and appreciate, perhaps for the very first time, what it feels like to have enough.

OUR BROKEN MENTAL HEALTH SYSTEM

The Nation, 2007

On April 16, 2007, a withdrawn, silent kid named Cho Seung-Hui opened fire on the Virginia Tech campus, killing thirty-two people. Leaving aside the issue of WMM (Weapons of Mass Murder, aka guns), the massacre has something to teach us about the American mental health system. It's farcically easy for an American to be diagnosed as mentally ill: All you have to do is squirm in your fourth-grade seat and you're likely to be hit with the label of ADHD and a prescription for an antipsychotic. But when a genuine whack job comes along—the kind of guy who calls himself "Question Mark" and turns in essays on bloodbaths—there's apparently nothing to be done.

While Cho Seung-Hui quietly—very quietly—pursued his studies, millions of ordinary, nonviolent folks were being subjected to heavy-duty labels ripped from the DSM-IV. An estimated 20 percent of American children and teenagers are diagnosed as mentally ill in the course of a year, and adults need not feel left out of the labeling spree: Watch enough commercials and you'll learn that you suffer from social phobia, depression, stress, or some form of sexual indifference (at least I find it hard to believe that all this "erectile dysfunction" is purely physical in origin).

Consider the essay "Manufacturing Depression" that appeared in *Harper's*. Hoping to qualify for a study on "Minor Depression" at the Massachusetts General Hospital, the author, Gary Greenberg, presented a list of his problems, including "the stalled writing projects and the weedy garden, the dwindling bank accounts and the difficulties of parenthood," in other words, "the typical plaint and worry and disappointment of a middle-aged, middle-class American life." Alas, it turned out he did not qualify for the Minor Depression study. "What you have," the doctor told him, "is Major Depression."

A number of psychiatrists have pointed out that the real business of the mental health system is social control. Normal, physically active nine-year-olds have to be taught to sit still. Adults facing "dwindling bank accounts" have to be drugged or disciplined into accepting their fate. What therapy aims to achieve is not "health" but compliance with social norms. The idea still rings true every time I've been confronted with a "pre-employment personality test" that reads like a police interrogation: How much have you stolen from previous employers? Do you have any objections to selling cocaine? Is it "easier to work when you're a little bit high"?

Then there is the ubiquitous Myers-Briggs test, which seems obsessed with weeding out loners. Presumably, someone in the HR department can use your test results to determine whether you're a good "fit." (Incidentally, Myers-

Briggs possesses no category for and no means of detecting the person who might show up at work one day with an automatic weapon.)

But for all the attention to "personality" and garden-variety neurosis, we are left with the problem of the afore-mentioned psychotics, and the painful question remains: If Cho Seung-Hui's oddities had been noted earlier—say, when he was still under eighteen—could he have been successfully diagnosed and treated? Journalist Paul Raeburn's 2004 book, *Acquainted with the Night: A Parent's Quest to Understand Depression and Bipolar Disorder in His Children*, suggests that the answer is a resounding no.

When his own children started acting up, Raeburn found that there are scores of therapists listed in the Yellow Pages, as well as quite a few inpatient facilities for the flamboyantly symptomatic. But nothing linked these various elements of potential care into anything that could be called a "system." The therapists, who all march to their own theoretical and pharmaceutical drummers, have no reliable connections to the hospitals, nor do the hospitals have any means of providing follow-up care for patients after they are discharged.

Then there is the matter of payment. As managed-care plans gained ground in the health care system in the 1990s, Raeburn reports, they cut their spending on psychiatric treatment by 55 percent, putting mental health services almost out of the reach of the middle class, never mind the poor. Hence, no doubt, the fact that three-quarters of children and teenagers who receive a diagnosis of mental illness get no care for it at all.

If we have no working mental health system, and no means of detecting or treating the murderously disturbed, then here's yet another argument for doing what we should do anyway: Limit access to the tools of murder, end the casual sale of handguns.

LIPOSUCTION: THE KEY TO ENERGY INDEPENDENCE

The Nation, 2008

Everyone talks about our terrible dependency on oil—foreign and otherwise—but hardly anyone mentions what it *is*. Fossil fuel, all right, but whose fossils? Mostly tiny plants called diatoms, but quite possibly a few Barney-like creatures went into the mix, like stegosaurus, brontosaurus, or other giant reptiles that shared the Jurassic period with all those diatoms. What we are burning in our cars and using to heat or cool our homes is, in other words, a highly processed version of corpse juice.

Think of this for a moment, if only out of respect for the dead: There you were, about a hundred million years ago, maybe a contented little diatom or a great big brontosaurus stumbling around the edge of a tar pit—a lord of the earth. And what are you now? A sludge of long-chain carbon molecules that will be burned so that some mammalian biped can make a CVS run for Mountain Dew and chips.

It's an old human habit, living off the roadkill of the planet. There's evidence, for example, that early humans were engaged in scavenging before they figured out how to hunt for themselves. They'd scan the sky for circling vultures, dash off to the kill site—hoping that the leopard that did the actual hunting had sauntered off for a nap—and gobble up what remained of the prey. It was risky, but it beat doing your own antelope tracking.

We continue our career as scavengers today, attracted not by vultures but by signs saying Safeway or Giant. Inside these sites, we find bits of dead animals wrapped neatly in plastic. The killing has already been done for us—usually by underpaid immigrant workers rather than leopards.

I say to my fellow humans: It's time to stop feeding off the dead and grow up! I don't know about food, but I have a plan for achieving fuel self-sufficiency in less time than it takes to say "Arctic National Wildlife Refuge." The idea came to me from reports of the growing crime of french-fry-oil theft: Certain desperate individuals are stealing restaurants' discarded cooking oil, which can then be used to fuel cars. So the idea is this: Why not skip the french-fry phase and harvest high-energy hydrocarbons right from ourselves?

I'm talking about liposuction, of course, and it's a mystery to me why it hasn't occurred to any of those geniuses who are constantly opining about fuel prices on MSNBC. The average liposuction procedure removes about half a gallon of liquid fat, which may not seem like much. But think of the vast reserves our nation is literally sitting on! Thirty percent of Americans are obese, or about 90 million individuals or 45 million gallons of easily available fat—not from dead diatoms but from our very own bellies and butts.

This is the humane alternative to biofuels derived directly from erstwhile foodstuffs like corn. Biofuels, as you might have noticed, are exacerbating the global food crisis by turning edible plants into gasoline. But we could put humans back in the loop by first turning the corn into Fritos and hence into liposuctionable body fat. There would be a reason to live again, even a patriotic rationale for packing on the pounds.

True, liposuction is not risk-free, as the numerous doctors' websites on the subject inform us. And those of us who insist on driving gas guzzlers may quickly deplete their personal fat reserves, much as heroin addicts run out of usable veins. But the gaunt, punctured look could become a fashion statement. Already, the combination of a tiny waist and a huge carbon footprint—generated by one's Hummer and private jet—is considered a sign of great wealth.

And think what it would do for our nation's self-esteem. We may not lead the world in scientific innovation, educational achievement, or low infant mortality, but we are the global champions of obesity. Go to http://www.nation master.com/graph/hea_obe-health-obesity and you'll find America well ahead of the pack when it comes to personal body fat, while those renowned oil producers—Saudi Arabia, Venezuela, and Iran—aren't even among the top twenty-nine. All we need is a healthy dose of fat pride and for CVS to start marketing home liposuction kits. That run for Mountain Dew and chips could soon be an energy-neutral proposition.

THE SELFISH SIDE OF GRATITUDE

New York Times, 2015

This holiday season, there was something in the air that was even more inescapable than the scent of pumpkin spice: gratitude.

In November, NPR issued a number of brief exhortations to cultivate gratitude, culminating in an hourlong special on the "science of gratitude," narrated by Susan Sarandon. Writers in *Time* magazine, the *New York Times*, and *Scientific American* recommended it as a surefire ticket to happiness and even better health. Robert Emmons, a psychology professor at the University of California, Davis, who studies the "science of gratitude," argues that it leads to a stronger immune system and lower blood pressure, as well as "more joy and pleasure."

It's good to express our thanks, of course, to those who deserve recognition. But this holiday gratitude is all about you, and how you can feel better about yourself.

Gratitude is hardly a fresh face on the self-improvement scene. By the turn of the twenty-first century, Oprah Winfrey and other motivational figures were promoting an "attitude of gratitude." Martin Seligman, the father of "positive psychology," which is often enlisted to provide some sort of scientific basis for "positive thinking," has been offering instruction in gratitude for more than a decade. In the logic of positive self-improvement, anything that feels good—from scenic walks to family gatherings to expressing gratitude—is worth repeating.

Positive thinking was in part undone by its own silliness, glaringly displayed in the 2006 best seller *The Secret*, which announced that you could have anything, like the expensive necklace you'd been coveting, simply by "visualizing" it in your possession.

The financial crash of 2008 further dimmed the luster of positive thinking, which had done so much to lure would-be homeowners and predatory mortgage lenders into a speculative frenzy. This left the self-improvement field open to more cautious stances, like mindfulness and resilience, and—for those who could still muster it—gratitude.

Gratitude is at least potentially more prosocial than the alternative self-improvement techniques. You have to be grateful to *someone*, who could be an invisible God, but might as well be a friend, mentor, or family member. The gratitude literature often advises loving, human interactions: writing a "gratitude letter" to a helpful colleague, for example, or taking time to tell a family member how wonderful they are. These are good things to do, in a moral sense, and the new gratitude gurus are here to tell us that they also *feel* good.

But is gratitude always appropriate? The answer depends on who's giving it and who's getting it or, very commonly in our divided society, how much of the wealth gap it's expected to bridge. Suppose you were an $8-an-hour Walmart employee who saw her base pay elevated this year, by company fiat, to $9 an hour. Should you be grateful to the Waltons, who are the richest family in America? Or to Walmart's chief executive, whose annual base pay is close to $1 million and whose home sits on nearly 100 acres of land in Bentonville, Arkansas? Reflexively grateful people are easily dismissed as "chumps," and in this hypothetical case, the term would seem to apply.

Perhaps it's no surprise that gratitude's rise to self-help celebrity status owes a lot to the conservative-leaning John Templeton Foundation. At the start of this decade, the foundation, which promotes free-market capitalism, gave $5.6 million to Dr. Emmons, the gratitude researcher. It also funded a $3 million initiative called Expanding the Science and Practice of Gratitude through the Greater Good Science Center at the University of California, Berkeley, which coproduced the special that aired on NPR. The foundation does not fund projects to directly improve the lives of poor individuals, but it has spent a great deal, through efforts like these, to improve their attitudes.

It's a safe guess, though, that most of the people targeted by gratitude exhortations actually have something to be grateful for, such as Janice Kaplan, the author of the memoir *The Gratitude Diaries*, who spent a year appreciating her high-earning husband and successful grown children. And it is here that the prosocial promise of gratitude begins to dim. True, saying "thank-you" is widely encouraged, but much of the gratitude advice involves no communication or interaction of any kind.

Consider this, from a yoga instructor on CNN.com: "Cultivate your sense of gratitude by incorporating giving thanks into a personal morning ritual, such as writing in a gratitude journal, repeating an affirmation, or practicing a meditation. It could even be as simple as writing what you give thanks for on a sticky note and posting it on your mirror or computer. To help you establish a daily routine, create a 'thankfulness' reminder on your phone or computer to pop up every morning and prompt you."

Who is interacting here? "You" and "you."

The *Harvard Mental Health Letter* begins its list of gratitude interventions with the advice that you should send a thank-you letter as often as once a month, but all the other suggested exercises can be undertaken without human contact: "Thank someone mentally," "Keep a gratitude journal," "Count your blessings," "Meditate" and, for those who are so inclined, "Pray."

So it's possible to achieve the recommended levels of gratitude without spending a penny or uttering a word. All you have to do is to generate, within yourself, the good feelings associated with gratitude, and then bask in its warm, comforting glow. If there is any loving involved in this, it is self-love, and the current hoopla around gratitude is a celebration of onanism.

Yet there is a need for more gratitude, especially from those who have a roof over their heads and food on their table. Only it should be a more vigorous and inclusive sort of gratitude than what is being urged on us now. Who picked the lettuce in the fields, processed the standing rib roast, drove these products to the stores, stacked them on the supermarket shelves, and, of course, prepared them and brought them to the table? Saying grace to an abstract God is an evasion; there are crowds, whole communities of actual people, many of them with aching backs and tenuous finances, who made the meal possible.

The real challenge of gratitude lies in figuring out how to express our debt to them, whether through generous tips or, say, by supporting their demands for decent pay and better working conditions. But now we're not talking about gratitude, we're talking about a far more muscular impulse— and this is, to use the old-fashioned term, "solidarity"— which may involve getting up off the yoga mat.

MEN

HOW "NATURAL" IS RAPE?

Time, 2000

It was cute the first time around: when the president lost his head over Monica's thong undies, that is, and the evolutionary psychologists declared that he was just following the innate biological urge to, tee-hee, spread his seed. Natural selection favors the reproductively gifted, right? But the latest daffy Darwinist attempt to explain male bad behavior is not quite so amusing. Rape, according to evolutionary theorists Randy Thornhill and Craig T. Palmer, represents just another seed-spreading technique favored by natural selection. Sure it's nasty, brutish, and short on foreplay. But it gets the job done.

Thornhill and Palmer aren't endorsing rape, of course. In their article in the latest issue of the *Sciences*—which is already generating a high volume of buzz although their book, *A Natural History of Rape*, won't be out until April— they say they just want to correct the feminist fallacy that "rape is not about sex," it's about violence and domination. The authors argue, among other things, that since the majority of victims are women of childbearing age, the motive must be lust and the intent, however unconscious, must be to impregnate. Hence rape is not an act of pathology, but a venerable old strategy for procreation. What's "natural" isn't always nice.

Now, there are people who reject any attempt to apply evolutionary theory to human behavior, and, as far as I'm concerned, they can go back to composing their annual letters to Santa Claus. Obviously, humans have been shaped by natural selection (though it's not always so obvious how). We are not the descendants of the kindest or wisest of hominids—only of those who managed, by cunning or luck, to produce a few living offspring. But is rape really an effective strategy for guys who, deep down in their genes, just want to be fruitful and multiply?

There are plenty of evolutionary psychologists who would answer with a resounding no. They emphasize the evolutionary value of the human male's "parental investment"—his tendency to stick around after the act of impregnation and help out with the kids. Prehistoric dads may not have read many bedtime stories, but, in this account, they very likely brought home the occasional antelope haunch, and they almost certainly played a major role in defending the family from four-legged predators. In contrast, the rapist generally operates on a hit-and-run basis—which may be all right for stocking sperm banks, but is not quite so effective if the goal is to produce offspring who will survive in a challenging environment. The children of guys who raped-and-ran must have been a scrawny lot and doomed to end up on some leopard's lunch menu.

There's another problem with rape—again, from a

strictly Darwinian perspective. Even if it isn't "about violence," as feminists have claimed, it almost always involves violence or at least the threat thereof; otherwise, it isn't rape. Thornhill and Palmer downplay the amount of physical violence accompanying rape, claiming that no more than 22 percent of victims suffer any "gratuitous" violence beyond that necessary to subdue them. But we are still talking about appalling levels of damage to the mother of the rapist's prospective offspring. Most rape victims suffer long-term emotional consequences—like depression and memory loss—that are hardly conducive to successful motherhood. It's a pretty dumb Darwinian specimen who can't plant his seed without breaking the "vessel" in the process.

Thornhill and Palmer's insistence that the rapist isn't a psychopath, just an ordinary fellow who's in touch with his inner caveman, leads to some dubious prescriptions. They want to institute formal training for boys in how to resist their "natural" sexual impulses to rape. Well, sure, kids should learn that rape is wrong, along with all other forms of assault. But the emphasis on rape as a natural male sexual impulse is bound to baffle those boys—and I would like to think there are more than a few of them out there—whose sexual fantasies have never drifted in a rape-ward direction.

As for the girls, Thornhill and Palmer want them to realize that since rape is really "about sex," it very much matters how they dress. But where is the evidence that women in miniskirts are more likely to be raped than women in dirndls? Women were raped by the thousands in Bosnia, for example, and few if any of them were wearing bikinis or bustiers.

Yes, rape is "about sex," in that it involves a certain sexlike act. But it's a pretty dismal kind of "sex" in which one person's pain, and possible permanent injury, is the occasion for the other one's pleasure. What most of us mean by sex is something mutual and participatory, loving and uplifting, or at least flirty and fun. In fact, making the world safe for plunging necklines and thong undies is a goal that enlightened members of both sexes ought to be able to get behind. As for those guys who can't distinguish between sex and rape, I don't care whether they're as "natural" as granola, they don't deserve to live in the company of women.

THE WARRIOR CULTURE

Time, 1990

In what we like to think of as "primitive" warrior cultures, the passage to manhood requires the blooding of a spear, the taking of a scalp or head. Among the Masai of eastern Africa and dozens of other human cultures, a man could not marry until he had demonstrated his capacity to kill in battle. Leadership, too, in a warrior society is typically contingent on military prowess and wrapped in the mystique of death. In the Solomon Islands, a chief's importance could be reckoned by the number of skulls posted around his door, and it was the duty of the Aztec kings to nourish the gods with the hearts of human captives.

All warrior peoples have fought for the same high-sounding reasons: honor, glory, or revenge. The nature of their real and perhaps not conscious motivations is a subject of much debate. Some anthropologists postulate a murderous instinct, almost unique among living species, in human males. Others discern a materialistic motive behind every fray: a need for slaves, grazing land, or even human flesh to eat. Still others point to the similarities

between war and other male pastimes—the hunt and outdoor sports—and suggest that it is boredom, ultimately,
that stirs men to fight.

But in a warrior culture it hardly matters which motive is
most basic. Aggressive behavior is rewarded whether or not
it is innate to the human psyche. Shortages of resources are
habitually taken as occasions for armed offensives, rather
than for hard thought and innovation. And war, to a warrior people, is of course the highest adventure, the surest
antidote to malaise, the endlessly repeated theme of legend,
song, religious myth, and personal quest for meaning. It is
how men die and what they find to live for.

"You must understand that Americans are a warrior nation," Senator Daniel Patrick Moynihan told a group of
Arab leaders in 1990. He said this proudly, and he may,
without thinking through the ugly implications, have told
the truth. In many ways, in outlook and behavior, the
United States has begun to act like a "primitive" warrior
culture.

We seem to believe that leadership is expressed, in no
small part, by a willingness to cause the deaths of others.
After the US invasion of Panama, President Bush exulted
that no one could call him "timid"; he was at last a "macho
man." The press, in even more primal language, hailed him
for succeeding in an "initiation rite" by demonstrating his
"willingness to shed blood."

For lesser offices, too, we apply the standards of a warrior
culture. Female candidates are routinely advised to overcome the handicap of their gender by talking "tough." Thus,
for example, Dianne Feinstein embraced capital punish-

ment, while Colorado senatorial candidate Josie Heath found it necessary to announce that although she is the mother of an eighteen-year-old son, she is prepared to vote for war. Male candidates are finding their military records under scrutiny. No one expects them, as elected officials in a civilian government, to pick up a spear or a sling and fight. But they must state, at least, their willingness to have another human being killed.

More tellingly, we are unnerved by peace and seem to find it boring. When the cold war ended, we found no reason to celebrate. Instead we heated up the "war on drugs." What should have been a public-health campaign, focused on the persistent shame of poverty, became a new occasion for martial rhetoric and muscle flexing. Months later, when the Berlin Wall fell and communism collapsed throughout Europe, we Americans did not dance in the streets. What we did, according to the networks, was change the channel to avoid the news. Nonviolent revolutions do not uplift us, and the loss of mortal enemies only seems to leave us empty and bereft.

Our collective fantasies center on mayhem, cruelty, and violent death. Loving images of the human body—especially of bodies seeking pleasure or expressing love—inspire us with the urge to censor. Our preference is for warrior themes: the lone fighting man, bandoliers across his naked chest, mowing down lesser men in gusts of automatic-weapon fire. Only a real war seems to revive our interest in real events. With the Iraqi crisis, the networks report, ratings for news shows rose again—even higher than they were for Panama.

And as in any warrior culture, our warrior elite takes pride of place. Social crises multiply numbingly— homelessness, illiteracy, epidemic disease—and our leaders tell us solemnly that nothing can be done. There is no money. We are poor, not rich, a debtor nation. Meanwhile, nearly a third of the federal budget flows, even in moments of peace, to the warriors and their weaponmakers. When those priorities are questioned, some new "crisis" dutifully arises to serve as another occasion for armed and often unilateral intervention.

With Operation Desert Shield, our leaders were reduced to begging foreign powers for the means to support our warrior class. It does not seem to occur to us that the other great northern powers—Japan, Germany, the Soviet Union—might not have found the stakes so high or the crisis quite so threatening. It has not penetrated our imagination that in a world where the powerful, industrialized nation-states are at last at peace, there might be other ways to face down a pint-size third-world warrior state than with massive force of arms. Nor have we begun to see what an anachronism we are in danger of becoming: a warrior nation in a world that pines for peace, a high-tech state with the values of a roving warrior band.

A leftist might blame "imperialism"; a right-winger would call our problem "internationalism." But an anthropologist, taking the long view, might say this is just what warriors do. Intoxicated by their own drumbeats and war songs, fascinated by the glint of steel and the prospect of blood, they will go forth, time and again, to war.

AT LAST, A NEW MAN

New York Times, 1984

There have been waves of "new women" arriving on cue almost every decade for the last thirty years or so—from the civic-minded housewife, to the liberated single, to the dressed-for-success executive. But men, like masculinity itself, were thought to be made of more durable stuff. Change, if it came at all, would come only in response to some feminine—or feminist—initiative.

In the 1970s, for example, it had become an article of liberal faith that a new man would eventually rise up to match the new feminist woman, that he would be more androgynous than any "old" variety of man, and that the change, which was routinely expressed as an evolutionary leap from John Wayne to Alan Alda, would be an unambiguous improvement.

Today a new man is at last emerging, and I say this as someone who is not much given to such announcements. A new man, like a new sexuality or a new conservatism, is more likely to turn out to be a journalistic artifact than a cultural sea change.

But this time something has happened, both to our common expectations of what constitutes manhood and to the way many men are choosing to live.

I see the change in the popular images that define masculinity, and I see it in the men I know, mostly in their thirties, who are conscious of possessing a sensibility and even a way of life that is radically different from that of their fathers. These men have been, in a word, feminized, but without necessarily becoming more feminist. In fact, I do not think that those of us who are feminists either can or, for the most part, would want to take credit for the change.

If we had not all been so transfixed by the changes in women in the last fifteen or twenty years, far more attention would have been paid to the new man by this time. We can recall—with nostalgia or relief—the feminine ideal of less than a generation ago: the full-time homemaker who derived her status as well as her livelihood from her husband and considered paid employment a misfortune visited only on the opposite sex or the unwed. So sudden was her demise, at least as an ideal for most girls to aspire to, that we sometimes forget the notion of manhood that went along with that "feminine mystique."

I think of the men of my father's generation, men who came of age in the 1950s and who, like my own father, defined their masculinity, if not their identity, in terms of their ability to make a living and support a family. This was a matter of convention as much as of choice, for the man who failed to marry and become a reliable provider was considered a failure, and those who failed to marry at all (that is, by the age of thirty or so) were candidates for the label of "latent homosexual." Men of this generation were encouraged to equate effeminacy with un-Americanism and to use their leisure to escape—into sports, hunting, or simply the basement—from women and all things feminine.

We recognize that for the most part men aren't like that anymore and those who are seem grievously out of style. Usually, we think of the change simply as a movement away from the old norm—an opening up of possibilities. But the new man emerging today is not simply the old one minus the old prohibitions and anxieties. There is a new complex of traits and attitudes that has come to define manhood and a kind of new masculine gentility.

Taking his mid-1950s progenitor as a benchmark, the most striking characteristic of the new man is that he no longer anchors his identity in his role as family breadwinner. He may *be* the family breadwinner, or imagine becoming one someday, but his ability to do so has ceased to be the urgent and necessary proof of his maturity or of his heterosexuality. In fact, he may postpone or avoid marriage indefinitely—which is why the women's magazines complain so much about the male "lack of commitment" and "refusal to grow up."

But if the old responsibilities have declined, the pressure is not off: The old man expressed his status through his house and the wife who presided over it; the new man expects to express his status through his own efforts and is deeply anxious about the self he presents to the world. Typically, he is concerned—some might say obsessed—with his physical health and fitness. He is an avid and style-conscious consumer, not only of clothes but of food, home furnishings, and visible displays of culture. Finally, and in a marked reversal of the old masculinity, he is concerned that people find him, not forbearing or strong, but genuine, open, and sensitive.

These traits do not always occur together; in individual men, in fact, we are probably more used to encountering them separately, scattered among men of the middle and upper-middle classes. For example, on a spring lunch hour in the nation's capital, you will find scores of ruddy, middle-aged men, jogging resolutely on the banks of the Potomac, and I doubt that many of them are practitioners of the new sensitivity. On the other hand, sensitivity is now fairly well dispersed throughout the male population, so that it is not uncommon to encounter it in married breadwinners with children, where it may take the form of a somewhat fatuous volubility on the subject of fathering. Then, too, rejection of the breadwinner role—at least as reflected in the high rate of default on child-support payments by men who could well afford to pay them—is so endemic that it cannot be confined to a special new type of man. There are men who are otherwise old-fashioned but have taken up a formerly feminine activity like cooking; just as there must be (though I have not met one) upscale bachelors who eschew physical exercise and designer shirts.

But it is possible, increasingly, to find men who qualify as prototypical new males. They are likely to be from twenty-five to forty years old, single, affluent, and living in a city, for it is among such men that the most decisive break in the old masculine values is occurring. In these men, the traits that define the new masculinity are beginning to form a pattern and even to frame a new kind of conformity—one that is vastly different, however, from the gray-flannel blues that bedeviled an earlier generation of middle-class American men.

Jeffrey A. Greenberg was one of a number of young men interviewed by me and my assistant, Harriet Bernstein, a market researcher, who helped me locate single affluent men who were willing to discuss their interests and values. Greenberg is a thirty-two-year-old resident in neurosurgery who lives and works in Washington. He puts in eighty to a hundred hours a week as a doctor, works out in a gym three times a week, and otherwise devotes himself to "the study and acquisition of art." Cooking is his latest enthusiasm: "I thought I wasn't creative in that aspect, but I found that I'm definitely OK. I know what tastes good and I'm able to do that." He entertains at least once a week, which gives him a chance to show off his paintings and eclectic music collection. He indicated that, while there were women in his life, he did not yet "have the ability to make a firm commitment."

Thirty or even twenty years ago, a man like Jeffrey Greenberg would have been a self-conscious minority of "older" bachelors—probably envied by his married friends, and, at the same time, faintly suspected for his "effeminate" tastes.

Today [1984] he is part of a demographic trend that fascinates market researchers and delights the purveyors of upscale consumer goods. There are 7.5 million men living alone (twice as many as there were in 1970). And as the home-furnishings expert Joan Kron observes in her recent book *Home-Psych*, single men are less likely to view their condition as one of temporary deprivation, marked by canned-hash dinners and orange-crate furniture. They cook; they furnish; they may even decorate. *Home Furnishings Daily* has declared them the "New Target," and the magazines that guide their consumption decisions are proliferating and expanding. Significantly, the genre of men's magazine that has done the best in the last few years is the one (represented by *Esquire*, *GQ*, and *M*) that does not depend on the lure of sexy female images, only page after page of slender, confident-looking male models.

What accounts for this change in men? Or, perhaps I should ask more broadly, for this change in our notion of masculinity—a change that affects not only single, affluent young men but potentially the married, middle-aged, and financially immobile male? Sheldon Kotel, a Long Island accountant in his early forties who was my host on a local radio talk show, attributes any change in men to a prior revolution among women. From the early 1970s, he says, "You could see what was happening with women, and we had to get our act together, too. They didn't want to be in their traditional role anymore, and I didn't want to go on being a meal ticket for some woman."

Certainly the new man's unwillingness to "commit himself," in the old-fashioned sense, could be interpreted as a peevish reaction to feminist women—just as his androgynous bent could be interpreted as a positive adjustment, an attempt, as the advocates of men's liberation would say, to "get in touch with one's feminine side." Spokesmen for men's liberation, from Warren Farrell in the early 1970s to

Donald H. Bell, whose book *Being a Man: The Paradox of Masculinity*, was published in 1982, depict themselves and their fellows as wrestling with the challenge of feminism—giving up a little privilege here, gaining a little sensitivity there, to emerge more "whole" and "self-nurturing."

But for the most part, the new men one is likely to encounter today in our urban singles' enclaves (or on the pages of a men's fashion magazine) bear no marks of arduous self-transformation. No ideological struggle—pro- or antifeminist—seems to have shaped their decision to step out of the traditional male role; in a day-to-day sense, they simply seem to have other things on their minds. Stephen G. Dent, for example, is a twenty-nine-year-old member of a private New York investment firm who was also interviewed by Harriet Bernstein. Dent defines his goals in terms of his career and making money, "because that's how the score is kept." To this end, he rations his time carefully: more than ten hours a day for work and approximately half an hour a day for calisthenics and running. Women definitely figure in his life, and he is pleased to have reduced the time spent arranging dates to an efficient five minutes a day.

Dent feels that "Sensitivity is very important to being a man. It's easy for people to become so caught up in their career challenges that they don't stop to be sensitive to certain things." By that he said he meant "being able to appreciate things that girls appreciate. Like being able to window-shop, for example. An insensitive guy probably won't stop and look at a dress in a window."

For Brian Clarke, like Stephen Dent, the pressures of

upward mobility have pushed marriage into the distant future. He is thirty-three and works fourteen hours a day as a production assistant for a major network television show.

Feminism has not figured much in his life; he discussed it respectfully, but as if it were an idiosyncracy he had not encountered before. Yet he agreed enthusiastically to being identified as a new man. "I'm going uphill, and I don't see the top of the hill yet. So for now there is no one woman in my life.…I say it on the first date, 'No commitments!'" He is, furthermore, an ardent and tasteful consumer who remains au courant by reading *GQ*, *M*, *Interior Design*, and *Playboy*, this last, he reassured me, "for the fashions."

So I do not think there is a one-word explanation—like feminism—for the new manhood. Rather, I would argue, at least a part of what looks new has been a long time in the making and predates the recent revival of feminism by many decades. Male resistance to marriage, for example, is a venerable theme in American culture, whether in the form of low humor (Li'l Abner's annual Sadie Hawkins Day escape from Daisy Mae) or high art (the perpetual bachelorhood of heroes like Ishmael or the Deerslayer). As Leslie Fiedler argued in 1955 in *An End to Innocence*, the classics of American literature are, by and large, propaganda for boyish adventure rather than the "mature heterosexuality" so admired by mid-twentieth-century psychoanalysts.

The sources of male resentment are not hard to find: In a frontier society, women were cast as the tamers and civilizers of men; in an increasingly urban, industrial society, they became, in addition, the financial dependents of men. From a cynical male point of view, marriage was an arrangement through which men gave up their freedom for the dubious privilege of supporting a woman. Or, as H. L. Mencken put it, marriage was an occasion for a man "to yield up his liberty, his property, and his soul to the first woman who, in despair of finding better game, turns her appraising eye upon him." After all, the traditional female contributions to marriage have been menial, like housework, or intangible, like emotional support. The husband's traditional contribution, his wage or at least a good share of it, was indispensable, measurable, and, of course, portable—whether to the local tavern or the next liaison.

But before male resentment of marriage could become anything more than a cultural undercurrent of grumbling and misogynist humor, three things had to happen. First, it had to become not only physically possible but reasonably comfortable for men to live on their own. In nineteenth-century homes, even simple tasks like making breakfast or laundering a shirt could absorb long hours of labor. Bachelorhood was a privileged state, sustained by servants or a supply of maiden sisters; the average man either married or settled for boardinghouse life. As a second condition for freedom from marriage, men had to discover better ways of spending their money than on the support of a family. The historic male alternatives were drinking and gambling, but these have long been associated, for good reason, with precipitate downward mobility. Third, the penalties levied against the nonconforming male—charges of immaturity, irresponsibility, and latent sexual deviancy—had to be neutralized or inverted.

Within the last few decades, all of these conditions for male freedom have been met. Domestic appliances, plus a rapid rise in the number of apartment dwellings and low-price restaurants, made it possible for a man of average means to contemplate bachelorhood as something other than extended vagrancy. As Philip Roth observed of the 1950s in *My Life as a Man*, it had become entirely feasible—though not yet acceptable—for a young man to "eat out of cans or in cafeterias, sweep his own floor, make his own bed, and come and go with no binding legal attachments." In addition, that decade saw two innovations that boosted the potential autonomy of even the most domestically incompetent males—frozen foods and drip-dry clothes.

Perhaps more important, the consumer-goods market, which had focused on a bland assemblage of family-oriented products, began to show the first signs of serious segmentation. *Playboy*'s success in the 1950s instigated a revival of sophisticated men's magazines (sophisticated, that is, compared with *True, Police Gazette*, or *Popular Mechanics*) that delivered an audience of millions of independent-minded men to the advertisers of liquor, sports cars, stereo equipment, and vacations.

In *Playboy*'s case, the ads were complemented by editorial exhortations to male revolt and feature articles portraying wives as "parasites" and husbands as "slaves." There were better ways to spend money than on power mowers and patio furniture, as Hugh Hefner insinuated in his magazine's very first issue: "We like our apartment.... We enjoy mixing up cocktails and an hors d'oeuvre or two, putting a little mood music on the phonograph, and inviting in a female acquaintance for a quiet discussion of Picasso, Nietzsche, jazz, sex." And in case that sounded suspiciously effete for 1953, the centerfolds testified to an exuberant, even defiant, heterosexuality.

No sooner had the new, more individualistic male lifestyle become physically possible and reasonably attractive than it began also to gain respectability. Starting in the 1960s, expert opinion began to retreat from what had been a unanimous endorsement of marriage and traditional sex roles. Psychology, transformed by the human-potential movement, switched from "maturity" as a standard for mental health to the more expansive notion of "growth." "Maturity" had been a code word, even in the professional literature, for marriage and settling down; "growth" implied a plurality of legitimate options, if not a positive imperative to keep moving from one insight or experience to the next. Meanwhile, medicine—alarmed by what appeared to be an epidemic of male heart disease—had begun to speak of men as the "weaker sex" and to hint that men's greater vulnerability was due, in part, to the burden of breadwinning.

The connection was scientifically unwarranted, but it cast a lasting shadow over conventional sex roles: The full-time homemaker, who had been merely a parasite on resentful males, became a potential accomplice to murder, with the hardworking, role-abiding breadwinner as her victim. By the 1970s, no salvo of male resentment—or men's liberation—failed to mention that the cost of the traditional male role was not only psychic stagnation and sexual monotony, but ulcers, heart disease, and an early death.

Today, the old aspersions directed at the unmarried male have largely lost their sting. Images of healthy, hardworking men with no apparent attachments abound in the media, such as, for example, the genial-looking bicyclist in the advertisement for *TV Guide*, whose caption announces invitingly, "Zero Dependents."

Perhaps most important, a man can now quite adequately express his status without entering into a lifelong partnership with a female consumer. The ranch house on a quarter acre of grass is still a key indicator of social rank, but it is not the only one. A well-decorated apartment, a knowledge of wines, or a flair for cooking can be an equally valid proof of middle-class (or upper-middle-class) membership, and these can now be achieved without the entanglement of marriage or the risk of being thought a little "queer."

Certainly feminism contributed to the case against the old style of male conformity. On the ideological front, the women's movement popularized the sociological vocabulary of "roles"—a linguistic breakthrough that highlighted the social artifice involved in masculinity, as we had known it, as well as femininity. More practically, feminists envisioned a world in which neither sex would be automatically dependent and both might be breadwinners. Betty Friedan speculated that "Perhaps men may live longer in America when women carry more of the burden of the battle with the world, instead of being a burden themselves," and Gloria Steinem urged men to support the cause because they "have nothing to lose but their coronaries." Yet feminism only delivered the coup de grâce to the old man, who married young, worked hard, withheld his emotions, and "died in the harness." By the time of the feminist revival in the late 1960s and '70s, American culture was already prepared to welcome a new man, and to find him—not caddish or queer—but healthy and psychologically enlightened.

But if the new man's resistance to commitment grows out of longstanding male resentment, there are other features of the new manhood that cannot be explained as a product of the battle of the sexes, no matter which side is presumed to have taken the initiative. Married or single, the preoccupations of these men suggest anxiety rather than liberation, and I think the anxiety stems from very real and relatively recent insecurities about class.

The professional-managerial middle class, which is the breeding ground for social ideals like the new man or new woman, has become an embattled group. In the 1950s and '60s, young men of this class could look forward to secure, high-status careers, provided only that they acquired some credentials and showed up for work. Professional-level job slots were increasing, along with the expansion of corporate and governmental administrative apparatuses, and jobs in higher education increased to keep pace with the growing demand for managerial and "mental" workers.

Then came the long economic downturn of the 1970s and whole occupations—from public administration to college history teaching—closed their ranks and lost ground. One whole segment of formerly middle-class, educated youth drifted downward to become taxi drivers, waiters, or carpenters. As other people crowded into the most vocationally promising areas—medicine, law, management—those too became hazardously overpopulated. According to recent studies of the "disappearing middle class," the erstwhile middle-class majority is tumbling down and out (both because of a lack of jobs and because those that remain have not held their own against inflation), while a minority is scrambling up to become the new high-finance, high-tech gentry. Our new men are mainly in the latter category, or are at least holding on by their fingernails.

Times of rapid class realignment magnify the attention paid to class insignia—the little cues that tell us who is a social equal and who is not. In the prosperous 1960s and early '70s, the counterculture had temporarily blurred class lines among American men, mixing Ivy League dropouts with young veterans, hip professionals with unschooled street kids. Avant-garde male fashion was democratic: blue jeans, gold chains, and shoulder-length hair could equally well be affected by middle-aged psychiatrists, young truck drivers, or off-duty tax lawyers. Thanks to Army-surplus chic and its rock-star embellishments, there was no sure way to distinguish the upward bound from the permanently down-and-out.

By the insecure 1980s, class lines were being hastily redrawn, and many features of the new manhood can best be understood as efforts to stay on the right side of the line separating "in" from "out," and upscale from merely middle-class. The new male consumerism, for example, is self-consciously elitist: Italian-knit sweaters and double-breasted blazers have replaced the voluntary simplicity of flannel shirts and denim jackets. *Esquire* announced a "return to elegant dressing" that excludes not only the polyester set but the rumpled professor and any leftover bohemians.

Food fashions, too, have been steadily gentrified, and the traditional masculine culinary repertory of chili and grilled meats would be merely boorish today. A recent issue of *GQ* magazine gave its readers the following advice, which I would have thought almost too precious for the pages of *Gourmet*: "To turn dinner for two into an affair, break open the caviar again—this time over oysters or spooned into baked potatoes with melted butter, a dollop of crème fraîche and a sprinkling of minced green onion. Or offer truffles—black or white…tossed with pasta, cream and butter." Real men may not eat quiche—which has been adopted by the proletariat anyway—but new men are enthusiasts of sushi and cold pasta salads, and are prepared to move on as soon as these, too, find their way to more plebeian palates. As *M* magazine half-facetiously warned its readers, sushi may already be "out," along with pesto dishes and white-wine spritzers.

Consumer tastes are only the most obvious class cues that define the new man and set him off, not only from the old white-collar man but from the less fortunate members of his own generation. Another is his devotion to physical exercise, especially in its most solitary and public form—running. Running is a new activity, dating from the 1970s, and it is solidly upscale. Fred Lebow, the president of the New York Road Runners Club, describes the average marathon runner as a male, "34 years old, college-educated, physically fit and well-off," and a *New York Times* poll found that 46 percent of the participants in the 1983 New York City Marathon earned more than $40,000 a year (85 percent of the participants were male). The old man smoked, drank martinis to excess, and puttered at golf. The new man is a nonsmoker (among men, smoking is becoming a blue-collar trait), a cautious drinker, and, if not a runner, a patron of gyms and spas.

I would not argue that men run in order to establish their social status—certainly not at a conscious level. Running is one manifestation of the general obsession with fitness that gripped the middle class in the 1970s and for which there is still no satisfactory sociological explanation. On one level, running is a straightforward response to the cardiac anxiety that has haunted American men since the 1950s; it may also be a response to the occupational insecurity of the 1970s and '80s. Then, too, some men run to get away from their wives—transforming Rabbit Angstrom's cross-country dash in the final scene of John Updike's *Rabbit, Run* into an acceptable daily ritual. Donald Bell says he took up running (and vegetarianism) "to escape somewhat from the pain and frustration which I felt in this less than perfect marriage."

But whatever the individual motivations, running has become sufficiently identified as an upper-middle-class habit to serve as a reliable insignia of class membership: Running is public testimony to a sedentary occupation, and it has all but replaced the more democratic sports, such as softball and basketball, that once promoted interclass male mingling.

Finally, there is that most promising of new male traits—sensitivity. I have no hesitation about categorizing this as an upscale-class cue if only because new men so firmly believe that it is. For more than a decade, sensitivity has been supposed to be the inner quality that distinguishes an educated, middle-class male from his unregenerate blue-collar brothers: "They" are Archie Bunkers; "we" are represented by his more liberal, articulate son-in-law. As thoughtful a scholar as Joseph H. Pleck, program director of the Wellesley College Center for Research on Women, who has written extensively on the male sex role, simply restates (in a 1976 issue of the *Journal of Social Issues*) the prejudice that blue-collar men are trapped in the "traditional" male role, "where interpersonal and emotional skills are relatively undeveloped."

No one, of course, has measured sensitivity and plotted it as a function of social class, but Judith Langer, a market researcher, reports that, in her studies, it is blue-collar men who express less "traditional" or "macho" values, both in response to products and in speaking of their relationships with women. "Certainly I'm not suggesting that *only* blue-collar men show such openness," she concludes, "but rather that the stereotype of blue-collar workers can be limited."

To the extent that some special form of sensitivity is located in educated and upwardly mobile males, I suspect it may be largely a verbal accomplishment. The vocabulary of sensitivity, at least, has become part of the new masculine politesse; certainly no new man would admit to being insensitive or willfully "out of touch with his feelings." Quite possibly, as sensitivity has spread, it has lost its moorings in the therapeutic experience and come to signify the heightened receptivity associated with consumerism: a vague appreciation that lends itself to aimless shopping.

None of these tastes and proclivities of the new man

serve to differentiate him from the occasional affluent woman of his class. Women in the skirted-suit set tend to postpone marriage and childbearing; to work long hours and budget their time scrupulously; to follow fashions in food and clothing; and to pursue fitness where once slimness would have sufficed. As Paul Fussell observes in *Class: A Guide through the American Status System*, the upper-middle class—and I would include all those struggling to remain in the upper part of the crumbling middle class—is "the most 'role reversed' of all." And herein lies one of the key differences between the old and the new versions of the American ideal of masculinity: The old masculinity defined itself against femininity and expressed anxiety—over conformity or the rat race—in metaphors of castration. The new masculinity seems more concerned to preserve the tenuous boundary between the classes than to delineate distinctions between the sexes. Today's upper-middle-class or upwardly mobile male is less terrified about moving down the slope toward genderlessness than he is about sliding downscale.

The fact that the new man is likely to remain single well into his prime career years—or, if married, is unlikely to be judged by his wife's appearance and tastes—only intensifies his status consciousness. The old man of the middle class might worry about money, but he could safely leave the details of keeping up with the Joneses to his wife. He did not have to comprehend casseroles or canapés, because she would, nor did he have to feel his way through complex social situations, since sensitivity also lay in her domain. But our new man of the 1980s, married or not, knows that he may be judged solely on the basis of his own savoir faire, his ability to "relate," his figure, and possibly his muscle tone. Without a wife, or at least without a visible helpmate, he has had to appropriate the status-setting activities that once were seen as feminine. The androgynous affect is part of making it.

The question for feminists is: Is this new man what we wanted? Just a few years ago, feminists were, on the whole, disposed to welcome any change in a direction away from traditional manhood. Betty Friedan, in *The Second Stage*, saw "the quiet movement of American men" as "a momentous change in their very identity as men, going beyond the change catalyzed by the women's movement," and she suggested that it might amount to a "massive, evolutionary development."

That was written in a more innocent time, when feminists were debating the "Cinderella complex," as Colette Dowling termed women's atavistic dependencies on men, rather than the "Peter Pan syndrome," which is how another best seller describes the male aversion to commitment. In recent months, there has been a small flurry of feminist attacks on the new male or on assorted new-male characteristics.

The *Washington City Paper* carried a much-discussed and thoroughly acid article on "Wormboys," described by writer Deborah Laake as men who are "passive" in relation to women, who "shrink from marriage" and children, and "cannot be depended on during tough times." According to one woman she quotes, these new men are so fearful of commitment that they even hesitate to ask a woman out to dinner: "They're more interested in saying, 'Why don't you meet me for a drink?' because it implies so much less commitment on their part." I wouldn't exaggerate the extent of the backlash, but it has been sufficient to send several male colleagues my way to ask, with nervous laughter, whether I was writing a new contribution to the "war on wimps."

I don't blame them for being nervous. My generation of feminists insisted that men change, but we were not always directive—or patient—enough to say how. We applauded every sign of male sensitivity or growth as if it were an evolutionary advance. We even welcomed the feminization of male tastes, expecting that the man who was a good cook and a tasteful decorator at twenty-five would be a devoted father and partner in midlife. We did not understand that men were changing along a trajectory of their own and that they might end up being less like what we *are* than like what we were once expected to be—vain and shallow and status-conscious.

But since these are times when any hint of revisionism easily becomes grist for conservatism, it is important to emphasize that if we don't like the new male, neither are we inclined to return to the old one. If the new man tends to be a fop, the old man was (and is), at worst, a tyrant and a bully. At best, he was merely dull, which is why, during the peak years of male conformity, when the test of manhood lay in being a loyal breadwinner, so many of us lusted secretly for those few males—from James Dean and Elvis Presley to Jack Kerouac—who represented unattainable adventure. In our fantasies, as least, we did not want to enslave men, as *Playboy*'s writers liked to think, but to share the adventure.

Today, thanks to the women's movement, we have half a chance: Individualism, adventure—that "battle with the world" that Friedan held out to women—is no longer a male prerogative. But if it is to be a shared adventure, then men will have to change, and change in ways that are not, so far, in evidence. Up until now, we have been content to ask them to become more like women—less aggressive, more emotionally connected with themselves and others. That message, which we once thought revolutionary, has gotten lost in the androgynous drift of the consumer culture. It is the marketplace that calls most clearly for men to be softer, more narcissistic and receptive, and the new man is the result.

So it is not enough, anymore, to ask that men become more like women; we should ask instead that they become more like what both men and women *might* be. My new man, if I could design one, would be capable of appreciation, sensitivity, intimacy—values that have been, for too long, feminine. But he would also be capable of commitment, to use that much-abused word, and I mean by that commitment not only to friends and family but to a broad and generous vision of how we might all live together. As a feminist, I would say that vision includes equality between men and women and also—to mention a social goal that seems almost to have been forgotten—equality among men.

PATRIARCHY DEFLATED

The Baffler, 2018

Sometimes it takes a slovenly alt-right "strategist" to put things in proper historical perspective. In a recent chat with a journalist, Steve Bannon called the #MeToo movement an "anti-patriarchy movement" that is "going to undo ten thousand years of recorded history." That much is true. But the implication that patriarchy is somehow the same as civilization gets more implausible with every me-too revelation.

We have been encouraged to think of patriarchy as a solemn undertaking, a millennia-old system designed to keep women down and young men from getting out of line. Its favorite notions, over the centuries, have been Honor, Tradition, Power, and Glory. Its material manifestations range from pyramids to skyscrapers, from the simple lines of ancient Greek temples to the neoclassical architectural majesty of nineteenth-century European capitals. It accessorizes its most hallowed rituals with columns of uniformed soldiers and stirring martial music.

The Naked and the Daft

But how silly patriarchy is looking at this moment, as one rich and powerful man after another falls victim to the #MeToo movement. We've learned that the fatuous centrist Charlie Rose, whose wardrobe includes Versace slacks, liked to swan around among his female office staff in the nude, as did the deep-closeted casino billionaire Steve Wynn. Matt Lauer, whose job was to lend gravitas to the *Today* show, kept a bag full of sex toys in his office, so he'd have something to play with should he manage to lure a young woman in. The president of the most powerful nation in the world, it has been alleged, employed prostitutes to pee on a Moscow hotel bed and enjoyed being spanked with a copy of *Forbes* magazine featuring his likeness on the cover.

Feminists have, of course, seen through the clouds of glory trailing patriarchy to expose its intrinsic cruelty and violence. But one thing we have seldom questioned is its seriousness. Consider the feminist dictum that rape is not about sex, but power. The rapist isn't having fun; he's simply enforcing the age-old power of men. That is, he's doing a kind of work—a service to the other elite men who are his peers. Sex, and hence the possibility of pleasure, at least for men, seldom enters into the feminist discourse on male violence, which has treated rape and sexual assault as an enactment of male domination, and perhaps a necessary warning to women—a kind of public service announcement.

But the mounting accusations of sexual harassment by

powerful men suggest that feminism has been taking patriarchy a bit too seriously. Maybe it's not about the endless
reproduction of power relationships; maybe it's about guys
just having fun. Out of sight of nannies and governesses
and wives, they are stealing treats. One of the accusers of
Hillary Clinton's lecherous former "faith consultant" says
he looked at her "like she was a snack"—not a person or
even a pretty girl but a handy between-meals treat. Certainly Harvey Weinstein treated women this way, hiring a
pimp disguised as a colleague to line up women in the foreign cities he visited so that the great mogul would never
have to go without sustenance. The sheer entitlement on
display here puts one in mind of Newt Gingrich's statement
that he feels like "a happy four-year-old who gets up every
morning hoping to find a cookie."

The Treats of Power

In theory, we might be able to extend a grudging smidgen
of sympathy to the downtrodden working-class man who
comes home to beat or rape his wife. How else is he going to
experience power? But many of the men starring in today's
sexual-harassment scandals already wield plenty of power,
through their positions or their money and can hardly
claim to be deprived of pleasure and flattery in their daily
lives. This is the class that stays in five-star hotels, flies in private jets, and expects their every whim to be gratified by a
staff of eager underlings.

Still, they need their sexual treats. The Presidents Club

in London drew hundreds of bankers and millionaires to pester the short-skirted young women who were paid to serve their drinks. Think, too, of Dominique Strauss-Kahn's sex parties, featuring pliant prostitutes for all-male groups of businessmen and IMF officials. The list goes on: Berlusconi's orgies. Trump's pussy-grabbing. Bill Clinton. Or, going back to the 1950s, Hugh Hefner's empire based on the idea that the "playboy" needs an endless supply of "playmates."

Fun has never been considered a major force in history, but perhaps it—and "the pursuit of pleasure" in general—should be. Gaze up again at the great architectural relics of empire you can find in London or Madrid. Where did the wealth come from to build these marvels? From war, of course—wars of conquest. And what is war? Well, it's hell, or so it is said. But it's also the supreme male adventure, especially for those males who get to ride, not tramp, to the battlefields.

For the last ten thousand years, from the Roman conquests through the Viking raids to the Crusades that followed them and on to the global wars of the twentieth century, war has been an opportunity for taking both treasure and pleasure—rape and pillage. It offers plenty of glory and honor, too, if only posthumously, but it hardly amounts to "civilization."

So, what is a twenty-first-century woman to think as she picks her way through the rubble of patriarchy? First, she should laugh out loud at every instance of male and class-based pomposity she encounters, remember that the president—or the esteemed artist or academic—likes to wag his penis at women in private. She should recall that the Wizard of Oz is an evil clown but still a clown. Then she might consider a suitable punishment for our dethroned patriarchs. Maybe they should be confined to one big locked room stocked with high-tech sex toys and left to fuck themselves sick.

With that accomplished, women—and male dissidents from patriarchy should be included here—might want to turn their attention to what a world shaped by the *female* pursuit of pleasure might look like. Would it be gentle and rainbow-colored? Or would it pulse with its own kinds of ecstasy and transgression?

WOMEN

ARE WOMEN GETTING SADDER? OR ARE WE ALL JUST GETTING A LOT MORE GULLIBLE?

Los Angeles Times, 2009

Feminism made women miserable. This, anyway, seems to be the most popular takeaway from "The Paradox of Declining Female Happiness," a recent study by Betsey Stevenson and Justin Wolfers, which purports to show that women have become steadily unhappier since 1972. Maureen Dowd and Arianna Huffington greeted the news with somber perplexity, but the more common response has been a triumphant: *I told you so.*

On Slate's DoubleX website, a columnist concluded from the study that "The feminist movement of the 1960s and 1970s gave us a steady stream of women's complaints disguised as manifestos...and a brand of female sexual power so promiscuous that it celebrates everything from prostitution to nipple piercing as a feminist act—in other words, whine, womyn, and thongs." Or as Phyllis Schlafly put it, more soberly: "The feminist movement taught women to see themselves as victims of an oppressive patriarchy in which their true worth will never be recognized and any success is beyond their reach...Self-imposed victimhood is not a recipe for happiness."

But it's a little too soon to blame Gloria Steinem for our dependence on SSRIs. For all the high-level head-scratching induced by the Stevenson and Wolfers study, hardly anyone has pointed out (1) that there are some issues with happiness studies in general, (2) that there are some reasons to doubt this study in particular, or (3) that, even if you take this study at face value, it has nothing at all to say about the impact of feminism on anyone's happiness.

For starters, happiness is an inherently slippery thing to measure or define. Philosophers have debated what it is for centuries, and even if we were to define it simply as a greater frequency of positive feelings than negative ones, when we ask people if they are happy, we are asking them to arrive at some sort of average over many moods and moments. Maybe I was upset earlier in the day after I opened the bills, but then was cheered up by a call from a friend, so what am I really?

In one well-known psychological experiment, subjects were asked to answer a questionnaire on life satisfaction, but only after they had performed the apparently irrelevant task of photocopying a sheet of paper for the experimenter. For a randomly chosen half of the subjects, a dime had been left for them to find on the copy machine. As two economists summarize the results: "Reported satisfaction with life was raised substantially by the discovery of the coin on the copy machine—clearly not an income effect."

As for the particular happiness study under discussion, the red flags start popping up as soon as you look at the data. Not to be anti-intellectual about it, but the raw data on how men and women respond to the survey reveal no discernible trend to the naked eyeball. Only by performing an occult statistical manipulation called "ordered probit estimates," do the authors manage to tease out any trend at all, and it is a tiny one: "Women were one percentage point less likely than men to say they were not too happy at the beginning of the sample [1972]; by 2006 women were one percentage point more likely to report being in this category." Differences of that magnitude would be stunning if you were measuring, for example, the speed of light under different physical circumstances, but when the subject is as elusive as happiness—well, we are not talking about paradigm-shifting results.

Furthermore, the idea that women have been sliding toward despair is contradicted by the one *objective* measure of unhappiness the authors offer: suicide rates. Happiness is, of course, a subjective state, but suicide is a cold, hard fact, and the suicide rate has been the gold standard of misery since sociologist Emile Durkheim wrote the book on it in 1897. As Stevenson and Wolfers report—somewhat sheepishly, we must imagine—"Contrary to the subjective well-being trends we document, female suicide rates have been falling, even as male suicide rates have remained roughly constant through most of our sample [1972–2006]." Women may get the blues; men are more likely to get a bullet through the temple.

Another distracting little data point that no one, including the authors, seems to have much to say about is that, while "women" have been getting marginally sadder, black women have been getting happier and happier. To quote the authors: "…happiness has trended quite strongly upward for both female and male African Americans… Indeed, the point estimates suggest that well-being may have risen more strongly for black women than for black men." The study should more accurately be titled "The Paradox of Declining White Female Happiness," only that might have suggested that the problem could be cured with melanin and Restylane.

But let's assume the study is sound and that (white) women have become less happy relative to men since 1972. Does that mean that feminism ruined their lives?

Not according to Stevenson and Wolfers, who find that "The relative decline in women's well-being…holds for both working and stay-at-home mothers, for those married and divorced, for the old and the young, and across the education distribution"—as well as for both mothers and the childless. If feminism were the problem, you might expect divorced women to be less happy than married ones and employed women to be less happy than stay-at-homes. As for having children, the presumed premier source of female fulfillment: They actually make women *less* happy.

And if the women's movement was such a big downer, you'd expect the saddest women to be those who had some direct exposure to the noxious effects of second wave feminism. As the authors report, however, "There is no evidence that women who experienced the protests and enthusiasm in the 1970s have seen their happiness gap widen by more than for those women who were just being born during that period."

What this study shows, if anything, is that neither marriage nor children make women happy. (The results are not in yet on nipple piercing.) Nor, for that matter, does there seem to be any problem with "too many choices," "work-life balance," or the "second shift." If you believe Stevenson and Wolfers, women's happiness is supremely indifferent to the actual conditions of their lives, including poverty and racial discrimination. Whatever "happiness" is...

So why all the sudden fuss about the Wharton study, which first leaked out two years ago anyway? Mostly because it's become a launching pad for a new book by the prolific management consultant Marcus Buckingham, best known for *First, Break All the Rules* and *Now, Discover Your Strengths*. His new book, *Find Your Strongest Life: What the Happiest and Most Successful Women Do Differently*, is a cookie-cutter classic of the positive-thinking self-help genre: First, the heart-wrenching quotes from unhappy women identified only by their email names (Countess1, Luveyduvy, etc.), then the stories of "successful" women, followed by the obligatory self-administered test to discover "the role you were bound to play" (Creator, Caretaker, Influencer, etc.), all bookended with an ad for the many related products you can buy, including a "video introduction" from Buckingham, a "participant's guide" containing "exercises" to get you to happiness, and a handsome set of "Eight Strong Life Plans" to pick from. The *Huffington Post* has given Buckingham a column in which to continue his marketing campaign.

It's an old story: If you want to sell something, first find the terrible affliction that it cures. In the 1980s, as silicone implants were taking off, the doctors discovered "micromastia"—the "disease" of small-breastedness. More recently, as big pharma searches furiously for a female Viagra, an amazingly high 43 percent of women have been found to suffer from "Female Sexual Dysfunction," or FSD. Now, it's unhappiness, and the range of potential "cures" is dazzling: Seagrams, Godiva, and Harlequin, take note.

OUR NEIGHBORHOOD PORN
COMMITTEE

Mother Jones, 1986

E ver since the attorney general declared open season on smut, I've had my work cut out for me. I'm referring, of course, to the Meese commission's report on pornography, which urges groups of private citizens to go out and fight the vile stuff with every means at hand—spray paint, acetylene torches, garlic, and crucifixes. In the finest spirit of grassroots democracy, the commission is leaving it up to us to decide what to slash and burn and what to leave on the library shelves. Not that we are completely without guidance in this matter, for Commissioner Frederick Schauer ("golden Schauer" to those wild and crazy boys at *Penthouse*) quotes approvingly a deceased judge's definition of hard-core porn: "I know it when I see it."

Well, so do I, thanks to the report's thoughtful assertions that pornography is something that "hurts women" and, in particular, "bears a causal relationship to the incidence of various nonviolent forms of discrimination against or subordination of women in our society." My little group of citizens—recruited from the PTA, Parents without Partners, and the YWCA aerobics class—decided to go straight to the heart of the matter: all written, scrawled, and otherwise-depicted manifestations of sexism, whether found on daytime TV, in the great classics of Western civilization, or in the published opinions of Donald ("Women can't understand arms control") Regan.

I can understand why the commission decided to restrict its own inquiry to the sexier varieties of sexism, commonly known as pornography. How often, after all, does a group composed largely of white male Republicans (you will pardon the redundancy) get to spend months poring over material that would normally only be available in dark little shops on the seamy, low-rent side of town, and to do so entirely at public expense?

But with all due respect, I believe they erred by so limiting themselves. Violence against women, to take the most unpleasant form of "subordination," predates the commercial porn industry by several millennia. Those Romans who perpetrated the rape of the Sabines, for example, did not work themselves up for the deed by screening *Debbie Does Dallas*, and the monkish types who burned thousands of witches in the Middle Ages had almost certainly not come across *Boobs and Buns* or related periodicals.

I thought my citizens' group should start its search for materials damaging to women with the Bible, on the simple theory that anything read by so many people must have something to do with all the wickedness in the world. "Gather around," I said to my fellow citizens. "If those brave souls on the Meese commission could wade through the likes of *Fellatio Frolics* and *Fun with Whips and Chains*, we can certainly get through Genesis."

It was rough going, let me tell you, what with the incest (Lot and his daughters), mass circumcisions, adultery, and various spillings of seed. But duty triumphed over modesty, and we were soon rewarded with examples of sexism so crude and so nasty that they would make *The Story of O* look like suffragist propaganda. There was the part about Eve and her daughters being condemned to bring forth their offspring in sorrow, and numerous hints that the bringing forth of offspring is in fact the only thing women have any business doing. There were injunctions against public speaking by women, and approving descriptions of a patriarchal dynasty extending, without the least concern for affirmative action, for countless generations from Isaac on. And then there were the truly kinky passages on the necessity of "submitting" to one's husband—an obvious invitation to domestic mayhem.

We wasted no time in calling the newly installed Meese commission hotline to report we had discovered material— widely advertised as "family" reading—that would bring a blush to the cheek of dear Dr. Ruth and worry lines to the smooth brow of Gloria Steinem. "Well, yes," said the commissioner who picked up the phone, "but could this material be used as a masturbatory aid? Is it designed to induce sexual arousal in all but the most priggish Presbyterian? Because it's the arousal, you know, that *reinforces* the sexism, transforming normal, everyday male chauvinism into raging misogyny."

We argued that we had seen a number of TV preachers

in states of arousal induced by this book, and that, furthermore, religious ecstasy might be far more effective at reinforcing sexism than any mere tickle of genital response. But we reluctantly agreed to stop our backyard Bible burnings and to try to focus on material that is more violent, up-to-date, and, preferably, with better visuals.

A week later we called the hotline to report we'd seen *Cobra*, *Raw Deal*, three episodes of *Miami Vice*, and a presidential address on the importance of Star Wars, and felt we now had material that was not only damaging to women but disrespectful of human life in all forms, male and female, born and unborn. "But is it dirty?" asked a weary commissioner. "You know, *sexy*?" And we had to admit that neither the sight of Arnold Schwarzenegger without a shirt nor the president in pancake makeup had ever aroused in us any feeling other than mild intestinal upset.

Now I think we're finally getting the hang of it. The problem, as identified by the Meese commission, isn't violence, sexism, or even sexual violence. The problem is sex, particularly those varieties of sex that might in any way involve women. So in the last few weeks, our citizens' anti-smut group has short-circuited six vibrators, burned three hundred of those lurid little inserts found in Tampax boxes, and shredded half the local supply of *Our Bodies, Ourselves*. It's a tough job, believe me, but as Ed Meese keeps telling us, someone's got to do it.

STRATEGIES OF
CORPORATE WOMEN

New Republic, 1986

S ome of us are old enough to recall when the stereotype of a "liberated woman" was a disheveled radical, notoriously braless, and usually hoarse from denouncing the twin evils of capitalism and patriarchy. Today the stereotype is more likely to be a tidy executive who carries an attaché case and is skilled in discussing market shares and leveraged buyouts. In fact, thanks in no small part to the anger of the earlier, radical feminists, women have gained a real toehold in the corporate world: About 30 percent of managerial employees are women, as are 40 percent of the current [1986] MBA graduates. We have come a long way, as the expression goes, though clearly not in the same direction we set out on.

The influx of women into the corporate world has generated its own small industry of advice and inspiration. Magazines like *Savvy* and *Working Woman* offer tips on everything from sex to software, plus the occasional instructive tale about a woman who rises effortlessly from managing a boutique to being the CEO of a multinational corporation. Scores of books published since the mid-1970s have told the aspiring managerial woman what to wear, how to flatter superiors, and, when necessary, fire subordinates. Even old-fashioned radicals like myself, for whom "CD" still means civil disobedience rather than an 8 percent interest rate, can expect to receive a volume of second-class mail inviting them to join their corporate sisters at a "networking brunch" or to share the privileges available to the female frequent flier.

But for all the attention lavished on them, all the six-figure promotion possibilities and tiny perks once known only to the men in gray flannel, there is a malaise in the world of the corporate woman. The continuing boom in the advice industry is in itself an indication of some kind of trouble. To take an example from a related field, there would not be a book published almost weekly on how to run a corporation along newly discovered Asian principles if American business knew how to hold its own against the international competition. Similarly, if women were confident about their role in the corporate world, I do not think they would pay to be told how to comport themselves in such minute detail. ("Enter the bar with a briefcase or some files...Hold your head high, with a pleasant expression on your face...After you have ordered your drink, shuffle through a paper or two, to further establish yourself [as a businesswoman]," advises *Letitia Baldrige's Complete Guide to Executive Manners*.)

Nor, if women were not still nervous newcomers, would there be a market for so much overtly conflicting advice:

how to be more impersonal and masculine (Charlene Mitchell and Thomas Burdick's *The Right Moves*) or more nurturing and intuitive (Marilyn Loden's *Feminine Leadership*); how to assemble the standard skirted, suited uniform (de rigueur until approximately 1982) or move beyond it for the softness and individuality of a dress; how to conquer stress or how to transform it into drive; how to repress the least hint of sexuality, or, alternatively, how to "focus the increase in energy that derives from sexual excitement so that you are more productive on the job" (Leslie Aldridge Westoff's *Corporate Romance*). When we find so much contradictory advice, we must assume that much of it is not working.

There is a more direct sign of trouble. A small but significant number of women are deciding not to have it all after all, and are dropping out of the corporate world to apply their management skills to kitchen decor and baby care. Not surprisingly, these retro women have been providing a feast for a certain "I told you so" style of journalism; hardly a month goes by without a story about another couple that decided to make do on his $75,000 a year while she joins the other mommies in the playground. But the trend is real. The editors of the big business–oriented women's magazines are worried about it. So is Liz Roman Gallese, the former *Wall Street Journal* reporter who interviewed the alumnae of Harvard Business School, class of '75, to write *Women Like Us*.

The women Gallese interviewed are not, for the most part, actual dropouts, but they are not doing as well as might have been expected for the first cohort of women to wield the talismanic Harvard MBA. Certainly they are not doing as well as their male contemporaries, and the gap widens with every year since graduation. Nor do they seem to be a very happy or likable group. Suzanne, the most successful of them, is contemptuous of women who have family obligations. Phoebe, who is perhaps the brightest, has an almost pathological impulse to dominate others. Maureen does not seem to like her infant daughter. Of the eighty-two women surveyed, thirty-five had been in therapy since graduation; four had been married to violently abusive men; three had suffered from anorexia or bulimia; and two had become Christian fundamentalists. Perhaps not surprisingly, given the high incidence of personal misery, two-fifths of the group were "ambivalent or frankly not ambitious for their careers."

What is happening to our corporate women? The obvious antifeminist answer, that biology is incompatible with business success, is not borne out by Gallese's study. Women with children were no less likely to be ambitious and do well than more mobile, single women (although in 1982, when the interviews were carried out, very few of the women had husbands or children). But the obvious feminist answer—that women are being discouraged or driven out by sexism—does gain considerable support from *Women Like Us*. Many of the women from the class of '75 report having been snubbed, insulted, or passed over for promotions by their male coworkers. Under these circumstances, even the most determined feminist would begin to suffer from what Dr. Herbert J. Freudenberger and Gail North (in their book *Women's Burnout*) call "business burnout." For nonfeminists, or, more precisely, postfeminists—like Gallese and her respondents, sexism must be all the more wounding for being so invisible and nameless. What you cannot name, except as apparently random incidents of "discrimination," you cannot hope to do much about.

Gallese suggests another problem, potentially far harder to eradicate than any form of discrimination. There may be a poor fit between the impersonal bureaucratic culture of the corporation and what is, whether as a result of hormones or history, the female personality. The exception that seems to prove the rule is Suzanne, who is the most successful of the alumnae and who is also a monster of detachment from her fellow human beings. In contrast, Gallese observes that men who rise to the top are often thoroughly dull and "ordinary"—as men go—but perhaps ideally suited to a work world in which interpersonal attachments are shallow and all attention must focus on the famed bottom line.

To judge from the advice books, however, the corporate culture is not as impersonal, in a stern Weberian sense, as we have been led to believe. For example, *The Right Moves*, which is a good representative of the "how to be more like the boys" genre of books for corporate women, tells us to "eliminate the notion that the people with whom you work are your friends"—sound advice for anyone who aspires to the bureaucratic personality. But it also insists that it is necessary to cultivate the "illusion of friendship," lest coworkers find you "aloof and arrogant." You must, in other words, dissemble in order to effect the kind of personality—

artificially warm but never actually friendly—that suits the corporate culture.

Now, in a task-oriented meritocratic organization—or, let us just say, a thoroughly capitalist organization dedicated to the maximization of profit—it should not be necessary to cultivate "illusions" of any kind. It should be enough just to get the job done. But as *The Right Moves* explains, and the stories in *Women Like Us* illustrate, it is never enough just to get the job done; if it were, far more women would no doubt be at the top. You have to impress people, win them over, and in general project an aura of success far more potent than any actual accomplishment. The problem may not be that women lack the capacity for businesslike detachment, but that, as women, they can never entirely fit into the boyish, glad-handed corporate culture so well described three decades ago in *The Lonely Crowd*.

There may also be a deeper, more existential, reason for the corporate woman's malaise. It is impossible to sample the advice literature without beginning to wonder what, after all, is the point of all this striving. Why not be content to stop at $40,000 or $50,000 a year, some stock options, and an IRA? Perhaps the most striking thing about the literature for and about the corporate woman is how little it has to say about the purposes, other than personal advancement, of the corporate "game." Not one among the Harvard graduates or the anonymous women quoted in the advice books ever voices a transcendent commitment to, say, producing a better widget. And if that is too much to expect from postindustrial corporate America, we might at least hope for some lofty organizational goals—to make X Corp. the biggest damn conglomerate in the Western world, or some such. But no one seems to have a vast and guiding vision of the corporate life, much less a fashionably conservative belief in the moral purposefulness of capitalism. Instead, we find successful corporate women asking, "Why am I doing what I'm doing? What's the point here?" or confiding bleakly that "Something's missing."

In fact, from the occasional glimpses we get, the actual content of an executive's daily labors can be shockingly trivial. Consider Phoebe's moment of glory at Harvard Business School. The class had been confronted with a real-life corporate problem to solve. Recognizing the difficulty of getting catsup out of a bottle, should Smucker and Co. start selling catsup out of a wide-mouthed container suitable for inserting a spoon into? No, was Phoebe's answer, because people like the challenge of pounding catsup out of the bottle; a more accessible catsup would never sell. Now, I am not surprised that this was the right answer, but I am surprised that it was greeted with such apparent awe and amazement by a professor and a roomful of smart young students. Maybe for a corporate man, the catsup problem is a daunting intellectual challenge. But a woman must ask herself: Is *this* what we left the kitchen for?

Many years ago, when America was more innocent but everything else was pretty much the same, Paul Goodman wrote, "There is nearly 'full employment'…but there get to be fewer jobs that are necessary or unquestionably useful; that require energy and draw on some of one's best capacities; and that can be done keeping one's honor and dignity."

Goodman, a utopian socialist, had unusually strict criteria for what counted as useful enough to be "man's work," but he spoke for a generation of men who were beginning to question, in less radical ways, the corporate work world described by William H. Whyte, David Riesman, Alan Harrington, and others. Most of the alienated white-collar men of the 1950s withdrew into drink or early coronaries, but a few turned to Zen or jazz, and thousands of their sons and daughters eventually joined with Goodman to help create the anticorporate and, indeed, anticareerist counterculture of the 1960s. It was the counterculture, as much as anything else, that nourished the feminist movement of the late 1960s and early 1970s, which is where our story began.

In the early years, feminism was torn between radical and assimilationist tendencies. In fact, our first sense of division was between the "bourgeois" feminists who wanted to scale the occupational hierarchy created by men, and the radical feminists who wanted to level it. Assimilation won out, as it probably must among any economically disadvantaged group. Networks replaced consciousness-raising groups; Michael Korda became a more valuable guide to action than Shulamith Firestone. The old radical, anarchistic vision was replaced by the vague hope (well articulated in *Feminine Leadership*) that, in the process of assimilating, women would somehow "humanize" the cold and ruthless world of men. Today, of course, there are still radical feminists, but the only capitalist institution they seem bent on destroying is the local adult bookstore.

*　　*　　*

As feminism loses its critical edge, it becomes, ironically, less capable of interpreting the experience of its pioneer assimilationists, the new corporate women. Contemporary mainstream feminism can understand their malaise insofar as it is caused by sexist obstacles, but has no way of addressing the sad emptiness of "success" itself. Even the well-worn term "alienation," as applied to human labor, rings no bells among the corporate feminists I have talked to recently, although most thought it an arresting notion. So we are in more or less the same epistemological situation Betty Friedan found herself in describing the misery—and, yes, alienation—of middle-class housewives in the early 1960s; better words would be forthcoming, but she had to refer to "the problem without a name."

Men are just as likely as women to grasp the ultimate pointlessness of the corporate game and the foolishness of many of the players, but only women have a socially acceptable way out. They can go back to the split-level homes and well-appointed nurseries where Friedan first found them. (That is assuming, of course, they can find a well-heeled husband, and they haven't used up all their childbearing years in the pursuit of a more masculine model of success.) In fact, this may well be a more personally satisfying option than a work life spent contemplating, say, the fluid dynamics of catsup. As Paul Goodman explained, with as much insight as insensitivity, girls didn't have to worry about "growing up absurd" because they had intrinsically meaningful work cut out for them—motherhood and homemaking.

There is no doubt, from the interviews in *Women Like*

Us as well as my own anecdotal sources, that some successful women are indeed using babies as a polite excuse for abandoning the rat race. This is too bad from many perspectives, and certainly for the children who will become the sole focus of their mothers' displaced ambitions. The dropouts themselves would do well to take a look at Peggy J. Berry's *Corporate Couple*, which advises executive wives on the classic problems such as: how to adjust to the annual relocation, how to overcome one's jealousy of a husband's svelte and single female coworkers, and how to help a husband survive his own inevitable existential crisis.

Someday, I believe, a brilliantly successful corporate woman will suddenly look down at her desk littered with spreadsheets and interoffice memos and exclaim, "Is this really worth my time?" At the very same moment, a housewife, casting her eyes around a kitchen befouled by toddlers, will ask herself the identical question. As the corporate woman flees out through the corporate atrium, she will run headlong into the housewife, fleeing into it. The two will talk. And in no time at all they will reunite those two distinctly American strands of radicalism—the utopianism of Goodman and the feminism of Friedan. They may also, if they talk long enough, invent some sweet new notion like equal pay for…meaningful work.

WHAT ABU GHRAIB TAUGHT ME

Los Angeles Times, 2004

Even those people we might have thought were impervious to shame, like the secretary of defense, admit that the photos of abuse in Iraq's Abu Ghraib prison turned their stomachs.

The photos did something else to me, as a feminist: They broke my heart. I had no illusions about the US mission in Iraq—whatever exactly it is—but it turns out that I did have some illusions about women.

Of the seven US soldiers now charged with sickening forms of abuse in Abu Ghraib, three are women: Specialist Megan Ambuhl, Private First Class Lynndie England, and Specialist Sabrina Harman.

It was Harman we saw smiling an impish little smile and giving the thumbs-up sign from behind a pile of hooded, naked Iraqi men—as if to say, "Hi Mom, here I am in Abu Ghraib!" It was England we saw with a naked Iraqi man on a leash. If you were doing PR for Al Qaeda, you couldn't have staged a better picture to galvanize misogynist Islamic fundamentalists around the world.

Here, in these photos from Abu Ghraib, you have everything that the Islamic fundamentalists believe characterizes Western culture, all nicely arranged in one hideous image—imperial arrogance, sexual depravity...and gender equality.

Maybe I shouldn't have been so shocked. We know that good people can do terrible things under the right circumstances. This is what psychologist Stanley Milgram found in his famous experiments in the 1960s. In all likelihood, Ambuhl, England, and Harman are not congenitally evil people. They are working-class women who wanted an education and knew that the military could be a stepping-stone in that direction. Once they had joined, they wanted to fit in.

And I also shouldn't be surprised because I never believed that women were innately gentler and less aggressive than men. Like most feminists, I have supported full opportunity for women within the military—(1) because I knew women could fight, and (2) because the military is one of the few options around for low-income young people.

Although I opposed the 1991 Persian Gulf War, I was proud of our servicewomen and delighted that their presence irked their Saudi hosts. Secretly, I hoped that the presence of women would over time change the military, making it more respectful of other people and cultures, more capable of genuine peacekeeping. That's what I thought, but I don't think that anymore.

A certain kind of feminism, or perhaps I should say a certain kind of feminist naiveté, died in Abu Ghraib. It was a feminism that saw men as the perpetual perpetrators, women as the perpetual victims and male sexual violence against women as the root of all injustice. Rape has repeatedly been an instrument of war and, to some feminists, it was beginning to look as if war was an extension of rape. There seemed to be at least some evidence that male sexual sadism was connected to our species' tragic propensity for violence. That was before we had seen female sexual sadism in action.

But it's not just the theory of this naive feminism that was wrong. So was its strategy and vision for change. That strategy and vision rested on the assumption, implicit or stated outright, that women were morally superior to men. We had a lot of debates over whether it was biology or conditioning that gave women the moral edge—or simply the experience of being a woman in a sexist culture. But the assumption of superiority, or at least a lesser inclination toward cruelty and violence, was more or less beyond debate. After all, women do most of the caring work in our culture, and in polls are consistently less inclined toward war than men.

I'm not the only one wrestling with that assumption today. Mary Jo Melone, a columnist for the *St. Petersburg* (Florida) *Times*, wrote on May 7, 2004: "I can't get that picture of England [pointing at a hooded Iraqi man's genitals] out of my head because this is not how women are expected to behave. Feminism taught me 30 years ago that not only had women gotten a raw deal from men, we were morally superior to them."

If that assumption had been accurate, then all we would have had to do to make the world a better place—kinder, less violent, more just—would have been to assimilate into what had been, for so many centuries, the world of men. We would fight so that women could become the generals, CEOs, senators, professors, and opinion-makers—and that was really the only fight we had to undertake. Because once they gained power and authority, once they had achieved a critical mass within the institutions of society, women would naturally work for change. That's what we thought, even if we thought it unconsciously—and it's just not true. Women can do the unthinkable.

You can't even argue, in the case of Abu Ghraib, that the problem was that there just weren't enough women in the military hierarchy to stop the abuses. The prison was directed by a woman, General Janis Karpinski. The top US intelligence officer in Iraq, who also was responsible for reviewing the status of detainees before their release, was Major General Barbara Fast. And the US official ultimately responsible for managing the occupation of Iraq since October 2003 was Condoleezza Rice. Like Donald H. Rumsfeld, she ignored repeated reports of abuse and torture until the undeniable photographic evidence emerged.

What we have learned from Abu Ghraib, once and for all, is that a uterus is not a substitute for a conscience. This doesn't mean gender equality isn't worth fighting for for its own sake. It is. If we believe in democracy, then we believe in a woman's right to do and achieve whatever men can do and achieve, even the bad things. It's just that gender equality cannot, all alone, bring about a just and peaceful world.

In fact, we have to realize, in all humility, that the kind of feminism based on an assumption of female moral superiority is not only naive; it also is a lazy and self-indulgent form of feminism. Self-indulgent because it assumes that a victory for a woman—a promotion, a college degree, the right to serve alongside men in the military—is by its very nature a victory for all of humanity. And lazy because it assumes that we have only one struggle—the struggle for gender equality—when in fact we have many more.

The struggles for peace and social justice and against imperialist and racist arrogance, cannot, I am truly sorry to say, be folded into the struggle for gender equality.

What we need is a tough new kind of feminism with no illusions. Women do not change institutions simply by assimilating into them, only by consciously deciding to fight for change. We need a feminism that teaches a woman to say no—not just to the date rapist or the overly insistent boyfriend but, when necessary, to the military or the corporate hierarchy within which she finds herself.

In short, we need a kind of feminism that aims not just to assimilate into the institutions that men have created over the centuries, but to infiltrate and subvert them.

To cite an old, and far from naive, feminist saying: "If you think equality is the goal, your standards are too low." It is not enough to be equal to men, when the men are acting like beasts. It is not enough to assimilate. We need to create a world worth assimilating into.

MAKING SENSE OF
LA DIFFÉRENCE

Time, 1992

F ew areas of science are as littered with intellectual rubbish as the study of innate mental differences between the sexes. In the nineteenth century, biologists held that woman's brain was too small for intellect, but just large enough for household chores. When the tiny-brain theory bit the dust (elephants, after all, have bigger brains than humans), scientists began a long, fruitless attempt to locate the biological basis of male superiority in various brain lobes and chromosomes. By the 1960s, sociobiologists were asserting that natural selection, operating throughout the long human prehistory of hunting and gathering, had predisposed males to leadership and exploration and females to crouching around the campfire with the kids.

Recent studies suggest that there may be some real differences after all. And why not? We have different hormones and body parts; it would be odd if our brains were a hundred percent unisex. The question, as ever, is, What do these differences augur for our social roles?—meaning, in particular, the division of power and opportunity between the sexes.

Don't look to the Flintstones for an answer. However human beings whiled away their first 100,000 or so years of existence, few of us today make a living by tracking down mammoths or digging up tasty roots. In fact, much of our genetic legacy of sex differences has already been rendered moot by that uniquely human invention: technology. Military prowess no longer depends on superior musculature or those bursts of aggressive fury that prime the body for combat at ax range. As for exploration, women—with their lower body weight and oxygen consumption—may be the more "natural" astronauts.

But suppose that the feminists' worst-case scenario turns out to be true, and that males really are better, on average, at certain mathematical tasks. If this tempts you to shunt the girls all back to Home Ec—the only acceptable realm for would-be female scientists eighty years ago—you probably need remedial work in the statistics of "averages" yourself. Just as some women are taller and stronger than some men, some are swifter at solid geometry and abstract algebra. Many of the pioneers in the field of x-ray crystallography—which involves three-dimensional visualization and heavy doses of math—were female, including biophysicist Rosalind Franklin, whose work was indispensable to the discovery of the double-helical structure of DNA.

Then there is the problem that haunts all studies of "innate" sex differences: the possibility that the observed differences are really the result of lingering cultural factors—pushing females, for example, to "succeed" by dummying up.

Girls' academic achievement, for example, usually takes a nosedive at puberty. Unless nature has selected for smart girls and dumb women, something is going very wrong at about the middle-school level. Part of the problem may be that males, having been the dominant sex for a few millennia, still tend to prefer females who make them feel stronger and smarter. Any girl who is bright enough to solve a quadratic equation is also smart enough to bat her eyelashes and pretend that she can't.

Teachers too may play a larger role than nature in differentiating the sexes. Studies show that they tend to favor boys by calling on them more often, making eye contact with them more frequently, and pushing them harder to perform. Myra and David Sadker, professors of education at American University, have found that girls do better when teachers are sensitized to gender bias and refrain from sexist language, such as the use of "man" to mean all of us. Single-sex classes in math and science also boost female performance, presumably by eliminating favoritism and male disapproval of female achievement.

The success, so far, of such simple educational reforms only underscores the basic social issue: Given that there may be real innate mental differences between the sexes, what are we going to do about them? A female advantage in reading emotions could be interpreted to mean that males should be barred from psychiatry—or that they need more coaching. A male advantage in math could be used to confine girls to essays and sonnets—or the decision could be made to compensate by putting more effort into girls' math education. In effect, we already compensate for boys' apparent handicap in verbal skills by making reading the centerpiece of grade-school education.

We are cultural animals, and these are cultural decisions of the kind that our genes can't make for us. In fact, the whole discussion of innate sex differences is itself heavily shaped by cultural factors. Why, for example, is the study of innate differences such a sexy, well-funded topic right now, which happens to be a time of organized feminist challenge to the ancient sexual division of power? Why do the media tend to get excited when scientists find an area of difference, and ignore the many reputable studies that come up with no differences at all?

Whatever science eventually defines it as, *la différence* can be amplified or minimized by human cultural arrangements: The choice is up to us, not our genes.

OUTCLASSED:
SEXUAL HARASSMENT

The Guardian, 2017

With Alissa Quart

The number of women in the entertainment industry coming forward with charges of sexual harassment is starting to feel endless. They include stars like Gwyneth Paltrow and Angelina Jolie but also heads of tech start-ups and journalists, gallerists, and producers.

But it is women working in far less glamorous occupations who really bear the brunt of male lechery and assault: the housekeepers, waitresses, and farmworkers. A paper in the journal *Gender, Work & Organization*, based on interviews with female workers at five-star hotels, found almost all experiencing some kind of inappropriate sexual advance from a guest. In another study, 80 percent of waitresses reported sexual harassment. A mind-boggling 88 percent of female construction workers did, too.

If you look at these numbers, you recognize that most victims are not so glamorous.

And yet, the current conversation about harassment is deeply skewed by social class. There are far too many think pieces about high-level actresses and far too few about the waitress at your local diner.

Why? For starters, most working-class women don't hire publicists or lawyers, and they aren't able to cultivate friends in high places. (They are very rarely applauded for that word of the year, "bravery," in public forums.) Most of these women never go public at all. After all, if you're earning $8 to $10 an hour, you cannot afford to go without a paycheck for the weeks it would take to find a new job. Any expression of dissatisfaction with a hostile workplace can lead to a legal firing on the grounds of, for example, having a bad attitude.

Blue-collar and retail workers may well be happy to see the issue of sexual harassment getting attention, yet they might also be irritated at celebs receiving all the attention and respond accordingly. Talk to a hairdresser, a waitress, or a domestic worker, and you're likely to encounter a deep vein of resentment.

We put the studies aside and actually heard from women on social media. "I've been sexually harassed in minimum and low-wage jobs: Choices were to put up with it or quit. Every single time, I quit. But I was young & single. Many women don't have that option," Pittsburgh artist Amie Gillingham wrote on Barbara's Twitter feed.

Or as writer Julie Rea put it to us, "When I was a waitress, there was sexual harassment/innuendo/verbal abuse from the chefs, the barmen, the kitchen porters, the drunk customers, AND the male managers!"

Another former waitress in Michigan wrote on Twitter, "As a waitress I experienced harassment daily. No HR dept to report it to. Manager & owner were biggest offenders. It was keep quiet or lose my job. Needed that job."

As Cecilia, who worked as a minibar attendant at a Chicago hotel, told the *Huffington Post*, she was asked to come into a room by a male guest who was masturbating to his computer when she entered. He wanted her to see him—this was by design.

Indeed, the "business trip" has gotten so hazardous that two cities—Seattle and New York—have passed initiatives that mandate that hotels supply their housekeepers with panic buttons. Harassment is so common that a hospitality careers website offers a checklist, albeit a toothless one, of what maids and cleaning women can do to protect themselves at work.

Threats involve creepy guests whacking off, grabbing them by their aprons, or throwing them down on the bed, as former IMF managing director Dominique Strauss-Kahn allegedly did to a hotel maid in 2011.

And if you think stronger unions always offer better protection for workers on this score, think again. According to a recent report, even staff at the Service Employees International Union (SEIU) have faced charges of sexual harassment—and that's the largest service workers' union.

There certainly is room for outrage about both the mistreatment of thespians and models, and the manhandling of waitresses or women picking berries in the fields. (We should try for a both/and campaign. It could be called #MostofThem!)

Then again, that inclusive strategy rests on a tacit assumption that the airing of the pain of, say, actor Mira

Sorvino will inevitably help less well-born women. And we think the associative property here is probably a fallacy. It's basically a trickle-down theory of female empowerment. We know how well trickle-down theories of all kinds tend to pan out.

So how can we excavate the vast iceberg of sexual harassment that lies beneath the glittering tip of celebrity abuse?

This is a powerful moment for sharing our stories, but it can sometimes feel like we are only reproducing class divisions that have long existed in the feminist movement— where we are aware of the elegant suffering of celebrity comics, businesswomen, and starlets but not those of the working mothers who are handing us our fries or fluffing our pillows. We are not seeing the way the latter are harassed in so many other ways. Working-class women regularly have their purses searched (ostensibly for stolen goods) or are expected to work overtime without pay. This kind of casual hassling is part of the general humiliation that most low-wage workplaces inflict.

Obviously, working women need safe spaces in which to share their experiences, which unions and affluent feminists could help provide—speak-outs and other public forums to spread the word that sexual harassment is not only pervasive but also, fortunately, illegal.

There is a statewide California bill requiring employers to train cleaning and security employees and managers in the basics of preventing sexual harassment. Not-for-profit organizations like Modern Alliance are working to bring many professions together against worker sexual harassment. The Local 1 union in Chicago has pushed for legislation with the brilliantly seamy hashtag #HandsOff PantsOn.

We should certainly put more pressure on local and federal government for similar bills and language in contracts around the country. But these are still small slaps at the many male hands groping at America's female workforce.

GOD, SCIENCE, AND JOY

MIND YOUR OWN BUSINESS

The Baffler, 2015

At about the beginning of this decade, mass-market mindfulness rolled out of the Bay Area like a brand-new app. Very much like an app, in fact, or a whole swarm of apps. Previous self-improvement trends had been transmitted via books, inspirational speakers, and CDs; now, mindfulness could be carried around on a smartphone. There are hundreds of them, these mindfulness apps, bearing names like Smiling Mind and Buddhify. A typical example features timed stretches of meditation, as brief as one minute, accompanied by soothing voices, soporific music, and images of forests and waterfalls.

This is Buddhism sliced up and commodified, and, in case the connection to the tech industry is unclear, a Silicon Valley venture capitalist blurbed a seminal mindfulness manual by calling it "the instruction manual that should come with our iPhones and BlackBerries." It's enough to make you think that the actual Buddha devoted all his time under the Bodhi Tree to product testing. In the mindfulness lexicon, the word "enlightenment" doesn't have a place.

In California, at least, mindfulness and other conveniently accessible derivatives of Buddhism flourished well before BlackBerries. I first heard the word in 1998 from a wealthy landlady in Berkeley, advising me to be "mindful" of the suffocating Martha Stewart-ish decor of the apartment I was renting from her, which of course I was doing everything possible to un-see. A possible connection between her "mindfulness" and Buddhism emerged only when I had to turn to a tenants' rights group to collect my security deposit. She countered with a letter accusing people like me—leftists, I suppose, or renters—of oppressing Tibetans and disrespecting the Dalai Lama.

During the same stint in the Bay Area, I learned that rich locals liked to unwind at Buddhist monasteries in the hills, where, for a few thousand dollars, they could spend a weekend doing manual labor for the monks. Buddhism, or some adaptation thereof, was becoming a class signifier, among a subset of Caucasians anyway, and nowhere was it more ostentatious than in Silicon Valley, where star player Steve Jobs had been a Buddhist or perhaps a Hindu—he seems not to have made much of a distinction—even before it was fashionable for CEOs to claim a spiritual life. Mindfulness guru and promoter Soren Gordhamer noticed in 2013 that tech leaders from Google, LinkedIn, Twitter, and other major tech companies seemed to be "tapped into an inner dimension that guides their work." He called it "wisdom" and named his annual conferences Wisdom 2.0—helpful shorthand, as it happens, for describing the inner smugness of the Bay Area elite.

Today, mindfulness has far outgrown Silicon Valley and its signature industry, becoming another numbingly ubiquitous feature of the verbal landscape, as "positive thinking" once was. While an earlier, more arduous, version of Buddhism attracted few celebrities other than Richard Gere, mindfulness boasts a host of prominent practitioners—Arianna Huffington, Gwyneth Paltrow, and Anderson Cooper among them. "Mindful leadership" debuted at Davos in 2013 to an overflow crowd, and Wisdom 2.0 conferences have taken place in New York and Dublin as well as San Francisco, with attendees fanning out to become missionaries for the new mind-set. This year's event in San Francisco advertises not only familiar faces from Google and Facebook, but also speeches by corporate representatives of Starbucks and Eileen Fisher. Aetna, a Fortune 100 health insurance company, offers its 34,000 employees a twelve-week meditation class, and its CEO dreams of expanding the program to include all its customers, who will presumably be made healthier by clearing their minds. Even General Mills, which dates back to the nineteenth century, has added meditation rooms to its buildings, finding that a seven-week course produces striking results. According to the *Financial Times*,

> 83 percent of participants said they were "taking time each day to optimize my personal productivity"—up from 23 percent before the course. Eighty-two percent said they now make time to eliminate tasks with limited productivity value—up from 32 percent before the course.

Productivity is only one objective of the new miniaturized meditation; there are also the more profound-sounding goals of "wisdom" and "compassion," which are not normally associated with Silicon Valley or American business in general. Just a few years ago, say in 2005, the tech industry exemplified a very different kind of corporate ideology, featuring multitasking and perpetually divided attention—think an incoming call conducted while scanning a new product design, checking email, and deflecting the interruptions of subalterns. It was madness, but the business self-help literature encouraged people to "surf the chaos," nourishing themselves on caffeine and adrenaline. If we needed to unclutter our minds, we were directed to the gym and an hour or so of intense physical activity. A trim muscular body, combined with an ever-flickering gaze, signified executive status.

The backlash against chaos surfing came on quickly, as if The Wolf of Wall Street had been forced to drink a soothing bowl of milk. Studies were piling up to suggest that a lifestyle dependent on multiple devices and double-shot espressos might be toxic to the human mind, impeding concentration and undermining human connectedness. There was wild talk of "unplugging" and fleeing offline. In northern California in 2013, a group called Digital Detox began offering Camp Grounded, a well-publicized summer camp for adults, at which all devices (and alcohol and children and real names) were prohibited, the better to encourage "play" and conversation. We had once imagined that human attention was infinitely divisible, with each particle of it potentially available to advertisers, entertainers, and employers. But it was turning out to be fragile, even endangered, and in need of constant repair.

Where brilliance and creativity had formerly reigned, there were, by the turn of the millennium, suspicions of pathology. Child psychiatrists began to drop "bipolarity" as a default diagnosis and turn their attention to attention itself. Too many children were deficient in it, just as their plugged-in parents were often guilty of "distracted parenting." The switch from bipolarity to attention deficit disorder is hard to date exactly, in part because these conditions are now said to be frequently "comorbid," or overlapping. But as we began to spend more and more of our time interacting with mood-less programs and devices, psychiatry seems to have turned from emotional concerns like bipolarity, which is a "mood disorder," to cognitive problems like ADD and ADHD.

At the same time, diagnoses of autism and Asperger's syndrome were skyrocketing—especially, as a 2001 article in *Wired* pointed out, in Santa Clara County, home of Silicon Valley. Among the adult population, surely something was wrong with Steve Jobs, who alternated between obsessive attention to details and complete withdrawal into himself, between a spiritual aloofness and uncontrolled temper tantrums. Some observers thought they detected a hint of autism in the unblinking, almost affect-free Bill Gates, and the characters in HBO's *Silicon Valley* are portrayed as well "within the spectrum."

So Silicon Valley embraced mindfulness with a twinge of contrition. Not only did its corporate culture encourage something called "geek syndrome," but its products seemed to spread that same derangement to everyone else. The devices that were supposed to make us smarter and more connected to other humans were actually messing with our minds, causing "net brain" and "monkey mind," as well as physical disorders associated with long hours of sitting. As we click between Twitter and Facebook, text and hypertext, one link and another, synapses are being formed and then broken with febrile inconstancy—or so a growing number of experts, such as MIT's Sherry Turkle, warn us—leaving the neuronal scaffolding too fragile to house large thoughts.

A less arrogant industry might have settled for warning labels on its phones and pads, but Silicon Valley wanted an instant cure, preferably one that was high-tech and marketable. The great advantage of mindfulness was that it seemed to be based firmly on science; no "hippie bullshit" or other "woo woo" was involved. A neuroscientist reported that Buddhist monks with about ten thousand hours of meditation under their belts had altered brain functions; shorter bouts of meditation seemed to work at least temporary changes in novices. The field of "contemplative neuroscience" was born, and Silicon Valley seized on it for a much-needed "neural hack." Through meditation, monastic or app-guided, anyone could reach directly into their own moist brain tissue and "resculpt" it in a calmer, more attentive direction. Mindfulness, as its promoters put it, fosters "neuroplasticity."

No one questions that the brain changes with the experiences the mind undergoes. If thought has a physical basis, as scientists assume, then it produces physical alterations in the brain. Trauma and addiction can lead to lasting problems; even fleeting events may leave the chemical changes in the brain that we experience as memory. In fact, "plasticity" is a pallid descriptor for the constant, ongoing transformation of brain tissue. Neurons reach out to each other through tiny membranous protrusions, often forming new synapses. Synapses that fire frequently grow stronger, while the inactive ones wither. Well-connected neurons thrive, while neglected ones die. There is even some evidence that neurons in mature animals can reproduce.

What there is no evidence for, however, is any particularly salubrious effect of meditation, especially in byte-sized doses. This was established through a mammoth, federally sponsored "meta-analysis" of existing studies, published in 2014, which found that meditation programs can help treat stress-related symptoms but are no more effective in doing so than other interventions, such as muscle relaxation, medication, or psychotherapy. There is no excuse for ignoring this study, which achieved worldwide attention. So maybe meditation does have a calming, "centering" effect, but so does an hour of concentration on a math problem or a glass of wine with friends. As for Silicon Valley's unique contribution, mindfulness apps, a recent study concluded that there is an almost complete lack of evidence supporting the usefulness of those applications. We found no randomized clinical trials evaluating the impact of these applications on mindfulness training or health indicators, and the potential for mobile mindfulness applications remains largely unexplored.

For an industry based on empirical science and employing large numbers of engineers, Silicon Valley has been remarkably incurious about the scientific basis of mindfulness, probably because the "neuroplasticity" concept is just too alluring. If the brain can be resculpted through conscious effort, then mindfulness is as imperative as physical exercise; the brain is a "muscle" and, like any muscle, in need of training. Google's chief motivator Chade-Meng Tan was an early adopter, setting up the company's mindfulness training program, Search Inside Yourself, in 2007, and later telling the *Guardian*:

> If you are a company leader who says employees should be encouraged to exercise, nobody looks at you funny.... The same thing is happening to meditation and mindfulness, because now that it's become scientific, it has been demystified. It's going to be seen as fitness for the mind.

One popular and highly rated mindfulness app, Get Some Headspace, advertises itself as a "gym membership for the mind." Only it's easier than working out, of course, or even yoga. As one enthusiastic software entrepreneur said of the Headspace app, "You don't have to sit in a lotus position. You just press 'play' and chill out."

Outside of meditation, which can take just a few minutes a day, the daily practice of mindfulness can be summarized as pay attention, or better yet, pay attention to one thing at a time. Take out the earphones when the children are trying to talk to you. Listen carefully to colleagues, look them in the eyes, and attempt to comprehend things from their point of view. Do not multitask; just sink yourself into "the moment," one task at a time. What could be simpler?

Left unanswered in all of this is the question of what to be mindful of. Yes, the children. But what do you do when one of them is trying to confide in you and the other one is screaming from the bedroom? Or say you're at a business lunch. You have to be mindful of your companion while simultaneously attempting to eat without spilling or choking—and I say you would be remiss if you failed to notice the sad-eyed busboy who is refilling the water glasses. Divided attention far predates the advent of smartphones and is intrinsic to many human activities, such as child-raising, cooking a large meal, and waiting on tables. Or take one of the most ancient human occupations—war—which is relevant because the mindfulness promoters are beginning to market their product to the US military. Incoming fire can come from any direction, at unexpected times and speeds. Morale must be considered, as well as changing instructions from the strategists in command. There is no danger of soldiers distractedly checking their Facebook pages; the issue is whether they have the mental bandwidth demanded by the exigencies of battle.

Silicon Valley got its own tiny taste of combat at the 2014 Wisdom 2.0 conference in San Francisco. The panel on "3 Steps to Build Corporate Mindfulness the Google Way" had just begun when a small group of protesters walked onstage and unfurled a banner saying "Eviction-Free San Francisco," a reference to the savage gentrification that Google, among others, has inflicted on the city. After security pushed the protesters offstage and started a tug-of-war for the banner, a Google mindfulness representative intoned, "We can use this as a moment of practice. Check in with your body and see what's happening, what it's like to be around conflict and people with heartfelt ideas that may be different than what we're thinking." Zen-like, the panel rolled on, undistracted by the brief glimpse of mass evictions and homelessness.

THE ANIMAL CURE

The Baffler, 2012

Encounters with lions, mountain goats, grizzly bears, dolphins, and whales are not least among the exotic experiences offered by the tourism industry. The attractions are obvious: a chance to be outdoors in stunning scenery, to see creatures you may have known only as two-dimensional images, and to feel ecologically high-minded in the process.

But current marketing for the wildlife encounter industry offers something grander, something that people have more commonly sought through meditation, fasting, or prayer. Surf the numerous websites for the booming worldwide whale-watching business, for example, and you will find companies from Baja to Sydney to Reykjavik promising whale-mediated "spiritual experiences."

Satisfied customers report having undergone life-altering changes, or at least fighting back tears: the vacation as vision quest. Or, within Britain, you can experience the "spiritual event" of a Big Cat Encounter—with the big cats conveniently caged. After treating wild animals as nuisances or meat for many centuries, humans are elevating them to the status of the numinous.

Fortunately, it is not necessary to spend a lot of money or endure seasickness to have a spiritual encounter with an animal. In a pinch, pets will do, and the internet offers a rich literature on the uplifting effects of ordinary dogs and cats. In her 2002 book *Mystical Dogs: Animals as Guides to Our Inner Life*, New Age writer Jean Houston promoted dogs not only for their ability to engender serenity in stressed humans, but to lead us to the experience of cosmic unity. As she instructs:

> Proceed with your dog guide down and down until you reach the deepest level of all, the spiritual realm....Often at this level one feels oneself in the presence of God or, if you prefer, the Mind of the Universe. In this realm, images, thoughts, body sensations, and emotions are fused in what is felt as a meaningful process culminating in a sense of self-understanding, self-transformation, spiritual enlightenment and possibly mystical union. Again, record your unique experience.

Cats, she said in an interview with Beliefnet, are "equally evocative of our spiritual depths," pointing out that the Dalai Lama's house is fairly crawling with them. For the spiritually attuned, almost any animal—insect, bird, butterfly—can serve as a doorman to the realm of enlightenment.

Dogs have been particularly nimble at seizing the new opportunities for animals as spirit guides, shamans, and healers. Long confined to blue-collar work as draft animals or security guards, they can now supplement their domestic roles with professional careers—for example, as "therapy dogs." One of the new canine professionals, Bella the Boxer, has written a business advice book titled *Secrets of a Working Dog: Unleash Your Potential and Create Success*, which recommends the power of "pawsitive" thinking. Her credentials? After bemoaning the limited opportunities formerly available to dogs, she urges the reader to shake off his stereotypes and wake up to the existence of a "new breed of working dog that relies on business savvy and brains. Rather than herd sheep, we're joining the human white-collar workforce."

One out of five corporations, Bella reports, now allows dogs at work, where they are tasked with raising human morale, increasing creativity, and reducing stress. Her own ambition is to become one of America's tens of thousands of registered therapy dogs and minister to patients in hospices and nursing homes.

Premonotheistic societies would have found nothing odd about animal healers or animal-induced epiphanies. They worshipped animals, animal-human hybrids (such as Sekhmet, the lion-bodied goddess of predynastic Egypt), and human-shaped deities with animal familiars (such as the Hindu goddess Durga, who rides a tiger). Even the anthropomorphized Greek deities could take animal form, as when Zeus became a swan to rape Leda, and seem to have originated as animal gods. Almost every large and potent animal species—bears, bulls, lions, sharks, snakes—have been an object of human cultic veneration. Before the

Christian missionaries arrived, my Celtic ancestors worshipped the goddess Epona, who took the form of a horse. The Makah people of Alaska worship "Whale," who provides them with both physical and spiritual sustenance.

In fact, the connection between animals and religiosity may predate fully evolved *Homo sapiens.* Why do humans tend to imagine that there are gods at all? Because, according to the latest from the field of cognitive science, there was a survival advantage in imagining that every stirring in the tall grass meant that a leopard—or some such potentially hazardous life-form—might be closing in for an attack. Our brains are what the cognitive scientists call "hyperactive agency detection devices": We see faces in clouds, hear denunciations in thunder, and sense transcendent beings all around us because we evolved on a planet densely occupied by other "agents"—animals that could destroy us with the slash of a claw or the splash of a fin, arbitrarily and in seconds.

The rise of the monotheistic religions, featuring either anthropomorphic gods like the Christian "father" or deities so abstract that they are impervious to representation, drove the animals, so to speak, from the temple of the human imagination. This change, occurring between roughly 2000 BCE and 700 CE, has long been celebrated as a huge step forward for humankind—the "axial transformation"— propelling us from the unseemly worship of savage beasts to the refined and dignified adoration of a god who is both perfect and perfectly good. But it was a tragic demotion for animals. The axial religions determined that some of them were ritually "unclean" and reclassified all of them as the inferiors of humans. In *The Others: How Animals Made Us Human*, Paul Shepard traced the "humanization" of the so-called world religions—the expunging of animal imagery from religious sites and the association, especially within Christianity, of animals with demons. There were exceptions like St. Francis of Assisi, but Shepard cites a thirteenth-century priest who defeathered a living sparrow in front of his congregation in order to punish the poor bird for being a bird, with all the innate wretchedness and iniquity that such status entails.

Are animals, at least those not designated as meat, finally making a comeback? We may not worship golden calves or offer human sacrifices to jaguar gods, but Americans spend approximately $50 billion a year on our pets. We have an animal rights movement dedicated loosely to the proposition that "animals are people too" and a burgeoning academic field of Animal Studies, which prepares students for careers in veterinary science or, less auspiciously, for fields like "swine management." There is serious talk of "rewilding" large sections of North American real estate by restoring the original Pleistocene flora and fauna—mastodons, or something resembling them, included.

Implicit in much of the new attention to animals is the commendably liberal idea that they are not—intellectually, emotionally, or morally—all that different from humans. Hollywood animal heroes like Remy the rat chef, Rango the cowboy chameleon, and the Kung Fu Panda aspire, scheme, set long-term goals, and, of course, communicate in the voices of human movie stars. In real life, as observed by scientists, animals have been found to be trespassing egregiously on capabilities once thought to be uniquely human: They can use simple tools; they can be altruistic; they can create what they seem to regard as works of art; they can reason and remember; they can fall into what looks like depression. Language is widespread in the nonhuman world, and not only among birds, dolphins, and whales. Very recent research reveals that American prairie dogs, who are closely related to squirrels, can issue calls informing each other about what kind of human, or other creature, might be approaching. "Here comes the tall human in the blue [shirt]," they can say, or "Here comes the short human in the yellow [shirt]." The human-animal distinction disappears almost completely within the new field of Critical Animal Studies, which seeks to advance "a holistic understanding of the commonality of oppressions, such that speciesism, sexism, racism, ableism, statism, classism, militarism, and other hierarchical ideologies and institutions are viewed as parts of a larger, interlocking, global system of domination." Animals are not only like humans, but they are also specifically like oppressed and marginalized categories of humans. One of the founders of Critical Animal Studies expects that, "within a decade [of 2009]," his field will take its "rightful place alongside women's studies, African-American studies, Chicano/a studies, disability studies, and queer studies."

But the current emphasis on animal-human similarities does not necessarily signal the approach of a new Eden, in which vegetarian lions will lie down with lambs. There is an unseemly coziness to much of this enlightened discourse, an assumption that animals are not only like humans, but that they *like* us, or at least bear no active grudges. Every-one has heard, as the Arlington (Virginia) Animal Welfare League puts it, that "there's no need to fear wildlife. If you don't bother them, they generally won't bother you." Hikers in the national parks are reassured that bears are unlikely to attack unless they are startled or have reason to fear a threat to their young. Even whales, who have suffered mightily at human hands, can be anthropomorphized and, at least in imagination, rendered completely tame. As the website for a Baja whale-watching service opines:

> Whales are amazing creatures. Not only are they among the largest creatures on Earth (Blue whales ARE the largest living creatures on the planet!) but they are also among the most gentle and friendly, and very family ori-ented. Whales were given a bad rap by whale hunters (who called them "devilfish") starting in the 1600s, be-cause some mother whales were violent in the water when protecting their young from harpoons, but what good mother WOULDN'T do anything to protect her baby?

Fortunately, "The whales have been very forgiving of their earlier slaughter by humans."

But when humans rest too much on the goodwill of an-imals, or simply let down their guard, things can go very wrong. The poster child for presumptuousness would have to be Timothy Treadwell, who was immortalized by Werner Herzog in the documentary *Grizzly Man*. Having spent thirteen summers living among grizzly bears in the Alaska wilderness—talking to them, reading to them, and occasionally petting them—he came to believe he was "a fully accepted wild animal—brother to these bears." A few weeks after arriving at that triumphant conclusion, he and his girlfriend were killed and partially eaten by one of his ursine siblings. Or we might cite the numerous humans in the life of chimpanzee Nim Chimpsky who taught him to sign more than one hundred words, while at the same time encouraging him to enjoy alcohol, marijuana, and light cross-species sexual intimacies. Perhaps frustrated by his inconsistent and ever-changing human companions, Nim attacked one and bit off nearly half her face.

Another well-documented case of human-animal intimacy gone wrong involves the novelist and short story writer Joy Williams and her German shepherd Hawk, whom she described in an essay as "my sweetie pie, my honey, my handsome boy, my love." As she was leading Hawk into a kennel for one of her rare trips without him, he suddenly leaped on her, biting her breast and hands until "there was blood everywhere." Hawk was subsequently "put down," but Joy survived to become a vegetarian and an animal rights advocate.

The problem is not that animals *are* different from humans in some generalizable way—less gracious, perhaps, or more impulsive and unpredictable—but that it makes very little sense to say what animals are like or not like. There are so many species of animals that any analysis based on the human-animal division is as eccentric, in its own way, as a hypothetical biology based on the jellyfish-nonjellyfish distinction would be. Within species, too, animals differ as individuals, just as humans differ—hence the difficulty in prescribing the best way to avoid a bear attack. Hikers are advised to deflect charging grizzlies by lying down and playing dead, but, sadly, some grizzlies are encouraged by this behavior. Nor can all cases of animal hostility be attributed to human error. Treadwell and Williams may have crossed a line into undue intimacy, but there is no such explanation for the fatal goring of a hiker by a mountain goat in 2011. The man was an experienced hiker, and the goat—who, it has been suggested, may have been harassed by a park ranger in the past—had no apparent proximate *casus belli*. And what are we to make of the occasional whale who attacks a boat—in some cases, even a whale-watching boat, brimming with interspecies goodwill?

So, before engaging a therapy dog, maybe especially a Jungian one, you might want to consider that, in addition to much friendly cooperation, there are serious issues between our species. Humans abuse dogs in many gratuitous ways and, despite much well-intentioned propaganda to the contrary, wolves—who are the ancestors of all dogs, including the "toy" ones—have long been a deadly threat to humans. From Russia to Italy, thousands of people—often children—were lost to wolves between the seventeenth and nineteenth centuries. In late eighteenth-century France, the frequency of wolf attacks on humans necessitated state-sponsored wolf hunts, and when these were suspended during the Revolution, the attacks resumed in full force.

More recently, in 1996, there was a rash of fatal wolf attacks on villagers in Uttar Pradesh. In early 2011 an unprecedented four-hundred-strong wolf pack—or, perhaps we should say army, since the horde represented an alliance of many packs—laid siege to a village in Siberia, although they restricted themselves to eating livestock. One wolf expert speculated that they were not wolves at all, but "a cross between domestic dogs and the wild animal." If so, he wrote, we are faced with "the nightmare possibility that an entirely new creature has been created which, while less wary of humans, also possesses the natural vulpine instinct for hunting and eating as a pack." And plenty of pet dogs other than Hawk have launched individual attacks on their apparently indulgent owners. To cite a couple of random examples, in the last five years a British woman lost her nose to her greyhound while she slept, and a Manhattan woman's scalp was torn open when she bent to give her Rottweiler a good-morning pat.

None of which is to say that animals may not make fine "spirit guides" or, to the extent that we need them, even deities. I once found myself well away from land and escorted by a couple of dolphins, each of them about the size of my kayak. They appeared to be playing with me, diving under the kayak and popping up on the other side, grinning their fixed, unreadable grins. It would have been easy enough for them to flip the kayak over and, if they were so minded, to push me under water until I drowned, but that was not the game they were playing that day. On another occasion, I had a chance to see a tiger, illuminated only by flashlight, at a distance of about three feet. Despite the sturdy fence between us, I found myself experiencing what zoologist Konrad Lorenz called the *heiliger Schauer*, or "holy shiver" of awe that predators inspire in their prey. There is something deeply uncanny about looking into the eyes of a powerful, intelligent, alien being. Maybe you could even call it spiritual.

Besides, it's long past time to admit that the "all-good" and "all-perfect" deities of monotheism have not worked out very well, discredited as they are by earthquakes, floods, tsunamis, and epidemics, not to mention all the murders committed in their names. And what about the built-in biological evil of predation, which has been a driving force of evolution at least since the Cambrian era, about 500 million years ago? If nature is "red in tooth and claw," it must be because the supreme deity, should there be one, prefers this color scheme.

You don't have to be an atheist to see that theodicy, or the effort to excuse God for evil, is a species of idiocy. There is no way to be both all good and all powerful, not in this region of the multiverse anyway. If there is a God or gods—a possibility I am not ruling out—clearly he, she, or they are not, in any human way, "good." At least with animals or zoomorphic deities we know where we are—which is with creatures in whom, as Michael Pollan puts it, we can glimpse "something unmistakably familiar (pain, fear, tenderness) and something irretrievably alien."

But these glimpses are rare. As the entrepreneurs of wildlife tourism understand, most of us are unlikely to encounter a free, self-determining animal larger than a raccoon unless we are willing to pay for the experience. The massive extinctions of megafauna—both through killing for food and killing for sport—that began twelve thousand years ago as humans spread out over the earth have accelerated drastically in the past century or two, leaving us a very lonely species. We try to compensate by seeking out the rare wild animals who have survived our depredations, or by imagining an invisible super being or God who will befriend and comfort us. Or we scan the galaxy for habitable planets, searching for the kind of company—quirky, diverse, and sometimes awe-inspiring—that we once found thick upon this earth.

THE MISSIONARY POSITION

The Baffler, 2012

M ost critics have regarded Ridley Scott's *Prometheus* in much the same way that Arthur Miller probably thought of Marilyn Monroe—gorgeous, but intellectually way out of her depth. No one denies the film's visual glory, which begins the moment a giant chalk-white alien strides out into the Icelandic wasteland, guzzles some gunk from a can, and splits open to release thousands of wriggling worm-like DNA strands into a waterfall. But when it comes to metaphysical coherence, the critical consensus is that *Prometheus* has nothing to offer. "There are no revelations," the *New York Times* opines, "only what are called, in the cynical jargon of commercial storytelling, 'reveals,' bits of momentarily surprising information bereft of meaning or resonance." In its refusal to offer an adequate accounting of the universe and our place in it, the film can even be accused of anti-intellectualism. "We were never really in the realm of working out logical solutions to difficult problems," Geoffrey O'Brien complains in the *New York Review of Books*, just a "cauldron" of "juicily irrational ingredients."

But *Prometheus* does have a clear-cut metaphysical proposition to offer, one so terrible as to be almost inadmissible. Consider the basic plot, minus the many alien invasions of human flesh, the references to corporate greed and alien WMDs, and the enigma of the devious HAL-like android: Guided by archeological clues found in prehistoric rock art, a group of humans set out on a trillion-dollar expedition to visit the planet (actually a moon) that the giant white alien came from. There, among innumerable horrors, since under its bleak surface this moon seems to be a breeding ground for lethal predators of the dark and squirmy variety, they find a cryogenically preserved clone or sibling of that original alien "creator" who seeded earth with DNA. The humans foolishly awaken him, perhaps expecting some sort of seminar on the purpose of life. Instead, the alien starts knocking heads off and strides away to resume his pre-nap project of traveling to and destroying the planet earth. This, and not the DIY abortion of a squid-like alien fetus, is the emotional climax of the film, the point when Noomi Rapace screams at the homicidal alien, "I need to know why! What did we do wrong? Why do you hate us?"

True, we don't know whether the big white aliens are gods, manifestations of a single God, or operatives working for some higher power. But just how much theological clarity can you expect from a Hollywood action film? It doesn't take any great imaginative leap to see that Scott and his writers are confronting us with the possibility that there may be a God, and that He (or She or It or They) *is not good*. This is not atheism. It is a strand of religious dissidence that usually flies well under the radar of both philosophers and cultural critics. For example, it took about five years before the critics noticed that Philip Pullman's popular trilogy *His Dark Materials* was not just about a dodgy or unreliable God, but about one who is actively malevolent. Atheism has become a respectable intellectual position, in some settings almost de rigueur, but as Bernard Schweizer explains in his enlightening 2010 book *Hating God: The Untold Story of Misotheism*, morally inspired opposition to God remains almost too radical to acknowledge. How many of Elie Wiesel's admirers know that he said, "Although I know I will never defeat God, I still fight him"? Or that Rebecca West declaimed that "the human will should [not] be degraded by bowing to this master criminal," and that she was echoing a sentiment already expressed by Zora Neale Hurston?

Barred from more respectable realms of speculation, the idea of an un-good God has been pretty much left to propagate in the fertile wetlands of science fiction. One of the early sci-fi classics of the twentieth century, H. P. Lovecraft's 1931 *At the Mountains of Madness*, offers a plotline that eerily prefigures Prometheus. An Antarctic expedition uncovers the ruins of a millions-of-years-old civilization created by extraterrestrial aliens, who awaken and kill most of the explorers. A couple of humans survive to determine, through a careful study of the ruins, that the aliens had "filtered down from the stars and concocted earth life as a joke or mistake." Not all sci-fi deities are so nasty. C. S. Lewis offered a Christ-like lion god in the Narnia series; *Battlestar Galactica*'s climax featured a vision of a benevolent, and oddly Luddite, god. But many of the great sci-fi epics derive their philosophical frisson from a callous or outright wicked deity: the impertinent Vulcan god of *Star Trek V: The Final Frontier*, the tyrannical worm-god of *God Emperor of Dune*, the trickster sea god of *Solaris*.

There are less satanic sci-fi gods too—more ethereal, universal, and even intermittently nonviolent. Olaf Stapledon's 1937 *Star Maker* ends with its far-traveling human protagonist encountering the eponymous "eternal spirit": "Here was no pity, no proffer of salvation, no kindly aid. Or here were all pity and all love, but mastered by a frosty ecstasy." In Arthur C. Clarke's 1953 short story "The Nine Billion Names of God," Tibetan monks who have set themselves the task of generating all the possible names of God finally get some assistance from a computer brought to them by Western technicians. As the technicians make their way back down the mountainside from the monastery, they look up at the night sky to see that "without any fuss, the stars were going out." The monks had been right: The universe existed for the sole purpose of listing the names of God and, once this task was accomplished, there was no reason for the universe to go on. The theme of an über-Being who uses humans for its own inscrutable purposes is developed more fully in Clarke's novel *Childhood's End*, in which an "Overmind" of remote extraterrestrial provenance sets humans on a course toward ecstatic communion with each other—and, somehow, at the same time, with it. When that goal is achieved, the earth blows itself up, along with the last human on it, after which the Overmind presumably moves on to find a fresh planet—and species—to fulfill its peculiar cravings.

The idea of an un-good God, whether indifferent or actively sadistic, flies in the face of at least two thousand years of pro-God PR, much of it irrational and coming from professed "people of faith." God is perfectly good and loving, they assert with an almost infantile sense of entitlement; he "has a plan" for us, no matter how murky or misguided that plan often seems. Otherwise, they ask, as if evaluating a health care provider, what comfort does he have to offer us? Or they petulantly demand a "perfect" God—all-good, omnipotent, and omniscient—in the name of what amounts to human vanity. If we, the top dogs on our planet, are to worship some invisible Other, he had better be unimaginably perfect.

But you don't have to be a theist to insist on the goodness of God. Generations of secular social scientists and others writing in the social-science tradition have insisted that a good God, whether He exists or not, is good for us. The argument takes the form of a historical narrative: In the ancient past—and its seeming equivalent in small-scale or "primitive" societies—deities were plural, female as well as male, and often of no detectable moral valence. The ancient deities of Mediterranean peoples, for example, a pantheon that ranges from Zeus to Yahweh and Baal, were psycho-gods—insatiable consumers of blood sacrifice, abettors of genocide, even, in the case of Zeus, a serial rapist. They offered no rationales for their behavior, and when Job insisted on an explanation for the travails visited upon him, he was told, in effect, "Because I can." Further back, in prehistory, lurk deities too wild and bloody-minded to take fully human form. They were predatory animals like Sekhmet, the lion-headed goddess of ancient Egypt, and the man-eating goddess Kali, who wears a tiger skin.

Then, the official narrative continues, somewhere between 900 and 200 BCE, the so-called "Axial Age," God underwent a major makeover. Blood sacrifice was gradually abandoned; diverse and multiple gods fused into a single male entity; a divine concern for peace and order supposedly came to permeate the universe. In the often-told story of divine redemption, Yahweh matures into the kindly shepherd of the Psalms and finally into the all-loving person of Jesus, who is himself offered up as a sacrifice. Comparable changes occur outside the Mediterranean world, including in persistently polytheistic Hinduism, which gives up animal sacrifice and reaches for a sublime über-Deity. What brought about this transformation?

Religious historian Karen Armstrong, probably the best-known living celebrant of axial progress, proposes in her 2006 book *The Great Transformation* that people simply got tired of the bad old gods' violence and immorality. Speaking of the late Vedic period in India, she writes that the traditional gods "were beginning to seem crude and unsatisfactory," leading to the search for a god "who was more worthy of worship." As people became nicer and more sensitive, they lost interest in the grand spectacles of animal sacrifice that constituted preaxial religious ritual and sought a more "spiritual" experience. (She also mentions, but only in passing, that in some parts of the world people had a less exalted reason for abandoning blood sacrifice: they were running out of animals to sacrifice.) To

Armstrong, the axial transformation had only one flaw—its "indifference to women," which is a pretty wan way to describe a theological shift that eliminated most of the planet's goddesses. But she humbly accepts the limits set by patriarchal monotheism: "Precisely because the question of women was so peripheral to the Axial Age, I found that any sustained discussion of this topic was distracting."

In his 2009 book *The Evolution of God*, the polymathic scholar Robert Wright offered what promised to be an even more objective and secular explanation for God's "transformation." He argues that, for various reasons, people, or at least key peoples, were becoming more cosmopolitan and tolerant, hence in need of a single, universal, morally admirable deity. This seems like a useful approach, until you recall that the ultracosmopolitan and theologically tolerant Romans readily absorbed the gods of conquered peoples into their own polytheistic pantheon. But Wright hardly needs any concrete historical forces, because "moral progress...turns out to be embedded in the very logic of religion as mediated by the basic direction of social evolution"—which I suppose is a way of saying that things could only get better, because such is their "logic" and "basic direction." As Wright informs us, "cultural evolution was all along pushing divinity, and hence humanity, toward moral enlightenment."

The "New Atheists"—Christopher Hitchens, Richard Dawkins, Sam Harris, and Daniel Dennett—easily flicked away the argument that God's axial upgrade was accompanied by a general increase in human goodness and mercy. They note that the new-model deities, with prophets like

Jesus and Muhammad, have proved just as effective at abetting cruelty and war as the old ones. If the gods have any of their reputed powers, and if they got nicer while humans did not, then we have to question the depth and sincerity of the gods' transformation—or whether it occurred at all. Interestingly, though, neither Armstrong nor Wright cedes any power or agency to the God whose growing goodness they applaud: To do so would be to give up their own claims to scholarly detachment. Their God is presented as nothing more than a projection of human needs and desires, an assessment no atheist could disagree with.

There is another theory of how humans became attached to "good" and increasingly monotheistic gods—and one that is refreshingly free of sweetness and optimism. As Jürgen Habermas and, more recently, in rich historical detail, Robert Bellah have pointed out, the "Axial Period" was a time of endemic warfare, intensified by the introduction of iron weapons across Eurasia. The maintenance of armies and the practice of war require strong central authorities— kings and eventually emperors—who discover that it is both risky and inefficient to try to rule their domestic populations entirely by force. Far easier to persuade the public that the king or the emperor is *deserving* of obedience because the deity he represents, or even embodies, is himself so transcendentally good. The autocrat who rules by divine right—from Constantine to Hirohito, the God-emperor of Japanese State Shintoism—demands not only obedience, but gratitude and love.

The good, post-axial God has not, of course, always been a reliable ally of tyrants. Christianity has again and again helped inspire movements against the powerful, such as the abolitionists and the twentieth-century civil rights movement. But this does not mean that the good God is necessarily good for us, or at least for the downtrodden majority of us. The unforgiveable crime of the post-axial religions is to encourage the conflation of authority and benevolence, of hierarchy and justice. When the pious bow down before the powerful or, in our own time, the megachurches celebrate wealth and its owners, the "good" God is just doing his job of what Habermas called "legitimation."

In 1974, Philip K. Dick experienced a theophany—a "self-disclosure by the divine"—which deftly summarizes science fiction's contribution to theology. It was a shattering revelation, leaving him feeling more like "a hit-and-run accident victim than a Buddha." He disintegrated into mental illness, at least to the point of earning a bed in a locked psychiatric ward for several weeks. As related in his novel *Valis*, in which the author figures as the protagonist, he fought back by working obsessively to understand and communicate his encounter with a deity of extraterrestrial origin that is "*in no way like mortal creatures*" (his italics). This deity or deities—for there may be at least a half dozen of them in Dick's idiosyncratic cosmogony—bear some resemblance to biological creatures: They have their own agendas, and what they seek, through their self-disclosures to humans, is "interspecies symbiosis."

If God is an alternative life-form or member of an alien species, then we have no reason to believe that It is (or They are), in any humanly recognizable sense of the word, "good." Human conceptions of morality almost all derive from the intensely social nature of the human species: Our young require years of caretaking, and we have, over the course of evolution, depended on each other's cooperation for mutual defense. Thus we have lived, for most of our existence as a species, in highly interdependent bands that have had good reasons to emphasize the values of loyalty and heroism, even altruism and compassion. But these virtues, if not unique to us, are far from universal in the animal world (or, of course, the human one). Why should a Being whose purview supposedly includes the entire universe share the tribal values of a particular group of terrestrial primates?

Besides, Dick may have been optimistic in suggesting that what the deity hungers for is "interspecies symbiosis." Symbiosis is not the only possible long-term relationship between different species. Parasitism, as hideously displayed in Ridley Scott's *Alien* series, must also be considered, along with its quicker-acting version, predation. In fact, if anything undermines the notion of a benevolent deity, it has to be the ubiquity of predation in the human and nonhuman animal worlds. Who would a "good" God favor—the antelope or the lion with hungry cubs waiting in its den, the hunter or the fawn? For Charles Darwin, the deal breaker was the Ichneumon wasp, which stings its prey in order to paralyze them so that they may be eaten alive by the wasp's larvae. "I cannot persuade myself," wrote Darwin, "that a beneficent and omnipotent God would have designedly created the Ichneumonidae with the express intention of their feeding within the living bodies of Caterpillars, or that a cat should play with mice." Or, as we may ask more generally: What is kindness or love in a biological world shaped by interspecies predation? "Morality is of the highest importance," Albert Einstein once said, "but for us, not for God."

In *Prometheus*, the first alien releases DNA on earth about 500 million years ago, on the eve, in many viewers' interpretation, of what has been called the Precambrian evolutionary explosion. If so, it was not life that the alien initiated on earth, because life predated the Precambrian. What he did may have been far worse; he may have infected the earth with the code or script for interspecies predation. Before the "explosion," terrestrial life was mostly unicellular and, judging from the low frequency of claws, shells, and other forms of weaponry found in the fossil record, relatively peaceful. Afterwards, living creatures became bigger, more diverse, better armed, and probably either meaner or a lot more frightened: The "arms race" between predator and prey had begun. The causality remains in question here, with scientists still puzzling over the origins of predation and its role in triggering the runaway evolutionary process that led, from the Cambrian on, to humans, to science fiction, and to the idea of God.

If the doughy aliens are not the ultimate deities whose morality we need to assess, then who or what is? Who do these aliens work for—or against? At the end of the movie, with all of their human comrades dead, the android and the Noomi Rapace character rebuild an alien spaceship and set off to find the planet that, according to the android's research, the aliens themselves originally came from. The possibility of a good God or gods, signaled by the cross

Noomi wears around her neck, remains open—as it must, of course, for the sequel.

But, contra so many of the critics, we have learned an important lesson from the magnificent muddle of *Prometheus*: If you see something that looks like a god—say, something descending from the sky in a flaming chariot, accompanied by celestial choir sounds and trailing great clouds of stardust—do not assume that it is either a friend or a savior. Keep a wary eye on the intruder. By all means, do not fall down on your knees.

THE NEW CREATIONISM:
BIOLOGY UNDER ATTACK

The Nation, 1997

With Janet McIntosh

When social psychologist Phoebe Ellsworth took the podium at a recent interdisciplinary seminar on emotions, she was already feeling rattled. Colleagues who'd presented earlier had warned her that the crowd was tough and had little patience for the reduction of human experience to numbers or bold generalizations about emotions across cultures. Ellsworth had a plan: She would preempt criticism by playing the critic, offering a social history of psychological approaches to the topic. But no sooner had the word "experiment" passed her lips than the hands shot up. Audience members pointed out that the experimental method is the brainchild of white Victorian males. Ellsworth agreed that white Victorian males had done their share of damage in the world but noted that, nonetheless, their efforts had led to the discovery of DNA. This short-lived dialogue between paradigms ground to a halt with the retort: "You believe in DNA?"

More grist for the academic right? No doubt, but this exchange reflects a tension in academia that goes far deeper than spats over "political correctness." Ellsworth's experience illustrates the trend—in anthropology, sociology, cultural studies, and other departments across the nation—to dismiss the possibility that there are any biologically based commonalities that cut across cultural differences. This aversion to biological or, as they are often branded, "reductionist" explanations, commonly operates as an informal ethos limiting what can be said in seminars, asked at lectures or incorporated into social theory. Extreme antiinnatism has had formal institutional consequences as well: At some universities, like the University of California, Berkeley, the biological subdivision of the anthropology department has been relocated to a separate building—a spatial metaphor for an epistemological gap.

Although some of the strongest rejections of the biological have come from scholars with a left or feminist perspective, antipathy toward innatist theories does not always score neatly along political lines. Consider a recent review essay by centrist sociologist Alan Wolfe in the *New Republic*. Wolfe makes quick work of Frank Sulloway's dodgy Darwinist claims (in *Born to Rebel: Birth Order, Family Dynamics, and Creative Lives*) about the influence of birth order on personality, but can't resist going on to impugn the motives of anyone who would apply biology to the human condition: In general, he asserts, "The biologizing of human beings is not only bad humanism, but also bad science."

For many social theorists, innate biology can be let in only as a constraint—"a set of natural limits on human functioning," as anthropologist Marshall Sahlins has written. It has, from this point of view, no positive insights to offer into how humans think, act, or arrange their cultures. For others, the study of innate human properties is not merely uninteresting but deeply misguided. Stanford philosopher of science John Dupré, for example, argues that it is "essentialist" even to think that we are a biological species in the usual sense—that is, a group possessing any common tendencies or "universal properties" that might shed some light on our behavior. As feminist theorist Judith Butler puts it, "The very category of the universal has begun to be exposed for its own highly ethnocentric biases."

But the notion that humans have no shared, biologically based "nature" constitutes a theory of human nature itself. No one, after all, is challenging the idea that chimpanzees have a chimpanzee nature—that is, a set of genetically scripted tendencies and potential responses that evolved along with the physical characteristics we recognize as chimpanzee-like. To set humans apart from even our closest animal relatives as the one species that is exempt from the influences of biology is to suggest that we do indeed possess a defining "essence," and that it is defined by our unique and miraculous freedom from biology. The result is an ideological outlook eerily similar to that of religious creationism. Like their fundamentalist Christian counterparts, the most extreme antibiologists suggest that humans occupy a status utterly different from and clearly "above" that of all other living beings. And, like the religious fundamentalists, the new academic creationists defend their stance as if all of human dignity—and all hope for the future—were at stake.

The new secular creationism emerged as an understandable reaction to excess. Since the nineteenth century, conservatives have routinely deployed supposed biological differences as immutable barriers to the achievement of a more egalitarian social order. Darwinism was quickly appropriated as social Darwinism—a handy defense of economic inequality and colonialism. In the twentieth century, from the early eugenicists to *The Bell Curve*, pseudo-biology has served the cause of white supremacy. Most recently, evolutionary psychology has become, in some hands, a font of patriarchal social prescriptions. Alas, in the past few years such simplistic biological reductionism has tapped a media nerve, with the result that, among many Americans, schlock genetics has become the default explanation for every aspect of human behavior from homosexuality to male promiscuity, from depression to "criminality."

Clearly science needs close and ongoing scrutiny, and in the past decade or two there has been a healthy boom in science studies and criticism. Scholars such as Evelyn Fox Keller, Sandra Harding, Emily Martin, and Donna Haraway have offered useful critiques of the biases and ethnocentric metaphors that can skew everything from hypothesis formation to data-collection techniques. Feminists (one of the authors included) have deconstructed medicine and psychology for patriarchal biases; left-leaning biologists such as Stephen Jay Gould, Richard Lewontin, and Ruth Hubbard have exposed misapplications of biology to questions of social policy. However, contemporary antibiologists decry a vast range of academic pursuits coming from very different theoretical corners—from hypotheses about the effects of genes and hormones, to arguments about innate cognitive modules and grammar, to explorations of universal ritual form and patterns of linguistic interaction. All these can be branded as "essentialist," hence wrongheaded and politically mischievous. Paradoxically, assertions about universal human traits and tendencies are usually targeted just as vehemently as assertions about differences: There are no differences between groups, seems to be the message, but there is no sameness among them, either.

Within anthropology, the social science traditionally friendliest to biology and now the one most bitterly divided over it, nineteenth-century claims about universal human nature were supplanted in the early twentieth century by Franz Boas and colleagues, who conducted detailed studies of particular cultures. By the mid-1960s, any role for biological commonalities in cultural anthropology was effectively foreclosed when Clifford Geertz remarked that "Our ideas, our values, our acts, even our emotions are, like our nervous system itself, cultural products."

As neo-Marxist and behaviorist theories of the tabula rasa human gained ground over the next decade, other disciplines followed anthropology's lead. So completely was sociology purged of biology that when Nicholas Petryszak analyzed twenty-four introductory sociology textbooks in 1979, he found that all assumed that "any consideration of biological factors believed to be innate to the human species is completely irrelevant in understanding the nature of human behavior and society." In general, by the seventies, antibiologism had become the rallying cry of academic liberals and feminists—and the apparent defense of human freedom against the iron chains of nature.

It was only with the arrival of the intellectual movements lumped under the term "postmodernism" that academic antibiologism began to sound perilously like religious creationism. Postmodernist perspectives go beyond a critique of the misuses of biology to offer a critique of biology itself, extending to all of science and often to the very notion of rational thought. In the simplified form it often takes in casual academic talk, postmodernism can be summed up as a series of tenets that include a wariness of metanarratives (meaning grand explanatory theories), a horror of essentialism (extending to the idea of any innate human traits), and a fixation on "power" as the only force limiting human freedom—which at maximum strength precludes claims about any universal human traits while casting doubt on the use of science to study our species or anything at all. Glibly applied, postmodernism portrays evolutionary theory as nothing more than a sexist and racist story line created by Western white men.

The deepest motives behind this new secular version of creationism are understandable. We *are* different from other animals. Language makes us more plastic and semiotically sophisticated, and renders us deeply susceptible to meanings and ideas. As for power, Foucault was right: It's everywhere, and it shapes our preferences and categories of thought, as well as our life chances. Many dimensions of human life that feel utterly "natural" are in fact locally constructed, a hard-earned lesson too easy to forget and too important not to publicize. The problem is that the combined vigor of antibiologism and simplified postmodernism has tended to obliterate the possibility that human beings have anything in common, and to silence efforts to explore this domain. Hence we have gone, in the space of a decade or two, from what began as a healthy skepticism about the misuses of biology to a new form of dogma.

As a biologically oriented researcher who has made controversial innatist claims, Rutgers social theorist Robin Fox notes with irony that secular creationist academics seem to have replaced the church as the leading opponents of Darwinism: "It's like they're responding to heresy." Stephen Jay Gould, who has devoted much of his career to critiquing misuses of biology, also detects parallels between religious and academic creationist zeal. While holding that many aspects of human life are local and contingent, he adds, "Some facts and theories are truly universal (and true)— and no variety of cultural traditions can change that…we can't let a supposedly friendly left-wing source be exempt from criticism from anti-intellectual positions."

The new creationism is not simply a case of well-intended politics gone awry; it represents a grave misunderstanding of biology and science generally. Ironically, the creationists invest the natural sciences with a determinative potency no thoughtful scientist would want to claim. Biology is rhetorically yoked to "determinism," a concept that threatens to clip our wings and lay waste to our utopian visions, while culture is viewed as a domain where power relations with other humans are the only obstacle to freedom.

But these stereotypes of biological determinism and cultural malleability don't hold up under scrutiny. For one thing, biology is not a dictatorship—genes work probabilistically, and their expression depends on interaction with their environment. As even Richard Dawkins, author of *The Selfish Gene* and a veritable Antichrist to contemporary creationists of both the secular and Christian varieties, makes clear: "It is perfectly possible to hold that genes exert a statistical influence on human behaviour while at the same time believing that this influence can be modified, overridden or reversed by other influences." And if biology is not a dictatorship, neither is culture a realm of perfect plasticity. The accumulated lessons of ethnography—and, paradoxically, postmodern theories of power themselves—suggest that even in the absence of biological constraints, it is not easy to remold human cultures to suit our utopian visions. In fact, in the extreme constructivist scenario borrowed by secular creationists, it's hard to imagine who would have the will or the ability to orchestrate real change: the people in power, who have no motivation to alter the status quo, or the oppressed, whose choices, preferences, and sentiments have been so thoroughly shaped by the cultural hegemony of the elite? Judged solely as a political stance, secular creationism is no less pessimistic than the biologism it seeks to uproot.

Milder versions of the "nature/nurture" debate begat a synthesis: "There is no biology that is not culturally mediated." But giving biology its due while taking cultural mediation into account requires inclusive and complex thinking—as Phoebe Ellsworth puts it: "You need a high tolerance of ambiguity to believe both that culture shapes things and that we have a lot in common." Despite the ham-fisted efforts of early sociobiologists, many (probably most) biologically based human universals are not obvious to the naked eye or accessible to common sense.

Finally, many secular creationists are a few decades out of date on the kind of "human nature" that evolutionary biology threatens to impose on us. Feminists and liberal academics were perhaps understandably alarmed by the aggressive "man the hunter" image that prevailed in the sixties and seventies; and a major reason for denying the relevance of evolution was a horror of the nasty, brutish cavemen we had supposedly evolved from. But today, evolutionary theory has moved to a more modest assessment of the economic contribution of big-game hunting (as opposed to gathering and scavenging) and a new emphasis on the cooperative— even altruistic—traits that underlie human sociality and intelligence. We don't have to like what biology has to tell us about our ancestors, but the fact is that they have become a lot more likable than they used to be.

In portraying human beings as pure products of cultural context, the secular creationist standpoint not only commits biological errors but defies common sense. In the exaggerated postmodernist perspective appropriated by secular creationists, no real understanding or communication is possible between cultures. Since the meaning of any human practice is inextricable from its locally spun semiotic web, to pluck a phenomenon such as "ritual" or "fear" out of its cultural context is, in effect, to destroy it. Certainly such categories have different properties from place to place, and careful contextualization is necessary to grasp their local implications. But as Ellsworth asks: "At the level of detail of 'sameness' that postmodernists are demanding, what makes them think that two people in the same culture will under-stand each other?" The ultimate postmodern retort would be, of course, that we do not, but this nihilism does not stand up to either common sense or deeper scrutiny. We manage to grasp things about each other—emotions, mo-tives, nuanced (if imperfect) linguistic meanings—that couldn't survive communicative transmission if we didn't have some basic emotional and cognitive tendencies in common.

The creationist rejection of innate human universals threatens not only an intellectual dead end but a practical one. In writing off any biologically based human common-ality, secular creationists undermine the very bedrock of the politics they claim to uphold. As Barbara Epstein of the History of Consciousness Program at the University of California, Santa Cruz, remarks: "If there is no human nature outside social construction, no needs or capacities other than those constructed by a particular discourse, then there is no basis for social criticism and no reason for protest or rebellion." In fact, tacit assumptions of human similarity are embedded in the theories of even such os-tensible social constructionists as Marx, whose theory of alienation assumes (in some interpretations, anyway) that there are authentic human needs that capitalism fails to meet.

Would it really be so destructive to our self-esteem as a species to acknowledge that we, like our primate relatives, are possessed of an inherited repertoire of potential re-sponses and mental structures? Would we forfeit all sense of agency and revolutionary possibility if we admitted that we, like our primate relatives, are subject to the rules of DNA replication (not to mention the law of gravity)? In their horror of "determinism," academic creationists seem to forget postmodernism's finest insight: that, whatever else we may be, we are indeed creatures of symbol and "text." We may be, in many ways, constrained by our DNA, but we are also the discoverers of DNA—and, beyond that, the only living creature capable of representing its biological legacy in such brilliant and vastly condensed symbols as "DNA."

The good news is that a break may be coming. In spite of the nose-thumbing inspired by the Alan Sokal/Social Text hoax, constructive debates and conversations between scientists and social theorists have been initiated in newsletters, journals, and conferences across the country. A few anthropology departments, including those at Northwestern, Penn State, and Emory, are encouraging communication between their cultural and biological subfields. And although interactionist work has not had adequate space to flourish, achievements so far suggest that, regardless of creationist disclaimers, biological and cognitive universals may be acutely relevant to social theory. Ann Stoler, an anthropologist, historian, and scholar of Foucault at the University of Michigan, agrees. By failing to take our innate cognitive tendencies seriously, she writes, social constructionists may be dodging the "uncomfortable question" as to whether oppressive ideologies like racism and sexism "acquire the weight…they do…because of the ways in which they feed off and build upon [universal] categories of the mind." As Ellsworth says, the meeting of human universals and culture is "where the interesting questions begin."

But for the time being it takes more than a nuanced mind to deal with the interface of culture and biology. It takes courage. This climate of intolerance, often imposed by scholars associated with the left, ill suits an academic tradition rhetorically committed to human freedom. What's worse, it provides intellectual backup for a political outlook that sees no real basis for common ground among humans of different sexes, races, and cultures.

UP CLOSE AT
TRINIDAD'S CARNIVAL

Smithsonian Magazine, 2009

When Northerners think of the Caribbean, Trinidad isn't usually the first place that comes to mind. Until recently, Trinidad had few tourist-oriented hotels or restaurants, and its crime rate is so high that visitors are advised not to venture outdoors wearing watches or jewelry, and definitely not at night. What Trinidad does have is carnival—a centuries-old blowout reputedly so wild and intense that it makes Mardi Gras look like a Veterans Day parade.

I had a reason beyond hedonism for making the trip. I'd spent nine years researching a book on the carnival tradition, *Dancing in the Streets: A History of Collective Joy*. Prehistoric rock drawings suggest that costuming and group dancing date back to the Paleolithic. In the nineteenth century, Western explorers found it going strong among indigenous peoples worldwide, including Polynesians, Inuits, West Africans, Aboriginal Australians, and villagers in India. In Europe, however, it had been suppressed when Protestantism and the Counter-Reformation wiped out most public festivities, which, over the years, had become flash points for popular unrest.

The European experience in Trinidad is a case in point: Eighteenth-century French settlers brought the tradition of a pre-Lenten festival, in which they found it amusing to dress up and dance like their African slaves. The enslaved peoples found it even more amusing to use the confusion of carnival as an occasion for uprisings. Long after slavery was abolished by the British in 1838, the colonial administration continued to fight the now-Africanized carnival piece by piece—banning, at one time or another, drums, masks, and dancing in the streets.

But carnival survived, and my question was: What compromises had it made to do so? I had watched Key West's version of carnival—October's Fantasy Fest—go downhill over the years, blanched by commercialization and robbed of artistry as the point of it became to bare one's (painted) breasts and drink oneself sick. Had Trinidad managed to keep carnival's traditional creativity and political charge alive? Most of my years of research had been sedentary, in hushed libraries and poorly lit archives. In February 2008 I decided to go dancing in the streets myself.

I arrived in Port of Spain two days before the official start of carnival, giving me plenty of time to see that "mas," as the Trinidadians call it (from "masquerade"), isn't just a diversion. It's practically a national mobilization. Tens of thousands of people poured into the squat, mountain-ringed city, most of them native-born "Trinis," home from other parts of the world, with a few European tourists thrown in. Banners flying over downtown streets advised, for safety's sake, to "stay with your lime," your lime being the friends you came with. Newspapers offered front-page reports of bitter rivalries in the pre-carnival soca music competitions, screaming headlines like "'No One Will Spoil Dis Mas,' Warns Police Commissioner Paul" and earnest editorials on exactly the kind of questions that concerned me, such as whether the predominance of foreign-made bikini costumes has reduced carnival to a girlie show.

The festivities begin at 4 a.m. on the Monday before Ash Wednesday with a ritual called Jouvay, from either the French *jour ouvert* ("opening day") or the Creole *jou ouvé?* ("Is it daybreak yet?"). I had no idea of what I was getting into when I "registered" at the 3canal storefront center the day before. 3canal is both a musical band and one of the many small production companies that stage carnival; the name, according to one of the musicians, Roger Roberts, derives from a type of machete used by cane cutters and, he says, is "a metaphor for cutting and clearing a path and space for vibes to flow and grow." Despite assurances that no one really has to pay, I'd plunked down 60 Trinidadian dollars (about $10 US) for a bag containing a 3canal badge, a white tank top, a square of silver lamé cloth and—ominously—a plastic water bottle filled with white paint.

A little after 4 a.m, I returned to the 3canal storefront with my little lime of four—two Trinis and two other Americans—to find hundreds of people milling around a flatbed truck from which the 3canal musicians were blasting the band's heavy beat into the darkness. Around Port of Spain, people were assembling into fourteen other Jouvay bands, each several hundred to a thousand strong, and each with its own music and colors.

When the flatbed truck started rolling, the crowd danced along behind it or, more precisely, "chipped," which is Trinidadian for moving individually to music. At first I chipped in my resolute white-lady way, conscious of my status as the only visible blue-eyed person in the crowd. But then the paint came into play, hurled from bottles and dabbed on any body at hand. A plastic bottle of rough whiskey was passed around. There was a moment of near-panic when a police car forced its way through the crowd, and I learned later that in the pushing and shoving a knife fight had broken out just behind us. But still, the vibe here was overwhelmingly sweet. A teenager planted himself in front of me and announced that I looked "too nice," a condition he corrected by gently anointing my face with fresh paint. I don't know the origins of this orgy of body-painting, and I am glad I hadn't joined one of the Jouvay bands that use chocolate or mud instead, but I know its effect: Race was dissolved; even age and gender became theoretical concepts.

In the tradition of Western sociology, crowds are dangerous because they can turn into mobs. So when a contingent from our procession broke away to chase a group of Chinese men watching from the sidelines, I ran along anxiously behind them. Was there resentment of these workers, imported to build downtown skyscrapers? No. Would there be violence? No, the Jouvay celebrants just wanted to cover the foreigners in paint, and the Chinese were doubling over with laughter as they escaped. This was the true and ancient spirit of carnival: There can be no spectators, only partici-pants, and everyone must be anointed.

Sunrise found us in a small public square, and in a con-dition far from the one we'd started in. We'd been moving through the streets for over three hours, powered by beers passed from hand to hand, and even my ultra-buff Ameri-can friend was beginning to sag. People were still chipping away, raising their heads toward the already-hot blue sky in a kind of triumph. Hardly anyone was noticeably drunk, but we were annihilated, as individuals anyway—footsore, bone-tired, dripping with paint and sweat. We were, in some transcendent way, perfected.

But carnival has many faces and many moods, with dif-ferent towns observing it in their own special ways. At dusk we were in the tiny mountain town of Paramin, sitting at an outdoor fried-chicken place. The townspeople were slowly assembling on the edge of the road, drinking beer and chip-ping to a sound system that had been erected just behind our table. At nightfall, the sound system fell silent, and ten men beating drums made out of biscuit tins emerged from the darkness—a reminder of the Trinidadian ingenuity at drawing music out of industrial detritus, like the island's steel drums, traditionally crafted from oil barrels. Behind the drummers came twenty people of indeterminate age and gender, covered in blue paint, some wearing grotesque devil masks, others leering hideously, leaping and writhing. Then another band of drummers, followed by another con-tingent from hell.

Some of the devils were pulling others on ropes or mock-beating them with sticks in what is thought to be an evocation of the work-'em-till-they-die slavery of early Trinidad. Certainly, there was an edge of menace here. When a Blue Devil approached and stabbed his finger at you, you had to give him a Trinidadian dollar (worth 16 US cents), or he would pull you up against his freshly painted body. The onlookers laughed and shrieked and ran, and in the end I didn't run fast enough. Having used up my dollars, partly in defense of two genuinely frightened little girls, I was slimed blue. As the devils eased up on their attacks, the crowd swelled and surged toward the town's central square, where vendors were selling beer and rum amid the ongoing chipping. But I was too sticky with paint to continue—and too shaken, I have to admit, by the mimed hostility of the devils, with its echoes of historical rage.

Shrove Tuesday, the second day, is when the mas bands parade through Port of Spain to be judged on their costumes and music. If there was a time to witness the corrupting effects of commercialism, this "pretty mas"—so called to distinguish it from the first day's "old mas"—would be it. There are about two hundred mas bands on the island, and each was offering, for the equivalent of several hundred US dollars, a costume and such essentials as a day's worth of food and drink and private security. A pre-carnival article in the *Sunday Express* estimated that the big bands, with 3,500 or more members, would each gross ten million Trinidadian dollars, not counting donations from corporate sponsors, such as the ubiquitous cell-phone company bmobile. This isn't just partying; this is business.

According to historian (and soca star) Hollis Liverpool, pretty mas grew out of the upper classes' efforts to tamp down the African-derived aspects of traditional mas, which they saw as vulgar and unruly. To an extent, they have succeeded: The price of admission limits participation to the more affluent, such as Nadia John, a thirty-year-old lawyer I met in her apartment on the Sunday before carnival. For John, it was all about the costume. She modeled the one she would wear with the Island People mas band: a bikini made of wire, feathers, and jewels, so minimal that she dared not let her mother see it.

Not that the poor don't try to crash the party—hence the need for all the private security that surrounds each band as it moves through the streets. According to Wyatt Gallery, one of the owners of the Island People band, this is because "We're very serious about the competition and don't want to look bad," as they might if a lot of uncostumed people slipped in.

So I wasn't expecting much, beyond a chance to see Nadia John in her glory, when we walked from our hotel to the part of town where the mas bands would march and found a place on the curb to sit. But it turned out that even pretty mas is impossible to tame. Despite all the "owners" and "producers," people were still creating carnival themselves, in the streets and on the sidelines—chipping, drinking, eating, and smoking ganja. Then the bands began to drift by, each with its own trucks for music, food, and drink. The marchers were chatting, chipping, and, most notably, "wining." This is like grinding in American dance culture, only the pelvic motions are quicker, more fluttery— an artistic rendition of sex rather than a simulation—and it can involve up to three people at a time. Probably not quite what the British meant by "pretty." One costumed woman sticks in my mind, lost in her own chip, throwing her head back, her face gleaming with exultation and sweat. As Goethe wrote of the eighteenth-century Roman carnival, it "is a festival that is not actually given to the people, but which the people give to themselves."

Yes, Trinidadian carnival has been commercialized—or "Brazilianized," as they say locally—with too much money and booty involved. But as Che Lovelace, a young artist told me, carnival "can't go back, it must go forward." The money helps support hundreds of Trinidadian artists, musicians, and entrepreneurs, and, he says, "helps drive the economy and create jobs." In Trinidad, commercialization is not the death of carnival, but part of how it perpetuates itself.

Scorecard for carnival 2008: In a win for Trinidad's persistent devils, a preliminary body count came to 5 dead and 20 others stabbed or shot. But in a triumph for artistry and social relevance, the title of best mas band went to the Mac-Farlane band with the apocalyptic theme "Earth: Cries of Despair, Wings of Hope." Its call for planetwide renewal and its towering, avant-garde costumes—giant structures pulled by the wearer and wreathed in colored smoke—stole the show.

BOURGEOIS
BLUNDERS

FAMILY VALUES

The Worst Years of Our Lives, 1990

S ometime in the eighties, Americans had a new set of "traditional values" installed. It was part of what may someday be known as the "Reagan renovation," that finely balanced mix of cosmetic refinement and moral coarseness that brought $200,000 china to the White House dinner table and mayhem to the beleaguered peasantry of Central America. All of the new traditions had venerable sources. In economics, we borrowed from the Bourbons; in foreign policy, we drew on themes fashioned by the nomad warriors of the Eurasian steppes. In spiritual matters, we emulated the braying intolerance of our archenemies and esteemed customers, the Shi'ite fundamentalists.

A case could be made, of course, for the genuine American provenance of all these new "traditions." We've had our own robber barons, military adventurers, and certainly more than our share of enterprising evangelists promoting ignorance and parochialism as a state of grace. From the vantage point of the continent's original residents, or, for example, the captive African laborers who made America a great agricultural power, our "traditional values" have always been bigotry, greed, and belligerence, buttressed by wanton appeals to a God of love.

The kindest—though from some angles most perverse—of the era's new values was "family." I could have lived with "flag" and "faith" as neotraditional values—not happily, but I could have managed—until "family" was press-ganged into joining them. Throughout the eighties, the winning political faction has been aggressively "profamily." They have invoked "the family" when they trample on the rights of those who hold actual families together, that is, women. They have used it to justify racial segregation and the formation of white-only, "Christian" schools. And they have brought it out, along with flag and faith, to silence any voices they found obscene, offensive, disturbing, or merely different.

Now, I come from a family—was raised in one, in fact—and one salubrious effect of right-wing righteousness has been to make me hew ever more firmly to the traditional values of my own progenitors. These were not people who could be accused of questionable politics or ethnicity. Nor were they members of the "liberal elite" so hated by our current conservative elite. They were blue-eyed, Scotch-Irish Democrats. They were small farmers, railroad workers, miners, shopkeepers, and migrant farmworkers. In short, they fit the stereotype of "real" Americans; and their values, no matter how unpopular among today's opinion-shapers, are part of America's tradition, too. To my mind, of course, the finest part.

But let me introduce some of my family, beginning with

my father, who was, along with my mother, the ultimate source of much of my radicalism, feminism, and, by the standards of the eighties, all-around bad attitude.

One of the first questions in a test of mental competency is "Who is the president of the United States?" Even deep into the indignities of Alzheimer's disease, my father always did well on that one. His blue eyes would widen incredulously, surprised at the neurologist's ignorance, then he would snort in majestic indignation, "Reagan, that dumb son of a bitch." It seemed to me a good deal—two people tested for the price of one.

Like so many of the Alzheimer's patients he came to know, my father enjoyed watching the president on television. Most programming left him impassive, but when the old codger came on, his little eyes twinkling piggishly above the disciplined sincerity of his lower face, my father would lean forward and commence a wickedly delighted cackle. I think he was prepared, more than the rest of us, to get the joke.

But the funniest thing was Ollie North. For an ailing man, my father did a fine parody. He would slap his hand over his heart, stare rigidly at attention, and pronounce, in his deepest bass rumble, "God Bless Am-ar-ica!" I'm sure he couldn't follow North's testimony—who can honestly say that they did?—but the main themes were clear enough in pantomime: the watery-eyed patriotism, the extravagant self-pity, the touching servility toward higher-ranking males. When I told my father that many people considered North a hero, a representative of the finest American traditions, he scowled and swatted at the air. Ollie North was the kind of man my father had warned me about, many years ago, when my father was the smartest man on earth.

My father had started out as a copper miner in Butte, Montana, a tiny mountain city famed for its bars, its brawls, and its distinctly unservile workforce. In his view, which remained eagle-sharp even after a stint of higher education, there were only a few major categories of human beings. There were "phonies" and "decent" people, the latter group having hardly any well-known representatives outside of Franklin Delano Roosevelt and John L. Lewis, the militant and brilliantly eloquent leader of the miners' union. "Phonies," however, were rampant, and, for reasons I would not understand until later in life, could be found clustered especially thick in the vicinity of money or power.

Well before he taught me other useful things, like how to distinguish fool's gold, or iron pyrite, from the real thing, he gave me some tips on the detection of phonies. For one thing, they broadened the *e* in "America" to a reverent *ahh*. They were the first to leap from their seats at the playing of "The Star Spangled Banner," the most visibly moved participants in any prayer. They espoused clean living and admired war. They preached hard work and paid for it with nickels and dimes. They loved their country above all, but despised the low-paid and usually invisible men and women who built it, fed it, and kept it running.

Two other important categories figured in my father's scheme of things. There were dumb people and smart ones: a distinction that had nothing to do with class or formal education, the dumb being simply all those who were taken in by the phonies. In his view, dumbness was rampant, and seemed to increase in proportion to the distance from Butte, where at least a certain hard-boiled irreverence leavened the atmosphere. The best prophylactic was to study and learn all you could, however you could, and, as he adjured me over and over: Always ask *why*.

Finally, there were the rich and the poor. While poverty was not seen as an automatic virtue—my parents struggled mightily to escape it—wealth always carried a presumption of malfeasance. I was instructed that, in the presence of the rich, it was wise to keep one's hand on one's wallet. "Well," my father fairly growled, "how do you think they got their money in the first place?"

It was my mother who translated these lessons into practical politics. A miner's daughter herself, she offered two overarching rules for comportment: Never vote Republican and never cross a union picket line. The pinnacle of her activist career came in 1964, when she attended the Democratic Convention as an alternate delegate and joined the sit-in staged by civil rights leaders and the Mississippi Freedom Democratic Party. This was not the action of a "guilt-ridden" white liberal. She classified racial prejudice along with superstition and other manifestations of backward thinking, like organized religion and overcooked vegetables. The worst thing she could find to say about a certain in-law was that he was a Republican and a churchgoer, though when I investigated these charges later in life, I was relieved to find them baseless.

My mother and father, it should be explained, were hardly rebels. The values they imparted to me had been "traditional" for at least a generation before my parents came along. According to my father, the first great steps out of mental passivity had been taken by his maternal grandparents, John Howes and Mamie McLaughlin Howes, sometime late in the last century. You might think their rebellions small stuff, but they provided our family with its "myth of origins" and a certain standard to uphold.

I knew little about Mamie McLaughlin except that she was raised as a Catholic and ended up in western Montana sometime in the 1880s. Her father, very likely, was one of those itinerant breadwinners who went west to prospect and settled for mining. At any rate, the story begins when her father lay dying, and Mamie dutifully sent to the next town for a priest. The message came back that the priest would come only if $25 was sent in advance. This being the West at its wildest, he may have been justified in avoiding house calls. But not in the price, which was probably more cash than my great-grandmother had ever had at one time. It was on account of its greed that the church lost the souls of Mamie McLaughlin and all of her descendents, right down to the present time. Furthermore, whether out of filial deference or natural intelligence, most of us have continued to avoid organized religion, secret societies, astrology, and New Age adventures in spirituality.

As the story continues, Mamie McLaughlin herself lay dying a few years later. She was only thirty-one, the mother of three small children, one of them an infant whose birth, apparently, led to a mortal attack of pneumonia. This time, a priest appeared unsummoned. Because she was too weak to hold the crucifix, he placed it on her chest and proceeded to administer the last rites. But Mamie was not dead yet. She pulled herself together at the last moment, flung the crucifix across the room, fell back, and died.

This was my great-grandmother. Her husband, John Howes, is a figure of folkloric proportions in my memory, well known in Butte many decades ago as a powerful miner and a lethal fighter. There are many stories about John Howes, all of which point to a profound inability to accept authority in any of its manifestations, earthly or divine. As a young miner, for example, he caught the eye of the mine owner for his skill at handling horses. The boss promoted him to an aboveground driving job, which was a great career leap for the time. Then the boss committed a foolish and arrogant error. He asked John to break in a team of horses for his wife's carriage. Most people would probably be flattered by such a request, but not in Butte, and certainly not John Howes. He declared that he was no man's servant, and quit on the spot.

Like his own wife, John Howes was an atheist or, as they more likely put it at the time, a freethinker. He, too, had been raised as a Catholic—on a farm in Ontario—and he, too, had had a dramatic, though somehow less glorious, falling out with the local clergy. According to legend, he once abused his position as an altar boy by urinating, covertly of course, in the holy water. This so enhanced his enjoyment of the Easter communion service that he could not resist letting a few friends in on the secret. Soon the priest found out and young John was defrocked as an altar boy and condemned to eternal damnation.

The full weight of this transgression hit a few years later, when he became engaged to a local woman. The priest refused to marry them and forbade the young woman to marry John anywhere, on pain of excommunication. There was nothing to do but head west for the Rockies, but not before settling his score with the church. According to legend, John's last act in Ontario was to drag the priest down from his pulpit and slug him, with his brother, presumably, holding the scandalized congregation at bay.

I have often wondered whether my great-grandfather was caught up in the radicalism of Butte in its heyday: whether he was an admirer of Joe Hill, Big Bill Haywood, or Mary "Mother" Jones, all of whom passed through Butte to agitate, and generally left with the Pinkertons on their tails. But the record is silent on this point. All I know is one last story about him, which was told often enough to have the ring of another "traditional value."

According to my father, John Howes worked on and off in the mines after his children were grown, eventually saving enough to buy a small plot of land and retire to farming. This was his dream, anyway, and a powerful one it must have been for a man who had spent so much of his life underground in the dark.

Far be it from me to interpret this gesture for my great-grandfather, whom I knew only as a whiskery, sweat-smelling, but straight-backed old man in his eighties. Perhaps he was enacting his own uncompromising version of Christian virtue, even atoning a little for his youthful offenses to the faithful. But at another level I like to think that this was one more gesture of defiance of the mine owners who doled out their own dollars so grudgingly—a way of saying, perhaps, that whatever they had to offer, he didn't really need all that much.

So these were the values, sanctified by tradition and family loyalty, that I brought with me to adulthood. Through much of my growing-up, I thought of them as some mutant strain of Americanism, an idiosyncrasy that seemed to grow rarer as we clambered into the middle class. Only in the sixties did I begin to learn that my family's militant skepticism and oddball rebelliousness were part of a much larger stream of American dissent. I discovered feminism, the antiwar movement, the civil rights movement. I learned that millions of Americans, before me and around me, were "smart" enough, in my father's terms, to have asked "Why?"—and, beyond that, the far more radical question, "Why not?"

These are also the values I brought into the Reagan-Bush era, when all the dangers I had been alerted to as a child were suddenly realized. The "phonies" came to power on the strength, aptly enough, of a professional actor's finest performance. The "dumb" were being led and abetted by low-life preachers and intellectuals with expensively squandered educations. And the rich, as my father predicted, used the occasion to dip deep into the wallets of the desperate and the distracted.

It's been hard times for a traditionalist of my persuasion. Long-standing moral values—usually claimed as "Judeo-Christian" but actually of much broader lineage—were summarily tossed, along with most familiar forms of logic. We were told, at one time or another, by the president or his henchpersons, that trees cause pollution, that welfare causes poverty, and that a bomber designed for mass destruction may be aptly named the *Peacemaker*. "Terrorism" replaced missing children to become our national bugaboo and—simultaneously—one of our most potent instruments of foreign policy. At home, the poor and the middle class were shaken down, and their loose change funneled blithely upward to the already overfed.

Greed, the ancient lubricant of commerce, was declared a wholesome stimulant. Nancy Reagan observed the deep recession of '82 and '83 by redecorating the White House, and continued with this Marie Antoinette theme while advising the underprivileged, the alienated, and the addicted to "say no." Young people, mindful of their elders' Wall Street capers, abandoned the study of useful things for investment banking and other occupations derived, ultimately, from three-card monte. While the poor donned plastic outerwear and cardboard coverings, the affluent ran nearly naked through the streets, working off power meals of goat cheese, walnut oil, and crème fraîche.

Religion, which even I had hoped would provide a calming influence and reminder of mortal folly, decided to join the fun. In an upsurge of piety, millions of Americans threw their souls and their savings into evangelical empires designed on the principle of pyramid scams. Even the sleazy downfall of our telemessiahs—caught masturbating in the company of $10 prostitutes or fornicating in their Christian theme parks—did not discourage the faithful. The unhappily pregnant were mobbed as "baby-killers"; sexual nonconformists—gay and lesbian—were denounced as "child molesters"; atheists found themselves lumped with "satanists," communists, and consumers of human flesh.

Yet somehow, despite it all, a trickle of dissent continued. There were homeless people who refused to be shelved in mental hospitals for the crime of poverty, strikers who refused to join the celebration of unions in faraway countries and scabs at home, women who insisted that their lives be valued above those of accidental embryos, parents who packed up their babies and marched for peace, students who protested the ongoing inversion of normal, nursery-school-level values in the name of a more habitable world.

I am proud to add my voice to all these. For dissent is also a "traditional value," and in a republic founded by revolution, a more deeply native one than smug-faced conservatism can ever be. Feminism was practically invented here, and ought to be regarded as one of our proudest exports to the world. Likewise, it tickles my sense of patriotism that insurgents in developing nations have often borrowed the ideas of our own civil rights movement. And in what ought to be a source of shame to some and pride to others, our history of labor struggle is one of the hardest-fought and bloodiest in the world.

No matter that patriotism is too often the refuge of scoundrels. Dissent, rebellion, and all-around hell-raising remain the true duty of patriots.

THE CULT OF BUSYNESS

New York Times, 1985

Not too long ago a former friend and soon-to-be acquaintance called me up to tell me how busy she was. A major report, upon which her professional future depended, was due in three days; her secretary was on strike; her housekeeper had fallen into the hands of the Immigration Department; she had two hours to prepare a dinner party for eight; and she was late for her time-management class. Stress was taking its toll, she told me: Her children resented the fact that she sometimes got their names mixed up, and she had taken to abusing white wine.

All this put me at a distinct disadvantage, since the only thing I was doing at the time was holding the phone with one hand and attempting to touch the opposite toe with the other hand, a pastime that I had perfected during previous telephone monologues. Not that I'm not busy, too: as I listened to her, I was on the alert for the moment the dryer would shut itself off and I would have to rush to fold the clothes before they settled into a mass of incorrigible wrinkles. But if I mentioned this little deadline of mine, she might think I wasn't busy enough to need a housekeeper, so I just kept on patiently saying "Hmm" until she got to her parting line: "Look, this isn't a good time for me to talk, I've got to go now."

I don't know when the cult of conspicuous busyness began, but it has swept up almost all the upwardly mobile, professional women I know. Already, it is getting hard to recall the days when, for example, "Let's have lunch" meant something other than "I've got more important things to do than talk to you right now." There was even a time when people used to get together without the excuse of needing something to eat—when, in fact, it was considered rude to talk with your mouth full. In the old days, hardly anybody had an appointment book, and when people wanted to know what the day held in store for them, they consulted a horoscope.

It's not only women, of course; for both sexes, busyness has become an important insignia of upper-middle-class status. Nobody, these days, admits to having a hobby, although two or more careers—say, neurosurgery and an art dealership—is not uncommon, and I am sure we will soon be hearing more about the tribulations of the four-paycheck couple. Even those who can manage only one occupation at a time would be embarrassed to be caught doing only one *thing* at a time. Those young men who jog with their headsets on are not, as you might innocently guess, rocking out, but are absorbing the principles of international finance law or a lecture on one-minute management. Even eating, I read recently, is giving way to "grazing"—the conscious ingestion of unidentified foods while drafting a legal brief, cajoling a client on the phone, and, in ambitious cases, doing calf-toning exercises under the desk.

But for women, there's more at stake than conforming to another upscale standard. If you want to attract men, for example, it no longer helps to be a bimbo with time on your hands. Upscale young men seem to go for the kind of woman who plays with a full deck of credit cards, who won't cry when she's knocked to the ground while trying to board the six o'clock Delta shuttle, and whose schedule doesn't allow for a sexual encounter lasting more than twelve minutes. Then there is the economic reality: Any woman who doesn't want to wind up a case study in the feminization of poverty has to be successful at something more demanding than fingernail maintenance or come-hither looks. Hence all the bustle, my busy friends would explain—they want to succeed.

But if success is the goal, it seems clear to me that the fast track is headed the wrong way. Think of the people who are genuinely successful—pathbreaking scientists, best-selling novelists, and designers of major new software. They are not, on the whole, the kind of people who keep glancing shiftily at their watches or making small lists titled "To Do." On the contrary, many of these people appear to be in a daze, like the distinguished professor I once had who, in the middle of a lecture on electron spin, became so fascinated by the dispersion properties of chalk dust that he could not go on. These truly successful people are childlike, easily dis-tractable, fey sorts, whose usual demeanor resembles that of a recently fed hobo on a warm summer evening.

The secret of the truly successful, I believe, is that they learned very early in life how *not* to be busy. They saw through that adage, repeated to me so often in childhood, that anything worth doing is worth doing well. The truth is, many things are worth doing only in the most slovenly, half-hearted fashion possible, and many other things are not worth doing at all. Balancing a checkbook, for example. For some reason, in our culture, this dreary exercise is regarded as the supreme test of personal maturity, business acumen, and the ability to cope with math anxiety. Yet it is a form of busyness which is exceeded in futility only by going to the additional trouble of computerizing one's checking account—and that, in turn, is only slightly less silly than taking the time to discuss, with anyone, what brand of personal computer one owns, or is thinking of buying, or has heard of others using.

If the truly successful manage never to be busy, it is also true that many of the busiest people will never be successful. I know this firsthand from my experience, many years ago, as a waitress. Any executive who thinks the ultimate in busyness consists of having two important phone calls on hold and a major deadline in twenty minutes, should try facing six tablefuls of clients simultaneously demanding that you give them their checks, fresh coffee, a baby seat, and a warm, spontaneous smile. Even when she's not busy, a waitress has to look busy—refilling the salt shakers and polishing all the chrome in sight—but the only reward is the minimum wage and any change that gets left on the tables. Much the same is true of other high-stress jobs, like working as a telephone operator, or doing data entry on one of the new machines that monitors your speed as you work: "Success" means surviving the shift.

Although busyness does not lead to success, I am willing to believe that success—especially when visited on the unprepared—can cause busyness. Anyone who has invented a better mousetrap, or the contemporary equivalent, can expect to be harassed by strangers demanding that you read their unpublished manuscripts or undergo the humiliation of public speaking, usually on remote Midwestern campuses. But if it is true that success leads to more busyness and less time for worthwhile activities—like talking (and listening) to friends, reading novels, or putting in some volunteer time for a good cause—then who needs it? It would be sad to have come so far—or at least to have run so hard—only to lose each other.

DEATH OF A YUPPIE DREAM

Journal der Rosa Luxemburg Stiftung, 2013

With John Ehrenreich

Every would-be populist in American politics purports to defend the "middle class," although there is no agreement on what it is. Just in the last couple of years, the "middle class" has variously been defined as everybody, everybody minus the 15 percent living below the federal poverty level; or everybody minus the very richest Americans. Mitt Romney famously excluded "those in the low end" but included himself (2010 income $21.6 million) along with "80 to 90 percent" of Americans. The Department of Commerce has given up on income-based definitions, announcing in a 2010 report that "middle class families" are defined "by their aspirations more than their income.... Middle class families aspire to home ownership, a car, college education for their children, health and retirement security and occasional family vacations"—which excludes almost no one.

Class itself is a muddled concept, perhaps especially in America, where any allusion to the different interests of different occupational and income groups is likely to attract the charge of "class warfare." If class requires some sort of "consciousness," or capacity for concerted action, then a "middle class" conceived of as a sort of default class—what you are left with after you subtract the rich and the poor—is not very interesting.

But there is another, potentially more productive, interpretation of what has been going on in the mid-income range. In 1977, we first proposed the existence of a "professional-managerial class," distinct from both the "working class," from the "old" middle class of small business owners, as well as from the wealthy class of owners.

The Origins of the Professional-Managerial Class

The notion of the "PMC" was an effort to explain the largely "middle-class" roots of the New Left in the sixties and the tensions that were emerging between that group and the old working class in the seventies, culminating in the political backlash that led to the election of Reagan. The right embraced a caricature of this notion of a "new class," proposing that college-educated professionals—especially lawyers, professors, journalists, and artists—make up a power-hungry "liberal elite" bent on imposing its version of socialism on everyone else.

The PMC grew rapidly. From 1870 to 1910 alone, while the whole population of the United States increased two-and-one-third times and the old middle class of business entrepreneurs and independent professionals doubled, the number of people in what could be seen as PMC jobs grew almost eightfold. And in the years that followed, that growth only accelerated. Although a variety of practical and theoretical obstacles keep us from making any precise analysis, we estimate that as late as 1930, people in PMC occupations still made up less than 1 percent of total employment. By 1972, about 24 percent of American jobs were in PMC occupations. By 1983 the number had risen to 28 percent and by 2006, just before the Great Recession, to 35 percent.

The relationship between the emerging PMC and the traditional working class was, from the start, riven with tensions. It was the occupational role of managers and engineers, along with many other professionals, to manage, regulate, and control the life of the working class. They designed the division of labor and the machines that controlled workers' minute-by-minute existence on the factory floor, manipulated their desire for commodities and their opinions, socialized their children, and even mediated their relationship with their own bodies.

At the same time, though, the role of the PMC as "rationalizers" of society often placed them in direct conflict with the capitalist class. Like the workers, the PMC were themselves employees and subordinate to the owners, but since what was truly "rational" in the productive process was not always identical to what was most immediately profitable, the PMC often sought autonomy and freedom from their own bosses.

By the mid-twentieth century, jobs for the PMC were

proliferating. Public education was expanding, the modern university came into being, local governments expanded in size and role, charitable agencies merged, newspaper circulation soared, traditional forms of recreation gave way to the popular culture, entertainment, and sports industries, etc.—and all of these developments created jobs for highly educated professionals, including journalists, social workers, professors, doctors, lawyers, and "entertainers" (artists and writers, among others).

Some of these occupations managed to retain a measure of autonomy and, with it, the possibility of opposition to business domination. The so-called "liberal professions," particularly medicine and law, remained largely outside the corporate framework until well past the middle of the twentieth century. Most doctors, many nurses, and the majority of lawyers worked in independent (private) practices.

In the 1960s, for the first time since the Progressive Era, a large segment of the PMC had the self-confidence to take on a critical, even oppositional, political role. Jobs were plentiful, a college education did not yet lead to a lifetime of debt, and materialism was briefly out of style. College students quickly moved on from supporting the civil rights movement in the South and opposing the war in Vietnam to confronting the raw fact of corporate power throughout American society—from the prowar inclinations of the weapons industry to the governance of the university. The revolt soon spread beyond students. By the end of the sixties, almost all of the liberal professions had "radical caucuses," demanding that access to the professions be opened up to those traditionally excluded (such as women and minorities), and that the service ethics the professions claimed to uphold actually be applied in practice.

The Capitalist Offensive

Beginning in the seventies, the capitalist class decisively reasserted itself. The ensuing capitalist offensive was so geographically widespread and thoroughgoing that it introduced what many left-wing theorists today describe as a new form of capitalism, "neoliberalism."

The new management strategy was to raise profits by single-mindedly reducing labor costs, most directly by simply moving manufacturing offshore to find cheaper labor. Those workers who remained employed in the United States faced a series of initiatives designed to discipline and control them ever more tightly: intensified supervision in the workplace, drug tests to eliminate slackers, and increasingly professionalized efforts to prevent unionization. Cuts in the welfare state also had a disciplining function, making it harder for workers to imagine surviving job loss.

Most of these antilabor measures also had an effect, directly or indirectly, on elements of the PMC. Government spending cuts hurt the job prospects of social workers, teachers, and others in the "helping professions," while the decimation of the US-based industrial working class reduced the need for mid-level professional managers, who found themselves increasingly targeted for downsizing. But there was a special animus against the liberal professions, surpassed only by neoliberal hostility to what conservatives

described as the "underclass." Crushing this liberal elite—
by "defunding the left" or attacking liberal-leaning nonprofit organizations—became a major neoliberal project.

Of course, not all the forces undermining the liberal professions since the 1980s can be traced to conscious neoliberal policies. Technological innovation, rising demand for
services, and ruthless profit-taking all contributed to an increasingly challenging environment for the liberal professions, including the "creative ones."

The internet is often blamed for the plight of journalists,
writers, and editors, but economic change preceded technological transformation. Journalism jobs began to disappear as corporations, responding in part to Wall Street
investors, tried to squeeze higher profit margins out of
newspapers and TV news programs. The effects of these
changes on the traditionally creative professions have been
dire. Staff writers, editors, photographers, announcers, and
the like faced massive layoffs (more than 25 percent of
newsroom staff alone since 2001), increased workloads,
salary cuts, and buyouts.

Then, in just the last dozen years, the PMC began to suffer
the fate of the industrial class in the 1980s: replacement by
cheap foreign labor. It came as a shock to many when, in the
2000s, businesses began to avail themselves of new high-
speed transmission technologies to outsource professional
functions.

By the time of the financial meltdown and deep recession
of the post-2008 period, the pain inflicted by neoliberal
policies, both public and corporate, extended well beyond

the old industrial working class and into core segments of the PMC. Unemployed and underemployed professional workers—from IT to journalism, academia, and eventually law—became a regular feature of the social landscape. Young people did not lose faith in the value of an education, but they learned quickly that it makes more sense to study finance rather than physics or "communications" rather than literature. The old PMC dream of a society ruled by impartial "experts" gave way to the reality of inescapable corporate domination.

But the PMC was not only a victim of more powerful groups. It had also fallen into a trap of its own making. The prolonged, expensive, and specialized education required for professional employment had always been a challenge to PMC families—as well, of course, as an often-insuperable barrier to the working class. Higher degrees and licenses are no longer a guarantee of PMC status. Hence the iconic figure of the Occupy Wall Street movement: the college graduate with tens of thousands of dollars in student loan debts and a job paying about $10 a hour, or no job at all.

Whither Class Consciousness?

So in the hundred years since its emergence, the PMC has not managed to hold its own as a class. At its wealthier end, skilled professionals continue to jump ship for more lucrative posts in direct service to capital: Scientists give up their research to become "quants" on Wall Street; physicians can double their incomes by finding work as investment analysts for the finance industry or by setting up "concierge" practices serving the wealthy. At the less fortunate end of the spectrum, journalists and PhDs in sociology or literature spiral down into the retail workforce. In between, health workers and lawyers and professors find their work lives more and more hemmed in and regulated by corporation-like enterprises. The center has not held. Conceived as "the middle class" and as the supposed repository of civic virtue and occupational dedication, the PMC lies in ruins.

More profoundly, the PMC's original dream—of a society ruled by reason and led by public-spirited professionals—has been discredited. Globally, the socialist societies that seemed to come closest to this goal either degenerated into heavily militarized dictatorships or, more recently, into authoritarian capitalist states. Within the United States, the grotesque failure of socialism in China and the Soviet Union became a propaganda weapon in the neoliberal war against the public sector in its most innocuous forms and a core argument for the privatization of just about everything.

But the PMC has also managed to discredit itself as an advocate for the common good. Consider our gleaming towers of medical research and high-technology care—all too often abutting urban neighborhoods characterized by extreme poverty and foreshortened life spans.

Should we mourn the fate of the PMC or rejoice that there is one less smug, self-styled, elite to stand in the way of a more egalitarian future? On the one hand, the PMC has played a major role in the oppression and disempowering of the old working class. It has offered little resistance to (and, in fact, supplied the manpower for) the right's campaign against any measure that might ease the lives of the poor and the working class.

On the other hand, the PMC has at times been a "liberal" force, defending the values of scholarship and human service in the face of the relentless pursuit of profit. In this respect, its role in the last century bears some analogy to the role of monasteries in medieval Europe, which kept literacy and at least some form of inquiry alive while the barbarians raged outside.

As we face the deepening ruin brought on by neoliberal aggression, the question may be: Who, among the survivors, will uphold those values today? And, more profoundly, is there any way to salvage the dream of reason—or at least the idea of a society in which reasonableness can occasionally prevail—from the accretion of elitism it acquired from the PMC?

Any renewal of oppositional spirit among the professional-managerial class, or what remains of it, needs to start from an awareness that what has happened to the professional middle class has long since happened to the blue-collar working class. The debt-ridden unemployed and underemployed college graduates, the revenue-starved teachers, the overworked and underpaid service professionals, even the occasional whistle-blowing scientist or engineer—all face the same kind of situation that confronted skilled craft-workers in the early twentieth century and all American industrial workers in the late twentieth century.

In the coming years, we expect to see the remnants of the PMC increasingly making common cause with the remnants of the traditional working class for, at a minimum, representation in the political process. This is the project that the Occupy movement initiated and spread, for a time anyway, worldwide.

THE UNBEARABLE BEING
OF WHITENESS

Mother Jones, 1988

This column is addressed to my fellow white people and contains material that we would prefer to keep among ourselves. God knows we have suffered enough already from the unique problems that have confronted white people over the centuries: the burden of bringing Christianity to heathens so benighted that they usually preferred death. The agony of sunburn. But now we face what may be the biggest problem of all. You know what I mean, brothers and sisters, *low self-esteem*.

It started with the Asian menace. Many years ago, "Made in Japan" applied chiefly to windup toys and samurai movies. No one thought twice about sending their children off to school with the sons and daughters of laundrymen and chop suey chefs. But now, alas, the average white person cannot comprehend the inner workings of the simplest product from Asia, much less read the owner's manual.

In the realm of business, our most brilliant blue-eyed MBAs admit they are like children compared to the shoguns of Mitsubishi and Toshiba. As for education, well, the local high school is offering a full scholarship to the first Caucasian to make valedictorian. And what white parents have not—when pressed to the limit by their brutish, ignorant, dope-fiend children—screamed, "God-damn it, Stacey [or Sean], why can't you act more like an Asian-American?"

Yes, I know the conventional explanation: White people lack convincing role models. Consider President Reagan, whose own son grew up believing—hoping?—that his true parents were the black help. Or consider the vice president, George Bush, a man so bedeviled by bladder problems that he managed, for the last eight years, to be in the men's room whenever an important illegal decision was made. Or consider how long it took, following the defeat of Robert Bork [as a Supreme Court nominee], for the conservatives to find a white man who was clean-shaven, drug-free, and had also passed his bar exam.

Then there were the nonblack Democratic candidates, who might be considered the very flower of white man-hood. For months, none of them could think of anything to say. Political discourse fell to the level of white street talk, as in "Have a nice day."

Then, stealthily, one by one, they began to model them-selves after Jesse Jackson. Even the patrician Al Gore, surely one of the whitest men ever to seek public office, donned a windbreaker and declared himself the champion of the working people. Richard Gephardt borrowed Jackson's rhyme about how corporations "merge" with each other and "purge" the workers. Soon he was telling moving stories about his youth as a poor black boy in the South, and how he had inexplicably turned white, clear up to and including his eyebrows.

Confronted with the obvious superiority of the black candidate, many white voters became perplexed and withdrawn. We had liked to think of black people as simple folk with large thighs and small brains—a race of Head Start dropouts, suitable for sweeping floors and assisting blond cops on TV. In fact, there is clear evidence of black intellectual superiority: In 1984, 92 percent of black people voted to retire Ronald Reagan, compared to only 36 percent of white people.

Or compare the two most prominent men of television, Bill Cosby and Morton Downey Jr. Millions of white Americans have grown up with no other father figure than "Cos." Market researchers have determined that we would buy any product he endorses, even if it were a skin-lightener. No one, on the other hand, would buy anything from Downey, unless it was something advertised anonymously in the classified section of *Soldier of Fortune*.

Perhaps it is true, as many white people have secretly and shamefully concluded, that these facts can only be explained by resorting to genetic theories of IQ. But I still like to think there are environmental explanations. A generation ago, for example, hordes of white people fled the challenging, interracial atmosphere of the cities and settled in the whites-only suburbs. Little did we know that a lifestyle devoted to lawn maintenance and shrub pruning would, in no time at all, engender the thick-witted peasant mentality now so common among our people.

At the same time, the white elite walled themselves up in

places like Harvard to preserve white culture in its purest form. Still others, the brightest of our race, retired to Los Alamos to figure out how to bring the whole thing to a prompt conclusion. Unfortunately, our extreme isolation from people of alternative races meant there was never anyone around to point out the self-destructive tendencies inherent in white behavior, which is still known collectively as "Western civilization."

Let's face it, we became ingrown, clannish, and stupid. Cut off from the mainstream of humanity, we came to believe that pink is "flesh-color," that mayonnaise is a nutrient, and that Barry Manilow is a musician. Little did we know that all over the world, people were amusing each other with tales beginning, "Did you hear the one about the Caucasian who…"

I know. It hurts. Low self-esteem is a terrible thing. Some white men, driven mad by the feeling that people are laughing at them, have taken to running around the streets and beating on random people of color or threatening to vote Republican.

Believe me, that kind of acting out won't help. If white people are ever to stand tall, we're going to have to leave our cramped little ghetto and stride out into the world again. Of course, there'll be the inevitable embarrassments at first: the fear of saying the wrong thing, of making mathematical errors, of forgetting the geography of the southern hemisphere. But gather up little Sean and Stacey and tell them, "We can do it! If we study and try very hard, even we can *be somebody*!"

IS THE MIDDLE CLASS DOOMED?

New York Times, 1986

Most of us are "middle-class," or so we like to believe. But there are signs that America is becoming a more divided society: Over the last decade, the rich have been getting richer; the poor have been getting more numerous; and those in the middle do not appear to be doing as well as they used to. If America is "coming back," as President Reagan reassured us in the wake of the economic malaise of the early 1980s, it may be coming back in a harsh and alien form.

It was in the late sixties that American society began to lurch off the track leading to the American dream. No one could have known it at the time, but, according to the economists Bennett Harrison, Chris Tilly, and Barry Bluestone, those were the last years in which economic inequality among Americans declined. Since then, in a sharp reversal of the equalizing trend that had been under way since shortly after World War II, the extremes of wealth have grown further apart and the middle has lost ground. In 1984, according to a report by Congress's Joint Economic

Committee, the share of the national income received by the wealthiest 40 percent of families in the United States rose to 67.3 percent, while the poorest 40 percent received 15.7 percent (the smallest share since 1947); the share of the middle 20 percent declined to 17 percent.

Some economists have even predicted that the middle class, which has traditionally represented the majority of Americans and defined the nation's identity and goals, will disappear altogether, leaving the country torn, like many developing societies, between an affluent minority and a horde of the desperately poor.

At least in the area of consumer options, we seem already in the process of becoming a "two-tier society." The middle is disappearing from the retail industry, for example. Korvettes and Gimbels are gone. Sears, Roebuck and JCPenney are anxiously trying to reposition themselves to survive in an ever more deeply segmented market. The stores that are prospering are the ones that have learned to specialize in one extreme of wealth or the other: Nordstrom's and Neiman-Marcus for the affluent; Kmart for those constrained by poverty or thrift. Whether one looks at food, clothing, or furnishings, two cultures are emerging: natural fibers versus synthetics; handcrafted wood cabinets versus mass-produced maple; David's Cookies versus Mister Donuts.

The political implications of the shift toward a two-tier society—if this is what is really happening—are ominous. Felix Rohatyn, the investment banker and civic leader, has observed: "A democracy, to survive, must at the very least appear to be fair. This is no longer the case in America." We may have outgrown the conceit that America is a uniformly "middle-class" society, but we have expected the extremes of wealth and poverty to be buffered by a vast and stable middle class. If the extremes swell, and if the economic center cannot hold, then our identity and future as a nation may be endangered.

Because the stakes are so high, the subject of class polarization has itself become bitterly polarized. On what could be called the "pessimistic" side is a group of mostly young, though highly acclaimed, economists who tend to be based in the relatively prosperous state of Massachusetts. The other side, which is represented at two research organizations, the Brookings Institution, in Washington, and the Conference Board, in New York City, argues that there are no fundamental flaws in the economy, and that the shift toward greater inequality will be short-lived.

Though much of the debate has been numbingly technical, the differences sometimes seem to have more to do with ideology than statistics. Fabian Linden of the Conference Board, for example, says of "the pessimists": "There are always people who think that this is an imperfect world and has to be changed.... It's awfully arrogant, if you think about it."

But no one, however humble, denies that there has been a profound change in the class contours of American society. No matter how you slice up the population—whether you compare the top fifth to the bottom fifth, or the top 40 percent to the poorest 40 percent—and no matter whether you look at individual earnings or household earnings, the have-nots are getting by on less and the haves are doing better than ever.

The change is particularly striking when families with children are compared over time. In 1968, the poorest one-fifth of such families received 7.4 percent of the total income for all families; in 1983, their share was only 4.8 percent, down by one-third. During the same period, the richest fifth increased its share from 33.8 percent to 38.1 percent. The result, according to the Census Bureau, is that the income gap between the richest families and the poorest is now wider than it has been at any time since the bureau began keeping such statistics in 1947.

So far, the middle class is still a statistical reality. At least a graph of income distribution still comes out as a bell-shaped curve, with most people hovering near the mean income rather than at either extreme. (If the middle class disappeared, the curve would have two humps rather than one in the middle.) But in the last decade, the income distribution curve has slumped toward the lower end and flattened a little on top, so that it begins to look less like a weathered hill and more like a beached whale. To the un-trained eye, the shift is not alarming, but as economist Jeff Faux, president of the Economic Policy Institute in Washington, says: "These numbers are very slow to move, really glacial. So when you do get a change you better pay attention."

The optimists in the debate attribute the downward shift in earnings chiefly to the baby boomers—the 78-million-member generation that began to crowd into the labor market in the 1960s and '70s, presumably driving down wages by their sheer numbers. As the boomers age, the argument goes, their incomes will rise and America will once again be a solidly middle-class society. But a recent analysis by the economists Bennett Harrison and Chris Tilly at the Massachusetts Institute of Technology and Barry Bluestone at Boston College suggests that the bulge in the labor force created by the baby boom and business-cycle effects can account for less than one-third of the increase in income inequality that has occurred since 1978.

In fact, baby boomers may find it much more difficult to make their incomes grow over time than did their parents' generation. A study by the economists Frank S. Levy and Richard C. Michel shows that, in earlier decades, men could expect their earnings to increase by about 30 percent as they aged from forty to fifty. But men who became forty in 1973 saw their earnings actually decline by 14 percent by the time they reached fifty. If this trend continues, the baby boomers will find little solace in seniority.

The fate of the baby boomers is central to the debate about America's economic future in another way, too. Contrary to the popular stereotype, the baby boomers are not all upwardly mobile, fresh-faced consumers of mesquite cuisine and exercise equipment. The baby boom is defined as those born between 1946 and 1964, and only 5 percent of them qualify as "yuppies" (young urban professional or managerial workers earning over $30,000 a year each, or $40,000 or more for a couple). Most of them, like most Americans, are "middle-class," in the limited sense that they fall somewhere near the middle of the income distribution, rather than at either extreme. Whether they can hold on to, or achieve, middle-class status—however defined—will be a test of whether the

American middle class is still capable of reproducing itself from one generation to the next.

"Middle-class" can be defined in several ways. Statistically, the middle class is simply the part of the population that earns near the median income—say, the 20 percent that earns just above the median income plus the 20 percent whose earnings fall just below it. But in colloquial understanding, "middle-class" is a matter of status as well as income, and is signaled by subtler cues—how we live, what we spend our money on, what expectations we have for the future. Since the postwar period, middle-class status has been defined by home ownership, college education (at least for the children), and the ability to afford amenities such as a second car and family vacations.

In the matter of home ownership, the baby boomers are clearly not doing as well as their parents. Levy and Michel calculate that the typical father of today's boomers faced housing costs that were equivalent to about 14 percent of his gross monthly pay. In 1984, a thirty-year-old man who purchased a median-priced home had to set aside a staggering 44 percent of his income for carrying charges. The recent decline in interest rates has helped some, but it has been largely offset by continuing inflation in the price of homes. The problem is not only that housing costs have escalated, but that the median income has actually been declining. According to the National Association of Homebuilders, a family today [1986] needs an income of approximately $37,000 to afford a median-priced home. In 1985, according to census figures, the median family income was $27,735—almost $10,000 short.

*   *   *

If the baby-boom bulge in the workforce is not the cause—or the sole cause—of America's slide toward greater economic inequality, what is? Public policy is one obvious contributing factor. In the 1960s and early '70s, public policy—and political rhetoric—favored a downward redistribution of wealth. Ronald Reagan reversed the trend and instituted policies that resulted in the government's first major upward redistribution of wealth since World War II. As a result of the combination of reduced taxes for the better-off and reduced social spending for the poor, the richest one-fifth of American families gained $25 billion in disposable income between 1980 and 1984, while the poorest one-fifth lost $7 billion. The current [1986] tax-revision bill would correct some of these inequities. But at the same time, according to a number of the bill's critics, including Richard A. Musgrave, professor emeritus of political economy at Harvard, it also represents a retreat from the very principle of progressivity in taxation in that it reduces the maximum rate of taxation for the very rich.

The drift toward a two-tier society actually began before the Republicans took office in 1981, and must have been set in motion by changes that go deeper than political trends. Some of these changes may be more social than economic; divorce, for example, can have the effect of splitting the members of individual families into different social classes since, in most cases, the woman ends up with the children and most of the responsibility for supporting them. Single mothers now account for almost half the household heads in poverty.

But if divorce is a factor in the emerging pattern of inequality, so is marriage. Mimi Lieber, a New York–based marketing consultant who has been following the impact of class polarization on consumer choices, says that we are seeing "a changing pattern of marriage; today, the doctor marries another doctor, not a nurse." The result is that marriage is less likely to offer women a chance at upward mobility.

On the whole, however, marriage is probably a stabilizing factor, at least if it is a "nontraditional" form of marriage. Seventy percent of baby-boom women are in the workforce—compared with about 30 percent in their mothers' generation—and the earnings of working wives are all that hold a growing number of families in the middle class. A study prepared by Sheldon Danziger and Peter Gottschalk for the Joint Economic Committee of Congress shows that most of the income gains made by white two-parent families with children since 1967 can be accounted for by increased earnings by wives. On a husband's earnings alone, the average family (of any race) would fall below the median income; on the wife's earnings alone, it would fall to the poverty level of $10,990 for a family of four.

Whatever else is changing in our patterns of marriage and divorce, something has happened to the average American's ability to support a family. According to Bluestone and Harrison, the economy is simply not generating enough well-paying jobs anymore: Between 1963 and 1978, only 23 percent of all new jobs paid poverty-level or "near-poverty-level" wages; but of the jobs generated between 1978 and 1984, almost half—48 percent—paid near-poverty-level wages. Here again, public policy is partly to blame. The minimum wage has not gone up since 1981, and now amounts to $6,700 for full-time, year-round work—almost $4,000 short of the poverty level for a family of four.

There are no doubt deeper—or, as the economists say, "structural"—reasons for the average American's sagging earning power. For one thing, the economy has been "globalized." In some industries, such as garments, toys, and electronics, American workers are competing—directly or indirectly—with workers in the southern hemisphere whose wages are a few dollars per day, rather than per hour. In a related development, the American economy has been "deindustrializing," or shifting from manufacturing to services, fast enough to displace 11.5 million Americans from blue-collar jobs (many in highly paid, unionized industries, such as auto and steel) since 1979. For the most part, service jobs tend to be lower-paying and nonunionized. Finally, there has been the technological revolution. Computers are eating away at many skilled, mid-level occupations—middle managers, department store buyers, machinists—as well as traditionally low-paid occupations, such as bank teller and telephone operator.

It is on the role of the "structural" changes that the economists are most fiercely divided, and, it seems to me, confused. The optimists insist that the causes of class polarization are more ephemeral than structural—if not the baby-boom bulge, then the strong dollar, or some other factor equally likely to go away by itself. Not long ago, the pessimists were convinced that polarization was the straightforward result of globalization, deindustrialization, and high technology, the combination of which, at least theoretically, could be expected to produce a nation of low-skilled helots dominated by a tiny technical-managerial elite.

Now some of them are not so sure. "It's incontestable," says David Smith, an economist on Senator Edward M. Kennedy's staff, "that as a service economy, we won't be able to sustain the level of growth required to maintain our standard of living." But, he says, recent data suggest that high technology does not necessarily bring about occupational polarization. As for international competition, he asks sarcastically, "Who the hell are we competing with in the insurance industry?"

There is no question, though, that American workers are less able than they were in the recent past to hold their own at the bargaining table—and most of them (the more than 80 percent who are not union members) never even get to the bargaining table. In the last decade, citing the need to compete in the newly global marketplace, employers have launched an aggressive campaign to cut labor costs, demanding—and frequently getting—wage givebacks, two-tier contracts, and other concessions. While wage-earning workers tighten their belts, top executives are reaping salaries that might once have been considered obscenely high. According to the social critic Michael Harrington: "We're seeing a savage attack on workers' wages and living standards. In the long run, no one's going to win because a low-wage society cannot be an affluent society."

*   *   *

Whatever the reasons for the growing polarization of American society, polarization creates its own dynamics, and perversely, they tend to make things worse, not better. For one thing, the affluent (say, the upper fifth) do what they can to avoid contact with the desperate and the downwardly mobile. They abandon public services and public spaces—schools, parks, mass transit—which then deteriorate. One result is that the living conditions and opportunities available to the poor (and many in the middle range of income) worsen. And, of course, as the poor sink lower, the affluent have all the more reason to withdraw further into their own "good" neighborhoods and private services.

As the better-off cease to utilize public services, they also tend to withdraw political support for public spending designed to benefit the community as a whole. If you send your children to private school, commute to work by taxi, and find your clean air at Aspen, you are likely to prefer a tax cut to an expansion of government services. This may be one reason for the decline of liberalism among America's upper-middle class. The liberal "effete snobs" that Spiro T. Agnew railed against are as rare today as Republicans on the welfare rolls.

There is another way in which class polarization tends to become self-reinforcing. As the Columbia University economist Saskia Sassen says: "The growth of the new urban upper middle class stimulates the proliferation of low-wage jobs. We're seeing the growth in the cities of a kind of 'servant class' that prepares the gourmet take-out food for the wealthy, stitches their designer clothes, and helps manufacture their customized furniture."

Traditional middle-class patterns of consumption, she notes, had a more egalitarian impact. When everyone bought their furniture at Sears and their food at the A&P, they were generating employment for workers in mass-production industries that were likely to be unionized and to pay well. In contrast, today's upscale consumer shops are boutique-scale outlets for items that are produced, or prepared, by relatively small, nonunionized companies.

The polarization of the extremes—the urban upper-middle class versus the "underclass"—inevitably makes it harder for those in the middle range of income to survive. As the rich get richer, they are able to bid up the costs of goods that middle-income people also consume, particularly housing. Wildly inflated housing costs hurt the affluent upper fifth, too, but they are far more likely than middle-income people to be able to command salary increases to match their escalating cost of living.

For those in the "new collar class," as Ralph Whitehead Jr., a University of Massachusetts professor, terms the non-yuppie plurality of baby boomers, a mortgage may be out of reach, much less a designer style of consumption. But we are all subjected to the blandishments of the booming market for upscale goods.

To be demonstrably "middle-class" in today's culture, a family needs not only the traditional house and car, but at least some of the regalia of the well-advertised upscale lifestyle—beers that cost $5 a six-pack for guests, and $60 sweatshirts for the teenage and preteen children. In order to be "middle-class" as our culture is coming to understand the term, one almost has to be rich.

So far, the hard-pressed families in the middle range of income have found a variety of ways to cope. They delay childbearing; and, even after the children come, both spouses are likely to hold jobs. They are ingenious about finding Kmart look-alikes for Bloomingdale's status goods; and, for the really big expenditures, they are likely to turn to parents for help. But these stratagems have their own costs, one of them being leisure for the kind of family life many of us were raised to expect. "We are seeing the standard two-income family," says Ethel Klein, a Columbia University political-science professor, "and the next step will probably be the three-income family, with the husband having to take a second job in order to keep up."

Karl Marx predicted that capitalist society would eventually be torn apart by the conflict between a greedy bourgeoisie and a vast, rebellious proletariat. He did not foresee the emergence, within capitalism, of a mass middle class that would mediate between the extremes and create a stable social order. But with that middle class in apparent decline and with the extremes diverging further from each other, it would be easy to conclude that the Marxist vision at last fits America's future.

But America is unique in ways that still make any prediction foolhardy. For one thing, Americans are notorious for their lack of class consciousness or even class awareness. In the face of the most brutal personal dislocations, we lack a vocabulary to express our dismay. Furthermore, at least at this point, we seem to lack political leadership capable of articulating both the distress of the have-nots and the malaise in the middle.

Thus there is no sure way to predict which way America's embattled middle class will turn. Some groups that are being displaced from the middle class seem to be moving leftward. Downwardly mobile single mothers, for example, may have helped create the gender gap that emerged, for the first time, in 1980 and was still prominent in the 1984 election, in which a greater proportion of women than men voted for the losing Democratic ticket. But the nation's debt-ridden farmers, another formerly middle-class group, have gone in all directions: some responding to Jesse Jackson's liberal populist message; others moving toward extreme right-wing fringe groups. The financially squeezed middle-income baby boomers are perhaps the most enigmatic of all. After much lush speculation as to their political inclinations, we know only that they tend to be liberal on social issues and more conservative on economic issues, and that they admire both Ronald Reagan and Bruce Springsteen.

Only at the extremes of wealth is political behavior becoming true to Marxist form. Thomas Byrne Edsall, author of *The New Politics of Inequality*, has documented an "extraordinary intensification of class-voting" in the eighties as compared with the previous two decades. For example, in 1956 Dwight D. Eisenhower won by nearly the same margin in all income groups, but in 1980 Reagan won among the rich but was soundly rejected by those in the bottom 40 percent of the income distribution. Party affiliation is becoming equally polarized, with the haves more monolith-ically Republican than at any time since the 1930s, and the have-nots more solidly Democratic.

It is not clear that either party, though, is willing to ad-vance the kinds of programs that might halt America's slide toward a two-tier society. Admittedly, it will be hard to get at the fundamental causes of class polarization until we know what they are. But there is no question that the dominant policy direction of the last few years has only ex-acerbated the trend. If we want to avert the polarization of American society, there is no choice, it seems to me, but to use public policy to redistribute wealth, and opportunity, downward again: not from the middle class to the poor, as Lyndon B. Johnson's Great Society programs tended to do, but from the very rich to everyone else.

We could start, for example, by raising the minimum wage, which would not only help the working poor but would also have a buoyant effect on middle-level wages. We could enact long-overdue measures, such as national health insurance and a system of subsidized child care, to help struggling young families. We could institute tax reforms that would both generate income for federal spending *and* relieve those in the middle brackets. A truly progressive in-come tax, combined with more generous public spending for education and social-welfare programs, would go a long way toward smoothing out the widening inequalities of op-portunity.

Everyone has a stake in creating a less anxious, more egalitarian society. In fact, from the point of view of the currently affluent, the greatest danger is not that a class-conscious, left-leaning political alternative will arise, but that it will not. For without a potent political alternative, we are likely to continue our slide toward a society divided between the hungry and the overfed, the hopeless and the have-it-alls. What is worse, there will be no mainstream, peaceable political outlets for the frustration of the declining middle class or the desperation of those at the bottom. Instead, it is safe to predict that there will be more crime, more exotic forms of political and religious sectarianism, and ultimately, that we will no longer be one nation, but two.

WELCOME TO FLEECE U.

Mother Jones, 1987

T his fall, my lovely and brilliant daughter will matriculate at a famous Ivy League college. Naturally, I am brokenhearted. You see, this fabulously prestigious institution, which for purposes of anonymity, I will call "Fleece U.," charges $20,000 a year—or more than two-thirds the median annual family income—to provide one's child with a bunk bed, cafeteria meals, and a chance to socialize with the future arbitrageurs and racehorse breeders of America.

Like any thrifty parent, I had done everything I could to discourage her from turning into "college material." I hid her schoolbooks. I tried to interest her in cosmetology, teen pregnancy, televison viewing. I even took her to visit a few campuses in the hope that she would be repelled by the bands of frat boys chasing minority students and beating on them with their marketing textbooks. I warned her that collegiate sexism has gotten so bad that the more enlightened colleges are now offering free rape crisis counseling as part of the freshman orientation package. "Oh, Mom," is all I got, "why don't you lighten *up*?"

When the college acceptance letters started pouring in last April, I sent them back stamped "Addressee Unknown," little realizing how determined these places can be when they're closing in on a sale. Brooke Shields called from Princeton to invite my daughter to a taffy pull. Henry Kissinger dropped by in a Learjet to discuss the undergraduate curriculum at Harvard. Benno Schmidt offered her a 15 percent discount at Yale and a date with a leading literary deconstructionist. I was flattered, but I could see I was trapped, like the time I accepted a coupon for a free margarita and found out I had obligated myself to attend a six-hour presentation on time-sharing options in the Poconos.

And don't tell me about financial aid. I had high hopes for that until I started filling out the application form. Question 12 inquired whether I had, in addition to my present income and home furnishings, any viable organs for donation. Question 34 solicited an inventory of the silverware. Question 92 demanded a list of rock stars who could plausibly be hit with a paternity suit.

Why does college cost so much? Or, more precisely, just where is the money going? The mystery deepens when you consider that $20,000 a year is approximately what it would cost to live full time in a downtown hotel with color TV and complimentary continental breakfast. Yet Fleece U., I happen to know, does not even offer room service. Alternatively, $20,000 is what it would cost to institutionalize some poor soul in a facility providing twenty-four-hour nursing service. Yet Fleece U., as everyone knows, has extraordinarily high standards and accepts only those students who have already learned to wash and dress themselves with a minimum of help.

Certainly, the money is not going to enrich the faculty. Except for a few celebrity profs, who have their own gene-splicing firms on the side or who moonlight as Pentagon consultants, most college faculty are a scruffy, ill-nourished lot, who are not above supplementing their income by panhandling on the steps of the student union. Nor can the money be going to the support staff. Even at venerable Fleece U., which has an endowment the size of the federal deficit, secretaries' wages are calculated on the basis of the minimum daily caloric requirement of the human female—any larger sum being considered an incitement to immorality.

Finally, we can rule out the possibility that the money is being used to support poor students who might otherwise go straight into burger flipping. With tuition rising twice as fast as inflation, poor students are no longer welcome at places like Fleece U., even in token numbers. Nationwide, the enrollment of black students peaked in 1980 but is now in decline due to cutbacks in federal aid programs. Meanwhile, the upper-middle class is fleeing the private colleges and beginning to crowd the working class out of state universities, which—at the astonishingly low price of $10,000 or so a year—are the best bargain since double coupons.

This leaves two possibilities: One is that the money is finding its way into the Iran-contra-Brunei triangle, from which no money has ever been known to reemerge. Of course, I have no logical reason for suspecting this. It is just that so much money these days starts out in the checkbooks of wealthy Connecticut widows or the royal family of Saudi Arabia and ends up hovering inaccessibly between Panama, Georgetown, and Zurich—perhaps to turn up someday as an Italian silk suit for Adolfo Calero or a spray of gardenias for Fawn Hall.

The second possibility, and the one that I personally consider more likely, is that the money is going to Don Regan. Not just Don Regan, of course, but G. Gordon Liddy, H. R. Haldeman, and possibly, in a year or two, Oliver North. For what do these fellows do after a period of public service followed, in some cases, by a relaxing spell in a minimum security prison? They repair to the college lecture circuit where, as I read recently, Don Regan pulls down $20,000 a night—the exact amount of my daughter's tuition at Fleece U.!

You can imagine how I feel about paying a sum of this magnitude to the man who almost drove Nancy Reagan to join a feminist support group. Yet I am gradually beginning to believe that the college experience will be important for my daughter. I realize that, even if she never opens a book, college will give her an opportunity I was never able to provide in our home: the chance to be around rich people—almost all of them young and attractive—continuously, twenty-four hours a day. Nor do I have to fear that she will lose the common touch. By the time she graduates, there will be at least one desperately poor person in her circle of acquaintances—myself.

PREWATCHED TV

The Guardian, 1994

Everything else has been automated, so why not that most commonplace of human activities—watching TV? This is the true secret of *Beavis and Butt-Head*'s megasuccess: not that they satisfy a young person's normal interest in arson and the torture of small animals and elderly people—which they do, of course, as has often been noted—but that they take the last bit of effort out of watching TV. For anyone so culturally impaired as not yet to have seen it, their show consists largely of two cartoon figures watching TV on a screen that fills up one's own. *They* make the ironic comments; *they* change the channel whenever a video threatens to drag. Hence the little pimple-butts' great gift to humankind—prewatched TV.

They're beginning to make prewatched commercials, too. Just as one's index finger moves to ward off the oncoming "message"—"Zap!"—the channel appears to change to something more entertaining. Then another virtual zap, and the product, whatever it is, returns. This is automated channel surfing—TV-viewing minus the last little vestige of muscular exertion.

At first we loved channel surfing on our own, accessing the collective mind, as it were, by tapping the buttons on the remote. People took pride in their craftsmanship— splicing scenes of hyena predation from the Discovery Channel in with the president's State of the Union address, for example, or alleviating the gloom of Bosnia with nacho recipes from the nearby Food Channel. Creative viewers mixed Hillary on health care with Tonya on skates, or cut into their favorite televangelist with the human sacrifice scene from *The Temple of Doom*. It was all there at one's fingertips: sprightly political chatter, singing transvestites, warnings about Satan, instructions for making béchamel sauce or rehabilitating a codependent relationship.

But then we went into overload. In my neighborhood, the breaking point came when the cable TV company upgraded us from forty to sixty channels, which meant there would now be not only twenty-four-hour news channels but channels offering continuous weather, shopping-by-phone, and trials of celebrity felons. The first casualty was a neighbor who developed a repetitive stress injury by overusing his remote. Now both of his index fingers are in finger-sized casts, and he has been reduced to changing channels with his nose.

Plus, it must be acknowledged that channel surfing was one of the factors undermining the American family. Once, it had been a simple matter to settle on the evening's entertainment—sex or violence, X-rated or R. After a brief, usually bloodless tussle, the victors settled down to enjoy and the losers resigned themselves to making irritating comments and exotic eructations, much as Beavis and Butthead now do for us. But when viewing became surfing, the fights got nastier. Children demanded their own TVs, often at gunpoint; spouses dueled with matching his-and-hers remotes. One theory has it that Lorena Bobbitt only went for the penis because the index finger, grossly thickened through overuse, resisted the knife.

Channel surfing has been destroying the nation as well. What, after all, are the fissures that really divide us? White versus black, right versus left, or some such archaic dispute? No, of course not. The real divisions are between those who watch MTV and those who favor Christian broadcasting, between CNN viewers and fans of Fox Network. But why let these transitory preferences come between us? American culture is not one or the other—Christian programming or writhing pelvises, "hard" news or Michael Jackson. American culture is everything running in together—béchamel sauce mixed with the Red Hot Chili Peppers, Pat Robertson a microsecond away from RuPaul.

Some say we should throw our remotes into the recycling bin and go back to the old days, when changing a channel involved walking from couch to set, twisting a knob, and returning, on foot, to couch. But the national attention span has gotten much too short for such arduous interruptions. It's far better to have the channel switching done for us, by some godlike invisible hand. Families, communities, nations will draw closer together as we all watch, i.e., rewatch, the same even-handed, prewatched blur.

THE RECESSION'S RACIAL DIVIDE

New York Times, 2009

With Dedrick Muhammad

What do you get when you combine the worst economic downturn since the Depression with the first black president? A surge of white racial resentment, loosely disguised as a populist revolt. An article on the Fox News website has put forth the theory that health reform is a stealth version of reparations for slavery: White people will foot the bill and, by some undisclosed mechanism, black people will get all the care. President Obama, in such fantasies, is a dictator and, in one image circulated among the antitax, anti–health reform "tea parties," he is depicted as a befeathered African witch doctor with little tusks coming out of his nostrils. When you're going down, as the white middle class has been doing for several years now, it's all too easy to imagine that it's because someone else is climbing up over your back.

Despite the sense of white grievance, though, black people are the ones who are taking the brunt of the recession, with disproportionately high levels of foreclosures and unemployment. And they weren't doing so well to begin with. At the start of the recession, 33 percent of the black middle class was already in danger of falling to a lower economic level, according to a study by the Institute on Assets and Social Policy at Brandeis University and Demos, a nonpartisan public policy research organization.

In fact, you could say that for African Americans the recession is over. It occurred from 2000 to 2007, as black employment decreased by 2.4 percent and incomes declined by 2.9 percent. During those seven years, one-third of black children lived in poverty, and black unemployment—even among college graduates—consistently ran at about twice the level of white unemployment.

That was the black recession. What's happening now is more like a depression. Nauvata and James, a middle-aged African-American couple living in Prince George's County, Maryland, who asked that their last name not be published, had never recovered from the first recession of the '00s when the second one came along. In 2003 Nauvata was laid off from a $25-an-hour administrative job at Aetna, and in 2007 she wound up in a $10.50-an-hour job at a car-rental company. James has had a steady union job as a building equipment operator, but the two couldn't earn enough to save themselves from predatory lending schemes.

They were paying off a $524 dining set bought on credit from the furniture store Levitz when it went out of business, and their debt swelled inexplicably as it was sold from one creditor to another. The couple ultimately spent a total of $3,800 to both pay it off and hire a lawyer to clear their credit rating. But to do this they had to refinance their home—not once, but with a series of mortgage lenders. Now they face foreclosure.

Nauvata, who is forty-seven, has since seen her blood pressure soar, and James, fifty-six, has developed heart palpitations. "There is no middle class anymore," he told us, "just a top and a bottom."

Plenty of formerly middle- or working-class white people have followed similar paths to ruin: the layoff or reduced hours, the credit traps and ever-rising debts, the lost home. But one thing distinguishes hard-pressed African Americans as a group: Thanks to a legacy of a discrimination in both hiring and lending, they're less likely than white people to be cushioned against the blows by wealthy relatives or well-stocked savings accounts. In 2008, on the cusp of the recession, the typical African-American family had only a dime for every dollar of wealth possessed by the typical white family. Only 18 percent of black people and Latinos had retirement accounts, compared with 43.4 percent of white people.

Racial asymmetry was stamped on this recession from the beginning. Wall Street's reckless infatuation with subprime mortgages led to the global financial crash of 2007, which depleted home values and 401(k)s across the racial spectrum. People of all races got sucked into subprime and adjustable-rate mortgages, but even high-income black people were almost twice as likely to end up with subprime home-purchase loans as low-income white people—even when they qualified for prime mortgages, even when they offered down payments.

According to a 2008 report by United for a Fair Economy, a research and advocacy group, from 1998 to 2006 (before the subprime crisis), black people lost $71 billion to $93 billion in home-value wealth from subprime loans. The researchers called this family net-worth catastrophe the "greatest loss of wealth in recent history for people of color." And the worst was yet to come.

In a new documentary film about the subprime crisis, *American Casino*, solid black citizens—a high school social studies teacher, a psychotherapist, a minister—relate how they lost their homes when their monthly mortgage payments exploded. Watching the parts of the film set in Baltimore is a little like watching the TV series *The Wire*, except that the bad guys don't live in the projects; they hover over computer screens on Wall Street.

It's not easy to get people to talk about their subprime experiences. There's the humiliation of having been "played" by distant, mysterious forces. "I don't feel very good about myself," says the teacher in *American Casino*. "I kind of feel like a failure."

Even people who know better tend to blame themselves—like Melonie Griffith, a forty-year-old African American who works with the Boston group City Life/La Vida Urbana helping other people avoid foreclosure and eviction. She criticizes herself for having been "naive" enough to trust the mortgage lender who, in 2004, told her not to worry about the high monthly payments she was signing on for because the mortgage would be refinanced in "a couple of months." The lender then disappeared, leaving Griffith in foreclosure, with "nowhere for my kids and me to go." Only when she went public with her story did she find that she wasn't the only one. "There is a consistent pattern here," she told us.

Mortgage lenders like Countrywide and Wells Fargo sought out minority home buyers for the heartbreakingly simple reason that, for decades, black people had been denied mortgages on racial grounds, and were thus a ready-made market for the gonzo mortgage products of the mid-'00s. Banks replaced the old racist practice of redlining with "reverse redlining"—intensive marketing aimed at black neighborhoods in the name of extending home ownership to the historically excluded. Countrywide, which prided itself on being a dream factory for previously disadvantaged home buyers, rolled out commercials showing canny black women talking their husbands into signing mortgages.

At Wells Fargo, Elizabeth Jacobson, a former loan officer at the company, recently revealed—in an affidavit in a lawsuit by the City of Baltimore—that salesmen were encouraged to try to persuade black preachers to hold "wealth-building seminars" in their churches. For every loan that resulted from these seminars, whether to buy a new home or refinance one, Wells Fargo promised to donate $350 to the customer's favorite charity, usually the church. (Wells Fargo denied any effort to market subprime loans specifically to black people.) Another former loan officer, Tony Paschal, reported that at the same time cynicism was rampant within Wells Fargo, with some employees referring to subprimes as "ghetto loans" and to minority customers as "mud people."

If any cultural factor predisposed black people to fall for risky loans, it was one widely shared with white people—

a penchant for "positive thinking" and unwarranted optimism, which takes the theological form of the "prosperity gospel." Since "God wants to prosper you," all you have to do to get something is "name it and claim it." A 2000 DVD from the black evangelist Creflo Dollar featured African-American parishioners shouting, "I want my stuff—right now!"

Joel Osteen, the white megachurch pastor who draws 40,000 worshippers each Sunday, about two-thirds of them black and Latino, likes to relate how he himself succumbed to God's urgings—conveyed by his wife—to upgrade to a larger house. According to Jonathan Walton, a religion professor at the University of California, Riverside, pastors like Osteen reassured people about subprime mortgages by getting them to believe that "God caused the bank to ignore my credit score and bless me with my first house." If African Americans made any collective mistake in the mid-'00s, it was to embrace white culture too enthusiastically, and substitute the individual wish fulfillment promoted by Norman Vincent Peale for the collective-action message of Martin Luther King.

But you didn't need a dodgy mortgage to be wiped out by the subprime crisis and ensuing recession. Black unemployment is now at 15.1 percent, compared with 8.9 percent for white people. In New York City, black unemployment has been rising four times as fast as that of white people. By 2010, according to Lawrence Mishel of the Economic Policy Institute, 40 percent of African Americans nationwide will have endured patches of unemployment or underemployment.

One result is that black people are being hit by a second wave of foreclosures caused by unemployment. Willett Thomas, a neat, wiry forty-seven-year-old in Washington who describes herself as a "fiscal conservative," told us that until a year ago she thought she'd "figured out a way to live my dream." Not only did she have a job and a house, but she had a rental property in Gainesville, Florida, leaving her with the flexibility to pursue a part-time writing career.

Then she became ill, lost her job, and fell behind on the fixed-rate mortgage on her home. The tenants in Florida had financial problems of their own and stopped paying rent. Now, although she manages to have an interview a week and regularly upgrades her résumé, Thomas cannot find a new job. The house she lives in is in foreclosure.

Mulugeta Yimer of Alexandria, Virginia, still has his taxi-driving job, but it no longer pays enough to live on. A thin, tall man with worry written all over his face, Yimer came to this country in 1981 as a refugee from Ethiopia, firmly believing in the American dream. In 2003, when Wells Fargo offered him an adjustable-rate mortgage, he calculated that he'd be able to deal with the higher interest rate when it kicked in. But the recession delivered a near-mortal blow to the taxi industry, even in the still relatively affluent Washington suburbs. He's now putting in nineteen-hour days, with occasional naps in his taxi, while his wife works thirty-two hours a week at a convenience store, but they still don't earn enough to cover expenses: $400 a month for health insurance, $800 for child care, and $1,700 for the mortgage. What will Yimer do if he ends up losing his house? "We'll go to a shelter, I guess," he said, throwing open his hands, "if we can find one."

So despite the right-wing perception of black power grabs, this recession is on track to leave black people even more economically disadvantaged than they were. Does a black president who is inclined toward bipartisanship dare address this destruction of the black middle class? Probably not. But if Americans of all races don't get some economic relief soon, the pain will only increase and, with it, perversely, the unfounded sense of white racial grievance.

DIVISIONS OF LABOR

New York Times, 2017

The working class, or at least the white part, has emerged as our great national mystery. Traditionally Democratic, they helped elect a flamboyantly ostentatious billionaire to the presidency. "What's wrong with them?" the liberal pundits keep asking. Why do they believe Trump's promises? Are they stupid or just deplorably racist? Why did the working class align itself against its own interests?

I was born into this elusive class and remain firmly connected to it through friendships and family. In the 1980s, for example, I personally anchored a working-class cultural hub in my own home on Long Island. The attraction was not me but my husband (then) and longtime friend Gary Stevenson, a former warehouse worker who had become an organizer for the Teamsters Union. You may think of the Long Island suburbs as a bedroom community for Manhattan commuters or a portal to the Hamptons, but they were then also an industrial center, with more than 20,000 workers employed at Grumman alone. When my sister moved into our basement from Colorado, she quickly found a job in a factory within a mile of our house, as did thousands of other people, some of them bused in from the Bronx. Mostly we hosted local residents who passed through our house for evening meetings or weekend gatherings—truck drivers, factory workers, janitors, and eventually nurses. My job was to make chili and keep room in the fridge for the baked ziti others would invariably bring. I once tried to explain the concept of "democratic socialism" to some machine-shop workers and went off on a brief peroration against the Soviet Union. They stared at me glumly across the kitchen counter until one growled, "At least they have health care over there."

By the time my little crew was gathering in the ranch house, working-class aspirations were everywhere being trampled underfoot. In 1981, President Reagan busted the air traffic controllers' union by firing more than 11,000 striking workers—a clear signal of what was to come. A few years later, we hosted a picnic for Jim Guyette, the leader of a militant meatpacking local in Minnesota that had undertaken a wildcat strike against Hormel (and, of course, no Hormel products were served at our picnic). But labor had entered into an age of givebacks and concessions. Grovel was the message, or go without a job. Even the "mighty mighty" unions of the old labor chant, the ones that our little group had struggled both to build and to democratize, were threatened with extinction. Within a year, the wildcat local was crushed by its own parent union, the United Food and Commercial Workers.

Steel mills went quiet, the mines where my father and

grandfather had worked shut down, factories fled south of the border. Much more was lost in the process than just the jobs; an entire way of life, central to the American mythos, was coming to an end. The available jobs, in fields like retail sales and health care, were ill paid, making it harder for a man without a college education to support a family on his own. I could see this in my own extended family, where the grandsons of miners and railroad workers were taking jobs as delivery-truck drivers and fast-food restaurant managers or even competing with their wives to become retail workers or practical nurses. As Susan Faludi observed in her 1999 book *Stiffed*, the deindustrialization of America led to a profound masculinity crisis: What did it mean to be a man when a man could no longer support a family?

It wasn't just a way of life that was dying but also many of those who had lived it. Research in 2015 by Angus Deaton, a Nobel laureate in economics, with his wife, economist Anne Case, showed that the mortality gap between college-educated and non-college-educated had been widening rapidly since 1999. A couple of months later, economists at the Brookings Institution found that for men born in 1920, there was a six-year difference in life expectancy between the top 10 percent of earners and the bottom 10 percent. For men born in 1950, that difference more than doubled, to 14 years. Smoking, which is now mostly a working-class habit, could account for only a third of the excess deaths. The rest were apparently attributable to alcoholism, drug overdoses, and suicide, usually by gunshot—what are often called "diseases of despair."

In the new economic landscape of low-paid service jobs,

some of the old nostrums of the left have stopped making sense. "Full employment," for example, was the mantra of the unions for decades, but what did it mean when so many jobs no longer paid enough to live on? The idea had been that if everyone who wanted a job could get one, employers would have to raise wages to attract new workers. But when I went out as an undercover journalist in the late 1990s to test the viability of entry-level jobs, I found my coworkers—waitstaff, nursing-home workers, maids with a cleaning service, Walmart "associates"—living for the most part in poverty. As I reported in the resulting book, *Nickel and Dimed*, some were homeless and slept in their cars, while others skipped lunch because they couldn't afford anything more than a snack-size bag of Doritos. They were full-time workers, and this was a time, like the present, of nearly full employment.

The other popular solution to the crisis of the working class was job retraining. If ours is a "knowledge economy"—which sounds so much better than a "low-wage economy"—unemployed workers would just have to get their game on and upgrade to more useful skills. President Obama promoted job retraining, as did Hillary Clinton as a presidential candidate, along with many Republicans. The problem was that no one was sure what to train people in; computer skills were in vogue in the '90s, welding has gone in and out of style, and careers in the still-growing health sector are supposed to be the best bets now. Nor is there any clear measure of the effectiveness of existing retraining programs. In 2011, the Government Accountability Office found the federal government supporting forty-seven job-training projects as of 2009, of which only five had been evaluated in the previous five years. Paul Ryan has repeatedly praised a program in his hometown, Janesville, Wisconsin, but a 2012 ProPublica study found that laid-off people who went through it were less likely to find jobs than those who did not.

No matter how good the retraining program, the idea that people should be endlessly malleable and ready to recreate themselves to accommodate every change in the job market is probably not realistic and certainly not respectful of existing skills. In the early '90s, I had dinner at a Pizza Hut with a laid-off miner in Butte, Montana (actually, there are no other kinds of miners in Butte). He was in his fifties, and he chuckled when he told me that he was being advised to get a degree in nursing. I couldn't help laughing, too—not at the gender incongruity but at the notion that a man whose tools had been a pickax and dynamite should now so radically change his relation to the world. No wonder that when blue-collar workers were given the choice between job retraining, as proffered by Clinton, and somehow, miraculously, bringing their old jobs back, as proposed by Trump, they went for the latter.

Now when politicians invoke "the working class," they are likely to gesture, anachronistically, to an abandoned factory. They might more accurately use a hospital or a fast-food restaurant as a prop. The new working class contains many of the traditional blue-collar occupations—truck driver, electrician, plumber—but by and large its members are more likely to wield mops than hammers, and bedpans rather than trowels. Demographically, too, the working class has evolved from the heavily white male grouping that used to assemble at my house in the 1980s; black and Hispanic people have long been a big, if unacknowledged, part of the working class, and now it's more female and contains many more immigrants as well. If the stereotype of the old working class was a man in a hard hat, the new one is better represented as a woman chanting, "*El pueblo unido jamás será vencido!*" (The people united will never be defeated!)

The old jobs aren't coming back, but there is another way to address the crisis brought about by deindustrialization: Pay all workers better. The big labor innovation of the twenty-first century has been campaigns seeking to raise local or state minimum wages. Activists have succeeded in passing living-wage laws in more than a hundred counties and municipalities since 1994 by appealing to a simple sense of justice: Why should someone work full time, year-round, and not make enough to pay for rent and other basics? Surveys found large majorities favoring an increase in the minimum wage; college students, church members, and unions rallied to local campaigns. Unions started taking on formerly neglected constituencies like janitors, home health aides, and day laborers. And where the unions have faltered, entirely new kinds of organizations sprang up: associations sometimes backed by unions and sometimes by philanthropic foundations—Our Walmart, the National Domestic Workers Alliance, and the Restaurant Opportunities Centers United.

Our old scene on Long Island is long gone: the house sold, the old friendships frayed by age and distance. I miss it. As a group, we had no particular ideology, but our vision, which was articulated through our parties rather than any manifesto, was utopian, especially in the context of Long Island, where if you wanted any help from the county, you had to be a registered Republican. If we had a single theme, it could be summed up in the old-fashioned word "solidarity": If you join my picket line, I'll join yours, and maybe we'll all go protest together, along with the kids, at the chemical plant that was oozing toxins into our soil—followed by a barbecue in my backyard. We were not interested in small-P politics. We wanted a world in which everyone's work was honored and every voice heard.

I never expected to be part of anything like that again until, in 2004, I discovered a similar, far-better-organized group in Fort Wayne, Indiana. The Northeast Indiana Central Labor Council, as it was then called, brought together Mexican immigrant construction workers and the native-born building-trade union members they had been brought in to replace, laid-off foundry workers and Burmese factory workers, adjunct professors and janitors. Their goal, according to the president at the time, Tom Lewandowski, a former General Electric factory worker who served in the 1990s as the AFL-CIO's liaison to the Polish insurgent movement Solidarnosc, was to create a "culture of solidarity." They were inspired by the realization that it's not enough to organize people with jobs; you have to organize the unemployed as well as the "anxiously employed"—meaning potentially the entire community. Their not-so-secret tactic was parties and picnics, some of which I was lucky enough to attend.

The scene in Fort Wayne featured people of all colors and collar colors, legal and undocumented workers, liberals and political conservatives, some of whom supported Trump in the last election. It showed that a new kind of solidarity was within reach, even if the old unions may not be ready. In 2016, the ailing AFL-CIO, which for more than six decades has struggled to hold the labor movement together, suddenly dissolved the Northeast Indiana Central Labor Council, citing obscure bureaucratic imperatives. But the labor council was undaunted. It promptly reinvented itself as the Workers' Project and drew more than 6,000 people to the local Labor Day picnic, despite having lost its internet access and office equipment to the AFL-CIO .

When I last talked to Tom Lewandowski, in early February 2017, the Workers' Project had just succeeded in organizing twenty Costco contract workers into a collective unit of their own and were planning to celebrate with, of course, a party. The human urge to make common cause—and have a good time doing it—is hard to suppress.

THROW THEM OUT WITH THE TRASH: WHY HOMELESSNESS IS BECOMING AN OCCUPY WALL STREET ISSUE

Huffington Post, 2011

As anyone knows who has ever had to set up a military encampment or build a village from the ground up, occupations pose staggering logistical problems. Large numbers of people must be fed and kept reasonably warm and dry. Trash has to be removed; medical care and rudimentary security provided—to which ends a dozen or more committees may toil night and day. But for the individual occupier, one problem often overshadows everything else, including job loss, the destruction of the middle class, and the reign of the 1 percent. And that is the single question: *Where am I going to pee?*

Some of the Occupy Wall Street encampments now spreading across the United States have access to Port-o-Potties (Freedom Plaza in Washington, DC) or, better yet, restrooms with sinks and running water (Fort Wayne, Indiana). Others require their residents to forage on their own. At Zuccotti Park, just blocks from Wall Street, this means long waits for the restroom at a nearby Burger King or somewhat shorter ones at a Starbucks a block away.

At McPherson Square in DC, a twenty-something occupier showed me the pizza parlor where she can cop a pee during the hours it's open, as well as the alley where she crouches late at night. Anyone with restroom-related issues—arising from age, pregnancy, prostate problems, or irritable bowel syndrome—should prepare to join the revolution in diapers.

Of course, political protesters do not face the challenges of urban camping alone. Homeless people confront the same issues every day: how to scrape together meals, keep warm at night by covering themselves with cardboard or tarp, and relieve themselves without committing a crime. Public restrooms are sparse in American cities—"as if the need to go to the bathroom does not exist," travel expert Arthur Frommer once observed. And yet to yield to bladder pressure is to risk arrest. A report titled "Criminalizing Crisis," released by the National Law Center on Homelessness and Poverty, recounts the following story from Wenatchee, Washington:

> Toward the end of 2010, a family of two parents and three children who had been experiencing homelessness for a year and a half applied for a two-bedroom apartment. The day before a scheduled meeting with the apartment manager during the final stages of acquiring the lease, the father of the family was arrested for public urination. The arrest occurred at an hour when no public restrooms were available for use. Due to the arrest, the father was unable to make the appointment with the apartment manager and the property was rented out to another person. As of

March 2011, the family was still homeless and searching for housing.

What the Occupy Wall Streeters are beginning to discover, and homeless people have known all along, is that most ordinary, biologically necessary activities are illegal when performed in American streets—not just peeing, but sitting, lying down, and sleeping. While the laws vary from city to city, one of the harshest is in Sarasota, Florida, which passed an ordinance in 2005 that makes it illegal to "engage in digging or earth-breaking activities"—that is, to build a latrine—cook, make a fire, or be asleep and "when awakened state that he or she has no other place to live."

It is illegal, in other words, to be homeless or live outdoors for any other reason. It should be noted, though, that there are no laws requiring cities to provide food, shelter, or restrooms for their indigent citizens.

The current prohibition on homelessness began to take shape in the 1980s, along with the ferocious growth of the financial industry (Wall Street and all its tributaries throughout the nation). That was also the era in which we stopped being a nation that manufactured much beyond weightless, invisible "financial products," leaving the old industrial working class to carve out a livelihood at places like Walmart.

As it turned out, the captains of the new "casino economy"—the stock brokers and investment bankers—were highly sensitive, one might say finicky, individuals, easily offended by having to step over the homeless in the streets or bypass them in commuter train stations. In an economy where a centimillionaire could turn into a billionaire overnight, the poor and unwashed were a major buzzkill. Starting with Mayor Rudy Giuliani in New York, city after city passed "broken windows" or "quality of life" ordinances, making it dangerous for the homeless to loiter or, in some cases, even look "indigent," in public spaces.

No one has yet tallied all the suffering occasioned by this crackdown—the deaths from cold and exposure—but "Criminalizing Crisis" offers this story about a homeless pregnant woman in Columbia, South Carolina:

> During daytime hours, when she could not be inside of a shelter, she attempted to spend time in a museum and was told to leave. She then attempted to sit on a bench outside the museum and was again told to relocate. In several other instances, still during her pregnancy, the woman was told that she could not sit in a local park during the day because she would be "squatting." In early 2011, about six months into her pregnancy, the homeless woman began to feel unwell, went to a hospital, and delivered a stillborn child.

Well before Tahrir Square was a twinkle in anyone's eye, and even before the recent recession, homeless Americans had begun to act in their own defense, creating organized encampments, usually tent cities, in vacant lots or wooded areas. These communities often feature various elementary forms of self-governance: food from local charities has to be distributed, latrines dug, rules—such as no drugs, weapons, or violence—enforced. With all due credit to the Egyptian democracy movement, the Spanish *indignados*, and rebels all over the world, tent cities are the domestic progenitors of the American occupation movement.

There is nothing "political" about these settlements of the homeless—no signs denouncing greed or visits from left-wing luminaries—but they have been treated with far less official forbearance than the occupation encampments of the "American autumn." LA's Skid Row endures constant police harassment, for example, but when it rained, Mayor Antonio Villaraigosa had ponchos distributed to nearby Occupy LA.

All over the country, in the last few years, police have moved in on the tent cities of the homeless, one by one, from Seattle to Wooster, Sacramento to Providence, in raids that often leave the former occupants without even their minimal possessions. In Chattanooga, Tennessee, last summer, a charity outreach worker explained the forcible dispersion of a local tent city by saying, "The city will not tolerate a tent city. That's been made very clear to us. The camps have to be out of sight."

What occupiers from all walks of life are discovering, at least every time they contemplate taking a leak, is that to be homeless in America is to live like a fugitive. The destitute are our own native-born "illegals," facing prohibitions on the most basic activities of survival. They are not supposed to soil public space with their urine, their feces, or their exhausted bodies. Nor are they supposed to spoil the landscape with their unusual wardrobe choices or body odors. They are, in fact, supposed to die, and preferably to do so without leaving a corpse for the dwindling public sector to transport, process, and burn.

But the occupiers are not from *all* walks of life, just from those walks that slope downwards—from debt, joblessness, and foreclosure—leading eventually to pauperism and the streets. Some of the present occupiers were homeless to start with, attracted to the occupation encampments by the prospect of free food and at least temporary shelter from police harassment. Many others are drawn from the borderline-homeless "nouveau poor," and normally encamp on friends' couches or parents' folding beds.

In Portland, Austin, and Philadelphia, the Occupy Wall Street movement is taking up the cause of the homeless as its own, which of course it is. Homelessness is not a side issue unconnected to plutocracy and greed. It's where we're all eventually headed—the 99 percent, or at least the 70 percent, of us, every debt-loaded college grad, out-of-work schoolteacher, and impoverished senior—unless this revolution succeeds.

ACKNOWLEDGMENTS

Grateful acknowledgment is made to the following for permission to reprint previously published material.

HAVES AND HAVE-NOTS

"Nickel-and-Dimed: On (Not) Getting By in America" (*Harper's Magazine*, 1999)

"How You Can Save Wall Street" (*Mother Jones*, 1988)

"S&M As Public Policy" (*The Guardian*, 1993)

"Going to Extremes: CEOs vs. Slaves" originally published as "CEOs vs. Slaves" (*The Nation*, 2007)

"Are Illegal Immigrants the Problem?" (*Barbara's Blog*, 2006)

"What's So Great about Gated Communities?" (*Huffington Post*, 2007)

"Is It Now a Crime to be Poor?" (*New York Times*, 2009)

"A Homespun Safety Net" (*New York Times*, 2009)

"Dead, White, and Blue" (*Guernica*, 2015)

HEALTH

"Welcome to Cancerland" (*Harper's Magazine*, 2001)

"The Naked Truth about Fitness" (*Lear's*, 1990)

"Got Grease?" (*Los Angeles Times*, 2002)

"Our Broken Mental Health System" (*The Nation*, 2007)

"Liposuction: The Key to Energy Independence" (*The Nation*, 2008)

"The Selfish Side of Gratitude" (*New York Times*, 2015)

MEN

"How 'Natural' is Rape?" (*Time*, 2000)

"The Warrior Culture" (*Time*, 1990)

"At Last, a New Man" originally published as "A Feminist's View of the New Man" (*New York Times*, 1984)

"Patriarchy Deflated" (*The Baffler*, 2018)

WOMEN

"Are Women Getting Sadder?" originally published as "The Sad Truth" (*Los Angeles Times*, 2009)

"Our Neighborhood Porn Committee" originally published as "The Story of Ed" (*Mother Jones*, 1986)

"Strategies of Corporate Women" (*New Republic*, 1986)

"Feminism's Assumptions Upended" originally published as "What Abu Ghraib Taught Me" (*Los Angeles Times*, 2004)

"Making Sense of la Différence" (*Time*, 1992)
"Outclassed: Sexual Harassment" originally published as "Sexual Harassment Doesn't Just Happen to Actors or Journalists. Talk to a Waitress, or a Cleaner" (*The Guardian*, 2017)

GOD, SCIENCE, AND JOY

"Mind Your Own Business" (*The Baffler*, 2015)
"The Animal Cure" (*The Baffler*, 2012)
"The Missionary Position" (*The Baffler*, 2012)
"The New Creationism: Biology under Attack" (*The Nation*, 1997)
"Up Close at Trinidad's Carnival" (*Smithsonian Magazine*, 2009)

BOURGEOIS BLUNDERS

"Family Values" (Introduction to *The Worst Years of Our Lives* [Pantheon, 1990])
"The Cult of Busyness" originally published as "Hers" (*New York Times*, 1985)
"Death of a Yuppie Dream" (*Journal der Rosa Luxemburg Stiftung*, 2013)
"The Unbearable Being of Whiteness" (*Mother Jones*, 1988)
"Is the Middle Class Doomed?" (*New York Times*, 1986)
"Welcome to Fleece U." (*Mother Jones*, 1987)

"Prewatched TV" (*The Guardian*, 1994)
"The Recession's Racial Divide" (*New York Times*, 2009)
"Divisions of Labor" (*New York Times*, 2017)
"Throw Them Out with the Trash: Why Homelessness Is Becoming an Occupy Wall Street Issue" (*Huffington Post*, 2011)

INDEX

ABOUT THE AUTHOR

BARBARA EHRENREICH is the author of more than a dozen books, including the *New York Times* bestsellers *Nickel and Dimed* and *Natural Causes*. She has a PhD in cellular immunology from Rockefeller University and writes frequently about health care and medical science, among many other subjects. She lives in Virginia.